A STUDY OF THE INTERPRETATION
OF NOAH AND THE FLOOD IN
JEWISH AND CHRISTIAN LITERATURE

A STUDY OF THE INTERPRETATION OF NOAH AND THE FLOOD IN JEWISH AND CHRISTIAN LITERATURE

BY

JACK P. LEWIS

Professor of Bible, Harding College Graduate School of Religion
Memphis, Tennessee

LEIDEN
E. J. BRILL
1968

TABLE OF CONTENTS

	Page
PREFACE	VII
LIST OF ABBREVIATIONS	IX
INTRODUCTION	1
I. NOAH AND THE FLOOD IN THE BIBLE	3
II. NOAH IN THE APOCRYPHA AND PSEUDEPIGRAPHA OF THE O.T.	10
III. THE FLOOD IN HELLENISTIC-JEWISH WRITERS	42
A. Philo of Alexandria	42
1. The Literal Noah	43
2. The Allegorical Noah	58
B. Pseudo-Philo	74
C. Josephus	77
IV. THE FLOOD IN THE EARLY VERSIONS	82
A. The Greek Versions	82
1. The Septuagint	82
2. Aquila	88
3. Theodotian	90
4. Symmachus	90
B. The Aramaic Versions	92
1. Targum of Onkelos	92
2. Targum of Pseudo-Jonathan	95
3. Jerusalem Targum	99
V. EARLY CHRISTIAN INTERPRETATIONS OF THE FLOOD	101
VI. THE RABBINIC NOAH	121

VII. The Flood and later Christian Spiritual Exegesis 156

Conclusion 181

Appendix

    A. Index of Scripture Passages on the Flood in the Works
       of Philo 183

    B. The Noah Commandments 186

    C. The Chronology of the Flood 190

Bibliography. 193

PREFACE

The following study which was first presented to Hebrew Union College-Jewish Institute of Religion, Cincinnati, Ohio, in 1962 in partial fulfillment of the requirements for the Ph.D. degree in Hebraic and Cognate Studies, is now presented to the public in hope that its collection of material may be of benefit to other scholars who are interested in this area of biblical studies.

I hereby acknowledge to the college a deep debt for the Louis M. Rabinowitz, J. Clarence Workum Memorial, and Mary E. Horowitz Foundation interfaith fellowships which were successively granted me in the three years 1951-1954, and which made my studies at the college possible. In addition to a lasting debt to all members of the faculty, I am further indebted to Dr. Samuel Sandmel who first suggested to me this area of study, who served as referee for the dissertation, and who made many helpful suggestions in the course of its preparation. Dr. Julius Lewy (now deceased), also on my committee, is remembered for his helpfulness.

I wish to thank the librarians at Hebrew Union College, Andover-Harvard Library, and Vanderbilt University Library for the use of their facilities and for kindnesses shown in the various stages of the preparation of this book. Mrs. Martha Sisson was kind enough to type the manuscript. Dr. William Green of Pepperdine College and Miss Annie May Alston, librarian of Harding College Graduate School of Religion, graciously read the manuscript. Remaining errors of the book are to be laid at my door, however, and not at theirs.

Kindest thanks are due to the Clarendon Press for permission to quote the R. H. Charles edition of *The Apocrypha and Pseudepigrapha of the O.T.*; to the American Biblical Encyclopedia Society for M. M. Kasher, *The Encyclopedia of Biblical Interpretation*; to the Division of Christian Education of the National Council of Churches of Christ for the R.S.V. edition of the Apocrypha; to the Society for Promoting Christian Knowledge for R. M. Grant, *Second Century Christianity*; and to A. Levene for his *The Syrian Fathers on Genesis*.

The compliment paid me by my friends and former students who responded to the invitation of Dr. George S. Benson, president of Harding College, to join him in furnishing the subsidy needed for the publication will not be forgotten. I am sure that they will find the book less enlightening than they had anticipated.

Compassion is extended to my wife, Lynell Carpenter Lewis, and to my two sons, John Robert and Jerry Wayne, who denied themselves attentions rightly theirs and who endured the trials of living with me during the long labors of preparing two doctoral dissertations, the second of which is this study. I only hope that they will not find their privations in vain.

Jack P. Lewis.

Memphis, Tennessee

August 28, 1965

LIST OF ABBREVIATIONS

A. and P.	*Apocrypha and Pseudepigrapha of the O.T. in English.*
AJSL.	*American Journal of Semitic Languages.*
ANF.	*Ante-Nicene Fathers.*
ARN.	*Aboth R. Nathan.*
A.V.	Authorized Version.
BA.	Babylonian Amora.
B.A.	*Biblical Archaeologist.*
Bar.	*Baruch.*
BDB.	F. Brown, S. R. Driver, C. A. Briggs, *Hebrew and English Lexicon of the O.T.*
Bib. Ant.	*Biblical Antiquities.*
CBQ.	*Catholic Biblical Quarterly.*
Const. Apost.	*Apostolic Constitutions.*
CSCO.	*Corpus scriptorum christianorum orientalium.*
CSEL.	*Corpus scriptorum ecclesiasticorum latinorum.*
EBI.	M. M. Kasher, *Ency. of Biblical Interpretation.*
E.V.	English Version.
F. of Ch.	*The Fathers of the Church.*
GCS.	*Die grieschischen christlichen Schriftsteller der ersten drei Jahrhunderte.*
GKC.	Gesenius-Kautzsch's *Hebrew Grammar*, A. E. Cowley, tr.
J.	*Jerusalem Talmud.*
JBL.	*Journal of Biblical Literature and Exegesis.*
JBR.	*Journal of Bible and Religion.*
J.E.	*Jewish Encyclopedia.*
JNES.	*Journal of Near Eastern Studies.*
JSOR.	*Journal of Society of Oriental Research.*
Jub.	*The Book of Jubilees.*
K-B.	Koehler, L., and Baumgartner, W., *Lexicon in Veteris Testamenti Libros.*
K.J.V.	King James Version.
LCC.	*Library of Christian Classics.*
LXX	The Septuagint.
M.	*Mishna.*
MT.	*Masoretic Text.*
Macc.	*Maccabees.*
N.T.	New Testament.
NPNF.	*A Select Library of Nicene and Post-Nicene Fathers of the Christian Church.*
Or. Sib.	*Sibylline Oracles.*
O.T.	Old Testament.

Philo:

Abr.	*De Abrahamo.*
Agr.	*De Agricultura.*
Conf.	*De Confusione Linguarum.*
Cong.	*De Congressu Eruditionis quaerendae gratia.*
Det.	*Quod Deterius Potiori insidiari solet.*
Ebr.	*De Ebrietate.*

Fug.	*De Fuga et Inventione (De Profugis).*
Gig.	*De Gigantibus.*
Heres	*Quis Rerum Divinarum Heres.*
Immut.	*Quod Deus immutabilis sit.*
LA.	*Legum Allegoria.*
Mig.	*De Migratione Abrahami.*
Mos.	*De Vita Mosis.*
Mut.	*De Mutatione Nominum.*
Plant.	*De Plantatione.*
Post.	*De Posteritate Caini.*
Praem.	*De Praemiis et Poenis.*
QG.	*Quaestiones et Solutiones in Genesin.*
Sob.	*De Sobrietate.*
Som.	*De Somniis.*
Virt.	*De Virtutibus.*

P.A.	Palestinian Amora.
PG.	*Patrologia Graeca.*
PL.	*Patrologia Latina.*
PRE.	*Pirke de R. Eliezer.*
R.	*Midrash Rabbah.*
R.B.	*Revue Biblique.*
R.S.V.	Revised Standard Version.
SC.	*Sources Chrétiennes.*
T.	Tanna.
T.B.	*Talmud Babli.*
Tos.	*Tosephta.*
T. Ps.-Jon.	*Targum of Pseudo-Jonathan.*
TU.	*Texte und Untersuchungen.*
V.T.	*Vetus Testamentum.*
Z.	*Zeitschrift.*

INTRODUCTION

This study limits itself in scope to a consideration of the biblical and post-biblical Jewish and Christian materials dealing with the flood. The writer feels justified in setting these limits, for ample literature is extant on the flood legends of the world which are at least sixty-eight in number.[1] Of these, only the accounts from the Mesopotamian regions show striking similarities to biblical material. Heidel [2] and Parrot [3] have recently dealt at length, though from widely different viewpoints, with these stories and with other archaeological finds alleged to confirm the Hebrew story. Likewise the efforts to make the most literal interpretation acceptable to the modern mind finds a representative in Rehwinkel,[4] though Rehwinkel has so allowed his imagination to play that he has damaged his case by considerable overstatement. All of these questions fall outside the limits here proposed: How did Hebrews and Christians of the early period deal with this enchanting episode of the early chapters of Genesis?

The enormous debt this investigation owes to its predecessors is obvious. Special use has been made of the collections of M. M. Kasher, *Torah Shelema*, and its English translation, *Encyclopedia of Biblical Interpretation*, and L. Ginzberg, *Legends of the Jews*. This study differs from those both in inclusion and in exclusion. Kasher limits himself to rabbinic materials. It is regrettable that his English translation does not indicate parallel passages to the ones he translates, for there is a great deal more repetition in rabbinic literature than one would surmise from the *Encyclopedia of Biblical Interpretation*. Ginzberg has considered some Christian materials, but chiefly from the viewpoint that they are illustrative of or parallel to rabbinic legends. Other ideas he neglects altogether. This is especially true in the allegorical and typological areas characteristic of certain periods of Christian exegesis. This study also differs from those of Kasher and

---

[1] H. Peake, *The Flood* (London: Kegan Paul, Trench,Trubner and Co., 1930), 124 pp.; J. G. Frazer, *Folklore in the O.T.* (London: Macmillan, 1919), I, 104-361.
[2] A. Heidel, *The Gilgamesh Epic* (Chicago: U. of Chicago Press, 1954), 269 pp.
[3] A. Parrot, *The Flood and Noah's Ark* (London: SCM. Press, 1955), 76 pp.
[4] A. M. Rehwinkel, *The Flood* (St. Louis: Concordia Pub. House, 1951), 372 pp.

Ginzberg in that, while their collections are in the nature of anthologies, this investigation considers motives lying back of interpretations.

Though there are a limited number of difficulties inherent in the text of the flood narrative, it is really the *Sitz im Leben* of the post-biblical writers that has determined their treatment of the flood story. Little interest is shown in giving "scientific exegesis." Even if the biblical difficulties are noticed, it is all too often to furnish support for a position already accepted on another basis. Since the presuppositions of the writers are different, it is obvious that their solutions will be different. This thesis will become all the more obvious as the investigation proceeds.

CHAPTER ONE

NOAH AND THE FLOOD IN THE BIBLE

The story of Noah is found in chapters 5:28-10:32 of Genesis. Noah was born in the 182nd year of his father's life (Gen. 5:28). Lamech also had other sons and daughters, though their names are not given. The basis for the choice of the name "Noah" is explained as: "out of the ground which the Lord cursed, this one shall bring us relief (ינחמנו) from our work and from the toil of our hands" (Gen. 5:29). The etymology seems to be a play on the root נוח, "to rest," and נח, "Noah," although the text actually used the root נחם which means "to comfort" or "to relieve."

Noah was the tenth generation from the creation.[1] After his five hundredth year he became the father of three sons: Shem, Ham, and Japheth (Gen. 5:32).

The circumstance which introduces the flood episode is the marriage of the sons of God (בני־האלהים) [2] and the daughters of men (בנות האדם).[3] These unions produced the mighty men (הגברים) of old. It is also stated that the נפלים were on the earth at that time (Gen. 6:4).[4] The Lord declared that His spirit would not always strive (ידון) with man.[5] His days would be limited to 120 years (Gen. 6:3).

---

[1] Adam, Seth, Enosh, Kenan, Mahalalel, Jared, Enoch, Methuselah, Lamech, and Noah, I Chron. 1:1-4; Lk. 3:36-38.

[2] Other books of the O.T. refer to angels as *bene-ha-'elohim* or בני־אלים, Job 1:6; 2:1; 38:7; Ps. 29:1; 89:7 (6); Dan. 3:25-28. N.T. references to a fall of angels are found in II Pet. 2:4; Jude 6. See the studies on this topic: Charles Robert, "Les Fils de Dieu et les Filles de L'Homme," *R.B.*, IV (1895), 340-373; Gustav E. Closen, *Die Sünde der "Söhne Gottes" Gen. 6:1-4* (Rome: Päpstliches Bibelinstitut, 1937), 258 pp.

[3] Though בנות האדם is an *hapax legomenon*, on an analogy with בני־האדם, there can be little doubt that human women are meant.

[4] C. A. Simpson, *The Early Traditions of Israel* (Oxford: Basil Blackwell, 1948), p. 61, argues that some such phrase as "they conceived and bare the Nephilim" has fallen out of the text. This is an unnecessary assumption; see W.H. Green, *The Unity of Genesis* (N.Y.: Scribner's, 1895), p. 58. The notion that נפלים are giants is probably borrowed from the one other occurrence of the root in Scripture, Num. 13:33, where their size frightens the Israelites into comparing themselves with grasshoppers. The efforts to arrive at an etymology for the word usually work from the root נפל, "to fall," but these are less than convincing; see *BDB.*, p. 658.

[5] The dictionaries either leave *yadon* unexplained, *K-B.*, p. 206; emend it to

The imagination of man's heart is described as only evil continually
(Gen. 6:5). The Lord was grieved to His heart that He had made man
(Gen. 6:6), and decided to blot out man, beast, creeping things, and
fowls of the air (Gen. 6:7). The terms "corrupt (תשחת)" and "filled
with violence (תמלא הארץ חמס)" describe the condition of the earth.

Noah, on the other hand, is described as "righteous, blameless in
his generation" (Gen. 6:9). He walked with God. God announced to
Noah His intention to destroy all life and commanded him to build an
ark of gopher wood (עצי־גפר),[1]) with rooms (קנים),[2]) covered inside
and out with pitch (Gen. 6:13-14). The length was to be 300 cubits;
the breadth, 50 cubits; the height, 30 cubits.[3]) There was to be a
"window (צהר; R.S.V., 'roof')"[4]) finished to a cubit above; a door
in the side; and a lower, second, and third deck (Gen. 6:15-16).

The decree of destruction included all flesh that had breath (Gen.
6:17), but a covenant was made with those in the ark: Noah, his
sons, and the wives of the four. Noah was commanded to take two
of every sort of flesh into the ark—male and female (זכר ונקבה)—
of birds, animals, and creeping things—that they might be kept alive
(Gen. 6:18-20). He was to take every sort of food that is eaten (Gen.

ידור; or trace it to לון, *BDB*., pp. 189, 192; see E. A. Speiser, "*Yḏwn*, Gen. 6:3,"
JBL., 75 (June, 1956), 126-129, for an effort to trace ידון to Akkadian *dinānu*;
see also A. Guillaume, "A Note on the Meaning of Gen. 6:3," *AJSL*., 56 (Oct.,
1939), 415-416; and G. R. Berry, "The Interpretation of Gen. 6: 3," *AJSL*., 16
(1899-1900), 47-49.

1) גפר is otherwise unknown as a Semitic word. Some would emend it to
כפר "pitch wood"; see *BDB*., p. 172, or merely say: "the wood of which the
ark was made," *K-B*., p. 191. For a conjecture that there may be a relationship
with the reed material known in Akkadian as *gipar*, see C. C. R. Murphy, "What
is Gopher Wood?" *Asiatic Review*, N.S., 42 (Jan., 1946), 79-81. Such boats are
known to the Arabs by the term *guffah* which in turn shows a sound resemblance
to "גפר." The Koran, Sura 54:13, describes the ark as made of planks and nails.

2) The dictionaries assume that קנים is derived from *ken*, "nest." This assumption would seem to lie back of the LXX reading. For an opinion that קנים
should be read "reeds"—that is the strips of papyrus between the boards—see
Cassuto (*EBI*. II, 11); and E. Ullendorff, "The Construction of Noah's Ark,"
V.T., IV (Jan., 1954), 95-96.

3) It has been estimated that this would give a ship with a displacement of
approximately 43,300 tons; see A. Heidel, *The Gilgamesh Epic* (Chicago: U.
Press, 1954), p. 236.

4) צהר is an *hapax legomenon*. "Window" of K.J.V. does not indicate that the
original here is any different from that of Gen. 8: 6 where חלון occurs. The
reading follows the Vulgate's *fenestram*. *BDB*., p. 844, and *K-B*., p. 796, suggest
from an analogy with roots from Arabic, Assyrian, and the Tel Amarna tablets
that the *ẓohar* is a roof. Cf. Shadal and Cassuto (*EBI*. II, 12).

6:21). It is tersely stated that Noah did what God commanded (Gen. 6:22; 7:5).

Chapter seven proceeds to give an additional order that seven (שבעה שבעה) [1]) clean animals—male and female (איש ואשתו)—were to be taken into the ark in addition to the pairs of those not clean. [2]) There were also to be seven birds (Gen. 7: 2-3). In seven days the rain would come and continue forty days and nights (Gen. 7:4).

When Noah was six hundred years old the flood came, and the men and their wives went into the ark. The account then states that clean and unclean animals went into the ark two and two (Gen. 7:8-9) and the same is repeated in vv. 13-16. The Lord shut Noah in the ark. Seven days later the rain came. The seventeenth day of the second month marks the beginning of the flood.

The sources of water were the fountains of the great deep and the windows of heaven (Gen. 7:11). Rain fell for forty days and nights (Gen. 7:12). The ark floated above the waters which covered the mountains fifteen cubits deep (Gen. 7:20). Everything in whose nostrils was the breath of life died: man, animals, creeping things, and birds of the air. The water prevailed on the earth 150 days. Then God made a wind blow on the earth and the water abated. The sources of water were restrained and the waters receded continuously. On the 17th day of the 7th month the ark came to rest on Mt. Ararat. [3]) On the first day of the tenth month the tops of the mountains were

---

[1]) The repetition expresses distribution; see *GKC.*, § 134 q.

[2]) The effort to solve problems by identification of sources, J and P, within the flood material was unknown in the period covered by this investigation. It is assumed without discussion by all writers that the story is a unit. In as far as the phenomena that are alleged to demand sources are noticed, it is considered that the numbers of ch. 7 supplement those of ch. 6; the divine name alternates to convey different aspects of the divine character; and the figures for the length of the flood supplement each other. Alleged differences in style were completely unnoticed.

[3]) Ararat is the name of a country in II K. 19:37; Is. 37:38; and Jer. 51:27. LXX transliterates the name except in Is. 37:38 where it renders it "Armenia." Modern students tend to identify Ararat with *Urartu* of the Assyrian inscriptions or with modern Armenia; see A. Parrot, *The Flood and Noah's Ark* (London: SCM. Press, 1955), p. 61. Students tend to identify the mountain itself with Massis, N. E. of Lake Van, which rises about 17,000 ft.; see A. Heidel, *The Gilgamesh Epic* (Chicago: U. Press, 1954), pp. 250-251.

The traditional view among the Moslems would identify the mountain with a spot S. W. of Lake Van at Gebel Gûdî; see J. Skinner, *A Critical and Exegetical Commentary on Genesis* (N.Y.: Scribner's, 1910), p. 166. The Koran, Sura 11:46, calls it Mt. Judi. Mt. Nisir of the cuneiform flood stories may be still further south at a spot between the lower Zab and the Adhem; see J. Skinner, *op. cit.*, p. 166, and A. Parrot, *op. cit.*, p. 62.

seen (Gen. 8:5). At the end of forty days Noah opened the window of the ark and sent forth a raven (הָעֹרֵב) [1] which went to and fro (וַיֵּצֵא יָצוֹא וָשׁוֹב) [2] until the waters dried. He then sent forth a dove which returned since she found no place to land. Water was still on the earth (Gen. 8:8-9). Seven days later he sent her forth again. This time she returned with an olive leaf (Gen. 8:10-11). Still seven days later she was again sent forth and did not return.

On the first day of the first month of his 601st year, Noah removed the covering from the ark. The ground was dry. On the 27th day of the second month God commanded that Noah go forth and that he bring the animals, the birds, and the creeping things out that they might breed, be fruitful, and multiply in the earth (Gen. 8:13-17). Noah then built an altar and took of every clean animal and bird and offered a burnt offering. God smelled the odor, was pleased, and said in His heart that He would never again curse the ground because the imagination of man's heart was evil, nor would He destroy every living creature again as He had done. Seed time and harvest, cold and heat, summer and winter, day and night would not cease while the world remains (Gen. 8:20-22).

God blessed Noah and his sons and commanded that they be fruitful, multiply, and fill the earth.[3] It was promised that all birds, animals, and creeping things would be afraid of them. As previously had been given them green plants, now every moving thing would be their food with the exception that the blood was not to be eaten.[4] Man's life blood would be required from the beasts and from man. Man should shed the blood of him who sheds man's blood, for God made man in His image.

---

[1] Hebrew may use an article to denote a person or thing which is as yet unknown as being present to the mind of the writer under given circumstances; see *GKC.*, § 126 q, r, t.

[2] The second infinitive absolute coordinated with the first expresses either accompanying or antithetical action to the first; see *GKC.*, § 113 s.

[3] The text presents the problem of whether the second person imperatives, פְּרוּ וּרְבוּ וּמִלְאוּ and what follows them, are a part of the spoken blessing of God or a statement separate from it with the exact words of the blessing, if any, left unquoted. The same verbs, but in the 3rd per. pl. ind., are used in connection with animals in Gen. 8:17 without a context of blessing; for though blessed at creation, there is no specific blessing on animals after the flood; see J. Skinner, *op. cit.*, p. 169. S. R. Driver, *Genesis* (Westminster Commentaries; London: Methuen, 1909), p. 95, treated the first seven verses of chapter nine as the wording of the blessing.

[4] The prohibition is repeated in the Law as applicable to Israelite and sojourner, Lev. 17:10-14; cf. Lev. 3:17; 7:26-27; Deut. 12:16, 23-25; Ez. 33:25.

God made a covenant with Noah, his sons, descendants, and the living creatures that came from the ark: birds, cattle, and beasts of the earth. Never again would there be a flood to cut off all flesh to destroy the earth (Gen. 9:8-11). God set a bow in the cloud to be a sign of the covenant.[1] It was promised that when clouds came and God saw the bow, He would remember the covenant. It was to be an everlasting covenant between God and every living creature on the earth (Gen. 9:12-27).

Noah now became a farmer and planted a vineyard.[2] He became drunken on the wine and lay uncovered in his tent. Ham saw him and told his two brothers who took a garment, walked backward so as to avoid seeing their father, and covered him with it. Noah awoke and cursed Canaan, Ham's son, that he should be a slave of slaves to his brothers, while they were to be blessed and enlarged (Gen. 9:20-27).

Noah lived 350 years after the flood and died at the age of 950 years. Chapter ten proceeds to enumerate the children born to Noah's sons after the flood. Only the line of Canaan, the son of Ham, need concern us here. His children were Sidon, Heth, the Jebusites, the Amorites, the Girgasites, the Hivites, the Arkites, the Sinites, the Arvadites, the Zemarites, and the Hamathites. The territory of the Canaanites extended from Sidon to Gaza in the direction of Gerar and to Lasha in the direction of Sodom, Gomorrah, Admah, and Zeboiim (Gen. 10:15-19). We note that these people are not said to inhabit Africa.

One further factor from the Bible which is decisive in post-biblical interpretation is the use made of the flood in biblical materials outside of Genesis. Biblical genealogies include the name of Noah in the tenth generation, while the names of his sons follow in immediate sequence (I Chron. 1:4; Lk. 3:36). In later literature Noah is frequently alluded to as an outstanding example of righteousness. Noah already plays this role as early as the time of Ezekiel, for Ezekiel declares that were Noah, Daniel, and Job in a land when God sends a famine, they would deliver but their own lives by their righteousness (Ez. 14:14). If it is pestilence that comes, they can deliver neither son

---

[1] For the rainbow as a natural phenomenon following a rain or for comparisons between the adornments of the throne of God and the colors of the rainbow, see Ez. 1:28; Rev. 4:3; 10:1; *Sir.* 43:11-12; 50:7.

[2] ויחל is likely a *hiph'il* of חלל. The root may either mean "to be profaned" or "to begin," *K-B.*, p. 303. ויחל נח איש האדמה ויטע coordinates a complementary verbal idea with a substantive; see *GKC.*, § 120 b.

nor daughter, but only their own lives (Ez. 14:20). Since Noah did deliver his sons in the days of the flood, this passage not only presents Noah as the righteous man, but it also makes it necessary to ask whether or not his sons were also righteous men.

The phrase "waters of Noah" is used in the book of Isaiah to introduce the idea of an unchangeable covenant. As God had promised Noah that the waters of the flood would no more cover the earth, so in the exile He swears that in days to come He will no more be angry with His people. The promise is as unchangeable as the hills (Is. 54:9-10).

In a context which praises the might of the Lord (Ps. 29:10), the Lord is said to sit enthroned above the flood (למבול). Since this is the one single occurrence in the MT. of the term מבול outside the flood section of Genesis, it is possible that Noah's flood is in the writer's view, despite the fact that the idea of God's throne over the waters is also found in Ps. 104:3.

The wickedness of the flood generation and its destruction may be alluded to in Job 22:15 ff. where wicked men were snatched away before their time as their foundation was washed away. Despite God's filling their homes with good things, they said to God, "Depart from us," and "What can the Almighty do to us?"

In addition to the above mentioned explicit references to Noah and the flood, certain poetic and apocalyptic sections of the Bible may borrow from the flood motif and combine it with pictures of an earthquake to give a picture of judgment. Isaiah announces that the Lord will lay waste the earth and make it desolate. The earth is staggering from transgression. Everlasting covenants have been broken (Is. 24:1, 4-5; cf. Gen. 9:16). The windows of heaven are opened and the foundations of the earth tremble (Is. 24:18; cf. Gen. 7:11; 8:2). A few are preserved by entering their chambers until the wrath is past (Is. 26:20-21). Other contributing elements to the concept would likely be the phrase "overflowing wrath (שצף קצף)" of Is. 54:8 (Isaiah's opponents thought it would affect the enemies of the nation, but the prophet makes clear that Israel is to suffer in her approaching defeat that led to exile [Is. 28:14-18; cf. 8:8]); שטף עבר (κατακλυσμός; "overflowing flood"), Nah. 1:8, describes the punishment of Nineveh; and the "flood (שטף, cf. κατακλυσμός)" of Dan. 9:26 destroys the city and sanctuary after the 62 weeks of Daniel's vision. In the metaphors used by the Psalmist, frequently a storm of great waters is used to express the tribulation of the righteous from which only the intervention of God can save them (Ps. 18:16; 65:5-8; 69:1; 89:9; 93:3).[1]) If the surmise is correct that these figures were suggested to the writer by Gen. 6-9,[2]) then we can see one stage by which the flood became a type of the end of the world in apocalyptic.

The treatment of the flood in Genesis and the later interpretations of it in biblical materials make up one important factor in the background of all writers included in this study. From this survey some questions present themselves as inherent in this narrative and also set the problems for the post-biblical commentators: (1) Who are the בני־האלהים? (2) What was the sin of the generation of the flood? (3) What was the character of Noah? (4) How was one ship able to hold the creatures prescribed? (5) How many of each sort of animal were in the ark—two, seven, or fourteen? (6) How widespread was the flood? (7) What is the significance of Noah's drunkenness? (8) What does the curse on Canaan imply?

As we proceed through the study, we shall see how the *Sitz im Leben* of the individual writers not only determines the treatment they give to minor details of the flood story but is especially determinative in the solutions they propose to these problems. Special attention is given by the sources to the motifs of Noah as the exemplary righteous man, the flood generation as the epitome of wickedness, and to the flood as a figure for God's punishment which destroys wicked humanity, but out of which a remnant is saved by grace to be the beginning of a new race. This last idea can refer to any great calamity, but easily lends itself in apocalyptic to pictures of the times of the end.

---

[1]) E. Hoskyns and N. Davey, *The Riddle of the N.T.* (London: Faber and Faber, Ltd., 1958), pp. 69-70.

[2]) S. H. Blank, *Prophetic Faith in Isaiah* (N. Y.: Harper and Bros., 1958), pp. 165-166; E. J. Kissane, *The Book of Isaiah* (Dublin: Browne and Nolan, Ltd., 1960), I, 275; J. Daniélou, *Sacramentum Futuri* (Paris: Beauchesne et ses fils, 1950), pp. 55 ff.

CHAPTER TWO

NOAH AND THE FLOOD AS INTERPRETED IN THE APOCRYPHA AND PSEUDEPIGRAPHA OF THE OLD TESTAMENT

When one turns from the Bible to the books of the Apocrypha and Pseudepigrapha he immediately recognizes that he has moved into a new realm of interpretation differing from that seen even in the later books of the O.T. No unity of thought is to be assumed for the Apocrypha and Pseudepigrapha. Certain common trends are observable, but each writer writes out of his own situation. The non-canonical writer assumes without discussion the historicity of the Pentateuchal narrative. Men of the past are his heroes and examples; embellishments are freely used; biblical materials are reworked to furnish descriptions of different situations from that to which they originally applied; and current day theological beliefs are read back into biblical narratives.

The first major question concerning the flood raised by the extra-canonical literature is: Is there a Book of Noah? In view of the tendency of pseudepigraphical writers to attribute books to most of the important O.T. characters, it would be exceedingly strange if Noah were overlooked. At the same time, it must be admitted that while ancient lists of Pseudepigrapha knew of a book of Lamech [1]) and of a book of Noria, the wife of Noah,[2]) no mention of a book of Noah survives in any ancient list now known to us.[3])

---

[1]) The list of Sixty Books has Lamech third in order; see M. R. James, *The Lost Apocrypha of the O.T.* (London: SPCK., 1920), pp. xii, 10-11. The Qumran scroll which before its unrolling was speculatively identified with the Lamech Apocalypse, see D. Barthélemy and J. T. Milik, *Discoveries in the Judean Desert, Qumran Cave I* (Oxford: Clarendon Press, 1955), I, 86, is now designated by its editors as the *Genesis Apocryphon*; see N. Avigad and Y. Yadin, *A Genesis Apocryphon* (Jerusalem: Magnes Press of the Hebrew University, 1956), pp. 7-8. We still do not have the Lamech Apocalypse and know nothing of its contents.

[2]) Epiphanius, *Pan. haer.* xxvi. I (*GCS*. 25. 275-276) quotes a Christian production, *The Book of Noria*, in which Noria the wife of Noah is the leading character. The work was produced by the Barbarite Gnostics and is of decided Gnostic tendencies. Noria repeatedly attempts to frustrate the building of the ark and even delays the process by burning it. Various forms of this legend were widespread in the Middle Ages; see M. R. James, *op. cit.*, pp. 12-15. In the Koran, Sura 66:10, she is finally condemned to Hell.

[3]) M. R. James, *op. cit.*, p. 11.

Of considerable importance in forming the case for the Noah book are three passages in the Pseudepigrapha in which appeal is made to the writings of Noah. The earliest allusions to such writings are in the *Bk. of Jubilees*. The first passage tells how Noah was taught the arts of healing by an angel that he might instruct his children how to overcome the evils begun by the evil spirits, the offspring of the Watchers. The book was then delivered to Shem (*Jub.* 10:13-14). The second allusion speaks of certain halachic matters dealing with regulations governing the eating of sacrificial meat found "written in the books of my forefathers, and in the words of Enoch, and in the words of Noah" (*Jub.* 21:10). Further halachic regulations demanding that the blood be covered in the earth before flesh is eaten are traced back to Abraham, in the Gk. fragment of *T. Levi*, to form the third passage. Abraham is said to have learned this rule from "the writing of the Book of Noah concerning the blood" (Gk. frag. *T. Levi* 56-57). The various passages present Noah as a transmitter of esoteric and halachic materials. It is to be noted, however, that the materials ordinarily ascribed to a Book of Noah hardly correspond to this description.

The view was popularized by R. H. Charles,[1]) though later denied by C. C. Torrey and S. Frost,[2]) that certain sections of I *Enoch* and *Jubilees* are to be traced back to a Noah book. The relevant sections are: I *Enoch* 6-11; 60; 65-69:25; 106-107; and *Jubilees* 7:20-39; 10:1-15. Probable also are I *Enoch* 39:1-2a; 41:3-8; 43-44; 54:7-55:2; and 59. It is widely believed that I *Enoch* is composite and thereby it is not difficult to conceive that the author could have used a Noah source. The material, however, has little in common with the material ascribed to Noah which was alluded to in the preceding paragraph of this study.[3]) A writer surveying Pentateuchal history as both *Jubilees* and *Enoch* do could hardly escape covering the flood. It is far from certain that these sections establish the existence of a Noah book.

Three divergent accounts are given of the origin and contents of the Hebrew Book of Noah, parts of which are extant.[4]) The first

---

[1]) R. H. Charles, *The Book of Enoch* (Oxford: Clarendon Press, 1912), pp. xlvi f.; *The Book of Jubilees* (London: A. and C. Black, 1902), pp. lxxi-lxxii.

[2]) C. C. Torrey, *The Apocryphal Literature* (New Haven: Yale U. Press, 1948), p. 112; S. Frost, *O.T. Apocalyptic* (London: Epworth Press, 1952), p. 166.

[3]) I *Enoch* 6-11; 39:1-2a; 67:4-69:29 deal with the fall of the angels; 41:3-9; 43-44; 59; 60 deal with astronomical secrets; and 10:1-3; 54:7-55:2; 65-67:3; and 106-107 deal with the flood itself.

[4]) The text is found in A. Jellinek, *Bet Ha-Midrasch* (Leipzig: C. W. Vollrath,

account, traceable back to the eleventh century and ordinarily known as the Book of Asaf the Jew, tells how the book was taken by the sages from a book of Shem's. After the flood it had been given to Shem by Noah on Mt. Lubar which belonged to the mountains of Ararat. At that time the unclean spirits began to overcome the sons of Noah through sickness and pain. The sons of Noah assembled and told their troubles to him. Noah knew that sickness came as a result of sin; hence he sanctified his descendants and made an offering and a supplication to God.

God sent the angel of the presence, named Raphael, to destroy the spirits from the earth so that they should bother man no more. After shutting them all up in the house of judgment, except for one-tenth which were left under the dominion of Mastema for the purpose of punishing evildoers with various sicknesses, the angel began the art of healing by the use of trees, plants, and roots. The chief of the remaining spirits was sent to Noah to teach him the art of such healings and the location where the proper herbs were to be found. Noah then wrote these things in a book and gave them to his eldest son Shem. From this source the knowledge of healing has dispersed to the Indians, Macedonians, and Egyptians.

Rönsch has correctly pointed out that the material in this first account agrees in all essentials with the story related in chapter ten of *Jubilees*.[1]) It is best thought of as a Hebrew fragment from that book,[2]) and for that reason is no independent evidence for a Noah book.

The second account of the book, borrowed from the collection of the ancient writings made by R. Elasar of Worms, tells how Adam prayed after being cast out of Eden. The angel Raziel gave him a book from which later generations, if worthy, could know all that was to happen. After the angel read the book to Adam, it was hidden. Later, the existence of the book was made known to Enoch in a dream, and he found it in a cave. From the book Enoch learned the course of the stars, the names of the ministering angels, the names of the earth, the heaven, the sun and the moon. Eventually there arose Noah, the

---

1857), III, 155-160, and in R. H. Charles, *The Ethiopic Versions of the Hebrew Book of Jubilees* (Oxford: Clarendon Press, 1895), p. 179. An analysis of the material is to be found in H. Rönsch, *Das Buch der Jubiläen* (Leipzig: Fues's Verlag, 1874), pp. 385-388.

[1]) H. Rönsch, *op. cit.*, pp. 387-388; cf. L. Ginzberg, *The Legends of the Jews* (Phila.: Jewish Pub. Soc., 1909-1955), I, 156-157; V, 177.

[2]) A. Jellinek, *op. cit.*, III, xxxi.

man righteous and perfect in his generation. In his 500th year the earth was destroyed by deeds of violence since all flesh had corrupted its way. The cry of the earth went up before the throne of the glory of God, but Noah found favor in the eyes of the Lord. The angel Raphael, the holy prince, was sent unto him to heal the earth. The angel gave him the book and made him understand what his task was. He reminded him that the book was given because God had found him perfect in his generation. Through it he would learn to make the ark (literally: "gopher wood") and to enter it, he and his family, to hide until the wrath should cease. Having understood from the book his obligation to take the two and the seven animals, Noah hid the book before he went into the ark. God closed him in and the flood was on for forty days and nights. Noah then blessed God in a blessing in which he stated that it was from the book that he had understood how to tell when it was day or night and what animals to feed at what time. God heard the prayer, made a wind dry the water, and the ark landed at Ararat. Noah handed the book on to Shem, and then it was passed on from generation to generation.[1])

The third account of the book, also stemming from R. Elasar of Worms, speaks of the book of secrets plainly written on sapphire stone given by Raziel to Noah in the year he entered the ark.[2]) From the book Noah learned things related to those spoken of in the second account just mentioned; but in addition, the book had the arts of healing, the interpretation of dreams, exorcism of spirits, and the meaning of thunder and lightning, as well as the means of discerning good and evil. From it Noah also learned to make an ark of gopher wood, to seal it from the waters of the flood, and to collect the animals and food. He put it into a golden box that he suspended in the ark in order that he might know day from night. After he went from the ark, the book aided him all his life and was then handed on in an unbroken succession until it came to Solomon who also made good use of it.

Jellinek saw in this Hebrew Noah material support for the contention that a book of Noah had been used to supplement the Ethiopic book of Enoch.[3]) We have seen, however, that the first account is to be considered a version of the tenth chapter of *Jubilees*. After the

---

[1]) *Ibid.*, III, xxxii, 157-159; cf. *Sefer Hayashar*, *Noah* (*EBI.* II, 18).
[2]) The connection with Enoch given in the second account is omitted in the third.
[3]) A. Jellinek, *op. cit.*, III, xxxii.

biblical and the Enoch materials have been eliminated from the other accounts, very little remains that cannot be paralleled in the Haggadah. Without an *a priori* judgment that a Noah book lay back of Enoch, it is difficult to see how more than folklore is needed to explain the source of these fragments. If this be true, then the fragments do not make impossible the case for a Noah book, but neither do they sustain it.

The most recent contribution to our problem is the material from the Qumran caves. The *Genesis Apocryphon* devotes considerable space to Noah. Since the scroll is as yet unpublished in its entirety, one is completely dependent upon the preliminary report which would indicate that columns II to XV deal with the birth of Noah, the flood, and its sequel.[1]) However, only column II of this material has been transcribed. In column II, Lamech is the speaker. Supposing that his child was begotten by the Watchers or fallen angels, he causes his wife, *BT'NWŠ*, to swear that the child is his.[2]) Lamech then goes to Methuselah, and Methuselah goes to Enoch to enquire of him.

Column III, though badly damaged, would seem to contain Enoch's answer. Line three has words about Enoch's father that correspond to I *Enoch* 107:13. The material seems to have little in common with Genesis 5 which reports the birth of Noah; but on the other hand, it is five times as long as the speech Enoch makes in I *Enoch*.

Column VI, line six, has Noah speak in the first person and tell of his marriage and of his taking wives for his sons. Column VII would seem to tell the story of the flood. Columns VIII and IX are damaged, but in column X, line twelve, the ark rests on a mountain in Ararat. Here Noah makes an atonement. Column XI reports a covenant God made with Noah in which the eating of blood is prohibited (cf. *Jub.* 6:13). In column XII the descendants of Noah are dealt with. Noah becomes a planter upon Mt. Lubar in line 13 (cf. *Jub.* 7). When the vines are ready, he makes a feast with his children. Other columns would perhaps contain the division of the earth among the sons of Noah.

Yadin notes repeated examples of parallels to *Jubilees*. There also the wife of Lamech is Betenos, though she is the daughter of his father's brother (or sister), while here she addresses him as "Lord and Brother." In *Jubilees*, also, the ark lands on Lubar. Yadin suggests that

---

[1]) N. Avigad and Y. Yadin, *A Genesis Apocryphon* (Jerusalem: Magnes Press of the Hebrew University, 1956), pp. 16-21.

[2]) Cf. *Jub.* 4:28.

since the *Apocryphon* is more detailed than *Jubilees*, it is a possible source from which *Jubilees* has drawn.[1])

Brief fragments, supposed by their editors to be remains of a Book of Noah that may have been the source for I Enoch, have been found in Qumran Cave I. Photographs, transcriptions, and a French translation have been published.[2]) The first of these fragments seems to describe the moral state of man and the decision to destroy the earth which material more or less corresponds to I *Enoch* 6-10. The second describes the intercession of the four angels.[3]) The third tells of the birth of Noah (cf. I *Enoch* 106); while the fourth group is perhaps a song of Methuselah.[4])

Starcky has reported that Cave IV has two fairly large fragments relating to Noah literature as well as some texts describing cosmological visions of the type found in I *Enoch*.[5])

Because of the fragmentary nature of the Qumran material, it is hazardous to venture guesses about its content and literary relationships. This is particularly true where the actual texts have not been published in full. We must conclude that as yet we do not have the Book of Noah and actually that beyond conjecture, we know very little about it; nor are we at all certain that such a book ever existed.

The idea of Noah as a writer belongs to the cycle of material which pictured the patriarchs as transmitters of esoteric materials. Also to this cycle belongs the warning given by Eve before her death of two judgments which were to come. The first would be by water, and the second by fire. She exhorted her children to make tablets of stone and brick upon which they inscribed their record so that it would survive either trial (*Vita Adae et Evae* 49:3 ff.).[6]) This passage is of considerable importance in the history of the idea of a flood of fire.[7])

Turning more directly to matters of interpretation, we will consider the flood as a hortatory device. The practice of drawing moral lessons from the details of episodes in the Pentateuch is the common heritage

---

[1]) N. Avigad and Y. Yadin, *op. cit.*, pp. 18-21.
[2]) D. Barthélemy and J. T. Milik, *Discoveries in the Judean Desert, Qumran Cave I* (Oxford: Clarendon Press, 1955), I, 84.
[3]) *Ibid.*, I, 152.
[4]) *Ibid.*, I, 84.
[5]) J. Starcky, "Cave 4 of Qumran," *B.A.*, XIX (1956), 94-96.
[6]) Warnings of approaching flood made by the antediluvian patriarchs are to be found in *Bk. of Adam and Eve* ii. 8, 21, 22; *T. Adam* iii. 15 and 1 *Enoch. Jub.* 8:3 speaks of records of patriarchs written on stone.
[7]) Cf. Josephus, *Ant.* i. 2. 3; *Mekilta, Amalek* iii. 14; *Or. Sib.* iii. 690; Philo, *Mos.* ii. 263.

of all Bible believing peoples. Each of the literary groups surveyed
in this study is interested in the flood from this viewpoint. It is in the
particular lesson drawn and the manner by which he arrives at that
lesson that each writer reveals his life situation.

Not every writer who deals with the בני־האלהים displays a primary
moral interest in the episode, but enough do to justify considering
the problem here. Each of the three historic interpretations of the
term can be seen in various passages of the Apocrypha and Pseudepigrapha. The earliest of these is that the בני־האלהים are angels. Sizeable
portions of the "Noah material" of I *Enoch*, filled with details of the
fall of angels and their activities on earth, serve only the purpose of
being a part of the survey of history revealed to Enoch in apocalyptic
fashion. These sections reveal the advanced angelology of the inter-
testamental period with specific names and functions assigned to each
angel. According to I *Enoch*, "the angels, the children of heaven,"
saw and lusted after the comely daughters of men, decided to choose
wives and beget children of them. Led by Semjaza, and nineteen
other chiefs, two hundred under oath to each other descended to Mt.
Hermon in the days of Jared (I *Enoch* 6:1-6; cf. 9:7-8; 10:11; 15:3-5;
64:1-2; 69:4). The fallen angels, known as Watchers,[1]) proceeded to
teach various arts, enchantments, sins, and other secrets to men (I
Enoch 8:1 f.; 9:8-9).[2]) Beyond the abyss at the end of the heaven,
Uriel showed Enoch the place of imprisonment of these angels in
eternal fire as they waited the judgment day and informed him that
the women with whom they had had connection became sirens (I
Enoch 19:1-2; 64:1-2). The fall of the angels is repeated in another
section of the book in apocalyptic symbolism. The daughters of men
are cows. Stars descend from heaven, become bulls, pasture with the
cows, and beget offspring which are elephants, camels, and asses.

---

[1]) I *Enoch* 1:5; 10:9, 15; 12:4; 13:10; 14:1, 3; 15:2; 16:1, 2; 91:15; cf.
"Watchful inventors because they had a sleepless mind," *Or. Sib.* i. 115.

[2]) References to women being taught cosmetics, adornments, and secrets
by angels are to be found in: Irenaeus, *Demonst.* 18; Clement of A., *Strom.* v.
10. 2 (*GCS.* 15. 332); Tertullian, *De cult. fem.* i. 2; ii. 10 (*CSEL.* 70. 60-62; 88-89);
Cyprian, *De hab. virg.* 14 (*CSEL.* 3. 1. 197); Ps.-Clem., *Hom.* viii. 14 (*GCS.*
42. 127); Julius Africanus, *Chron.* 2 (*PG.* 10. 65 C). References to angels as teachers
of astrology are to be found in Tertullian, *De idol.* 9 (*CSEL.* 20. 38), and Tatian,
Orat. ad Gr. 8. Tatian does not discuss the origin of demons, but has them teach
astrology. This must be premised on the same legend. In contrast, Serenius
has the line of Seth learn enchantment from the line of Cain. Ham inscribed these
superstitions on plates of metal and upon rocks, and then found them after the
flood; see John Cassian, *Collatio* VIII. 21 (*CSEL.* 13. 2. 240).

Following the great wickednesses which resulted, the stars are thrown into the abyss (I *Enoch* 86-88; cf. 90:21).

With only minor variations the same account of the angels—the Watchers—is given in the *Book of Jubilees* in another apocalyptic, but midrashic, survey of history. They descend in the days of Jared to instruct men to do judgment and uprightness (*Jub.* 4:15).[1]) By the days of Enoch they had united with the daughters of men so that Enoch testified against them (*Jub.* 4:22).[2])

Other surveys which assume this interpretation would be the *Gen. Apocryphon* where Lamech is afraid his child was begotten by the Watchers (*Gen. Apoc.* II, l. 16) and II *Baruch* where the history of the world is presented in symbolism of dark and bright rain. The darkness of darkness is reached following Adam's sin:

> For he became a danger to his own soul: even to the angels became he a danger. For, moreover, at the time when he was created, they enjoyed liberty. And some of them descended, and mingled with women. And then those who did so were tormented in chains. But the rest of the multitude of the angels, of which there is no number, restrained themselves. And those who dwelt on the earth perished together with them through the waters of the deluge (II *Bar.* 56:10-15).

Once an interpretation is established, it is only a short step to a homily based on that interpretation. This step is taken by the *Testaments of the 12 Patriarchs*. Reuben warns women to beware of external adornments:

> For thus they allured the Watchers who were before the flood; for as these continually beheld them, they lusted after them, and they conceived the act in their mind; for they changed themselves into the shape of men, and appeared to them when they were with their husbands. And the women lusting in their minds after their forms, gave birth to giants, for the Watchers appeared to them as reaching unto heaven (*T. Reub.* 5:6-7; cf. *Dam. Frag.* 3:2-5).

This writer seems to shy away from actually declaring that sexual union took place between angels and women, and makes the Watchers a sort of prenatal influence on the fetus when he says the women were "with their husbands." Naphtali makes the Watchers an example,

---

[1]) Cf. *Dam. Frag.* 3: 4-7; *Gen. Apoc.* col. 2; the angels come to earth to convict men of ingratitude toward God in Ps.-Clem., *Hom.* viii. 12 (*GCS.* 42. 126).

[2]) Ps.-Clem., *Recog.* I. 29 (*PG.* 1. 1223), has them appear in the ninth generation from Adam.

along with Sodom, in his warning against changing the order of
nature:

> In like manner the Watchers also changed the order of their nature,
> whom the Lord cursed at the flood, on whose account He made the earth
> without inhabitant and fruitless (*T. Naph.* 3:5).

In the *Damascus Fragment*, in the midst of a warning against evil
imagination, they become an example of stubbornness and failure to
keep the commandment of God:

> Because they walked in the stubbornness of their heart the Watchers
> of heaven fell. By them [in the thoughts of imagination] were they caught
> because they kept not the commandment of God (*Dam. Frag.* 3:4).

A textual variant found in the Syriac version of *Sirach* in a passage
discussing God's wrath against the wicked reads "ancient kings"
where the LXX reads "giants of old time (ἀρχαῖοι γίγαντες)" (*Sir.*
16:7). This Syriac reading possibly reflects a rabbinic view (*Gen. R.*
26. 5) that the בני־אלהים were the sons of the nobles.

The third interpretation of the בני־האלהים reflects a reaction against
identifying them with angels. As early as the time of Julius Africanus,
they were identified with the descendants of Seth.[1] In the Pseudepigrapha, this interpretation is found in *T. Adam* iii. 15 and in the *Bk.
of Adam and Eve* iii. 4, the latter of which while specifically rejecting
the angelic explanation goes some length to explain that the descendants of Seth remained on the Holy Mountain until the time of Enoch.
At that time one hundred men of them descended to the plain where
the daughters of Cain dwelt with beautiful figures, hands and feet
dyed with colors, and with tatooed ornaments on their faces. After
defiling themselves, the Sethites found it impossible to return to the
mountain (*Bk. of Adam and Eve* ii. 20). Though the book takes the
general pattern of a survey of history, implicit in its treatment of this
story is a warning against mixed marriages with ungodly people.

The treatment given the "mighty men of old (הגברים)," their
activities, and their fate reflects the *Sitz* of the writers in a very clear
way. For the extra-canonical writer, these men were giants (γίγαντες)
in agreement with the reading of the LXX, and were the offspring
of the בני־האלהים.[2] Enoch informs us that they were 3,000 ells in

---

[1] Julius Africanus, *Chron.* 2 (*PG.* 10. 65 B).
[2] *Sir.* 16:7; *Wisd.* 14:6; I *Bar.* 3:26; III *Macc.* 2:4; *T. Reub.* 5:7; *Or. Sib.*
i. 145. Other references to the giants as offspring of the Watchers are to be
found in I *Enoch* 106:17; Philo, *Gig.* 58; *QG.* i. 92; Josephus, *Ant.* i. 3. 1 f.;

height (I *Enoch* 7:2).¹) Three types of giants are assumed in the imagery of elephants, camels, and asses produced by the fallen stars (I *Enoch* 86:4; cf. 88:2).²) The giants consumed the acquisitions of men and then the men themselves. Next they sinned against birds, beasts, reptiles, and fish; and then they turned to cannibalism and blood drinking (I *Enoch* 7:4-5). Enoch sees in his sleep that the spirits of the giants would become evil spirits on earth to rise up against men and women (I *Enoch* 15:12).³)

The treatment of this theme in *Jubilees* is taken over from I *Enoch*. The offspring are Naphidim who are all unlike each other. They devour one another: the giants slay the Naphil, and the Naphil slay the Eljo, and the Eljo slay mankind (*Jub.* 7:22). Here also the evil demons are the sons of the Watchers (*Jub.* 10:1-7).

According to still another writer, 409,000 giants were destroyed in the flood (III *Bar.* 4:10).⁴)

For the writer interested in homilies, the punishment of these giants, "who revolted in their might," may serve as an example of God's wrath against the wicked (*Sir.* 16:7). The giants themselves may be an example of the lack of wisdom:

The giants were born there, who were famous of old, great in stature, expert in war. God did not choose them, nor give them the way to knowledge; so they perished because they had no wisdom, they perished through their own folly (I *Bar.* 3:26-28). ⁵)

Or again, the giants may illustrate the folly of arrogance and of trusting in one's own strength (III *Macc.* 2:4).⁶)

Dam. *Frag.* 3: 4-5; Athenagoras, *Supplic. pro Christ.* 24; Ps.-Clem., *Hom.* viii. 15 (*GCS.* 42. 127); and Sulpicius Severus, *Chron.* i. 2 (*CSEL.* 1. 5). The *Bk. of Adam and Eve* iii. 4 takes exception to it.

¹) Cf. *Dam. Frag.* 3:4-5 where their height was like the loftiness of cedars and their bodies were like mountains. Ps-Clem., *Hom.* viii. 15 (*GCS.* 42. 127), characterizes them as: "greater than men in size in as much as they were sprung of angels, yet less than angels in as much as they were born of women."

²) R. H. Charles, *The Bk. of Enoch* (Oxford: Clarendon Press, 1912), p. 18.

³) Other allusions to the spirits of the giants becoming demons are to be found in *Jub.* 10:1-9; cf. Tertullian, *Apol.* 22. 3-4 (*CSEL.* 69. 61); Justin M., *Apol.* ii. 5; Lactantius, *Div. inst.* ii. 14 (*CSEL.* 19. 162-163).

⁴) Cf. *Or. Sib.* ii. 283 for giants destroyed in the deluge. The *Bk. of Adam and Eve* iii. 4 speaks of "Garsina who were giants, mighty men of valor" unequalled in might.

⁵) This writer uses οἱ ὀνομαστοί to describe the fame of these giants just as does the LXX in Gen. 6:4; see H. St. John Thackeray, *The Septuagint and Jewish Worship* (London: Humphrey Milford, 1923), p. 98.

⁶) The giants are further alluded to in I *Bar.* 3:26-28, cited in Augustine, *Civ.*

Since the Scripture uses only general terms to describe the degradation of the flood generation, the bill of particulars furnished by any writer is an area in which he will reflect the religious mores of his time. While in the less descriptive accounts there are examples of very general statements as "deeds of violence since all flesh had corrupted his way" (Heb. *Bk. of Noah*), other writers become quite specific. In I *Enoch* a long list includes: practicing arts of metal work to furnish implements of war and ornaments (I *Enoch* 8:1; cf. 65); godlessness and fornication; enchantments and knowledge of signs (I *Enoch* 8:2-3); murder (I *Enoch* 9:9); idolatry (I *Enoch* 65:6 f.); sorceries (I *Enoch* 65:10); wickedness and deceit (I *Enoch* 93:4; cf. 86:5-6). A moral state somewhat comparable to this one is evidently reflected in the manuscript, fragments of which were found in Qumran Cave I.[1]) *Jubilees* is no less specific. The corruption of orders by all flesh, by which is probably meant interbreeding,[2]) brought on the decree of destruction—that God's spirit "should not always abide on man; for they are flesh, and their days shall be 120 years." In another passage we learn that fornication, uncleanness, and all impurity are the sins that brought the flood (*Jub.* 7:20-21).[3])

And everyone sold himself to work iniquity and to shed much blood, and the earth was filled with iniquity. And after this they sinned against the beasts and birds, and all that moves and walks on the earth: and much blood was shed on the earth, and every imagination and desire of men imagined vanity and evil continually (*Jub.* 7:23-24).

The *Sibylline Oracles* furnishes a list in a sermon by Noah: fighting and murder (*Or. Sib.* i. 180 f.), loving shame, tyrants, liars, filled with unbelief, adulterers, and flippant (*Or. Sib.* i. 205 f.).

The list of II *Enoch* has been handed down in two recensions:

They will not carry the yoke which I have laid upon them, nor sow the seeds which I have given them, but having cast off my yoke, they will take another yoke, and will sow empty seeds and will bow down to vain gods and reject my oneness, and the whole earth will quake with injustice, wrongs, and fornication and idolatry (II *Enoch* 34:1-2, text B).

Dei 15. 23 (*CSEL.* 40. 2. 114); III *Macc.* 2:3-4; *Wisd.* 14:6; Cyril of Jer., *De Catech.* ii. 8 (*PG.* 33. 392 B); John Cassian, *Collatio* VIII. 21 (*CSEL.* 13. 2. 240); and Jerome, *Ep.* 10. 1 (*CSEL.* 54. 35).

[1]) D. Barthélemy and J. T. Milik, *op. cit.*, I, 84.

[2]) Cf. *T. Naph.* 3:5 where the Watchers change the "order of nature."

[3]) Cf. *Gen. R.* 31. 6 where idolatry, impurity, and bloodshed bring the flood; and the *Bk. of Adam and Eve* iii. 25 which insists that adultery caused the flood and that idolatry started only after the flood.

More specific is the recension called "A" by R. H. Charles:

They would not bow down to me, but have begun to bow down to vain gods, and denied my unity, and have laden the whole earth with untruths, offences, abominable lecheries, namely one with another, and all manner of other unclean wickednesses, which are disgusting to relate (II *Enoch* 34:2, text A).

The picture of Noah as the exemplary righteous man of the past which earlier appeared in Ez. 14:14, 20 is carried further in the Apocrypha. *Sirach* proposes to "praise famous men . . . whose deeds of righteousness have not been forgotten . . . and their glory will not be blotted out." In the proposed list, Noah stands between Enoch and Abraham:

Noah was found perfect and righteous; in the time of wrath he was taken in exchange; [1]) therefore a remnant was left to the earth when the flood came. [2]) Everlasting covenants were made with him that all flesh should not be blotted out by a flood (*Sir.* 44:17).

In the midst of a description of a general resurrection for mankind, Benjamin continues this high estimate of Noah as he proclaims, "Ye shall see Enoch, Noah, and Shem and Abraham, and Isaac, and Jacob rising on the right hand in gladness" (*T. Benj.* 10:6). A unique turn is given to Noah's righteousness by Tobit when he makes Noah, Abraham, Isaac, and Jacob all examples of men who took wives of their kinsmen (*Tobit* 4:12). Tobit is in the midst of a warning against foreign marriages. Since Scripture has not one word on Noah's marriage, Tobit is obviously ascribing to the patriarch a virtue of his own day. The legend of his marriage to a relative is also to be found in *Jub.* 4:33.

No less obvious is the tendentious ascetic turn in the *Bk. of Adam and Eve* where Noah from youth afflicted his soul. When he was with his parents, he obeyed them. When apart from them he obeyed God. He maintained his chastity until his 500th year, at which time God commanded him to marry (*Bk. of Adam and Eve* iii. 1).

---

[1]) The translation of "taken in exchange" stems from LXX, ἀντάλαγμα. The Hebrew (perhaps תחליף) is problematical; see note of R. H. Charles, *A. and P.*, I, 483.

[2]) It is possible that *Sirach* knew the effort to obtain an etymology for Noah from ינוח, "to be left"; cf. I *Enoch* 83:8; 107:3; II *Enoch* 35:1; *Bk. of Adam and Eve* ii. 21; *Wisd.* 14:6; Ps.-Clem., *Recog.* iv. 12 (*PG.* 1. 1319). Origen reports that a Jew had used Ez. 14:14 in this sense, *Hom. Ez.* iv. 8 (*GCS.* 33. 369). This is an effort to project the doctrine of the remnant of the prophets; see J. Daniélou, *Sacramentum Futuri* (Paris: Beauchesne et ses Fils, 1950), p. 61.

In many other passages Noah's righteousness is noticed in passing, but with less obvious homiletical intent than in the cases just mentioned: I *Enoch* 67:1; cf. "the white bull," 89:1 ff.; "faithful and to all good works attentive" (*Or. Sib.* i. 148-149); and "faithful, just" (*Or. Sib.* i. 317).[1]

The writers find numerous other virtues illustrated in the flood episode. Wisdom is given credit for saving the earth:

> And when for his [Cain's] cause the earth was drowning with a flood, Wisdom again saved it, guiding the righteous man's course by a poor piece of wood (*Wisd.* 10:4).

On the other hand we have already seen that the giants are an example of those without wisdom (I *Bar.* 3:26-28).

Baruch finds an example of fidelity in Noah's dove and Elijah's raven by which he can admonish the eagle who is entrusted with his letter to the nine and one-half tribes who dwell beyond the Euphrates:

> Remember, moreover, that at the time of the deluge, Noah received from a dove the fruit of the olive, when he sent it forth from the ark (II *Bar.* 77:23).

The writer of IV *Maccabees*, interested in demonstrating that devout reason rules supreme over the passions,[2] finds the ark beset by the flood an example of the devout reason beset by the passions. With this figure he can praise the mother who saw her seven sons destroyed:

> O woman, nobler to resist than men, and braver than warriors to endure! For as the ark of Noah, with the whole living world for her burden in the world-whelming deluge, did withstand the mighty surges, so thou, the keeper of the Law, beaten upon every side by the surging waves of passions, and strained as with the strong blasts the tortures of thy sons did nobly weather the storms that assailed thee for religion's sake (IV *Macc.* 15:30-32). [3]

The vice of wine drinking finds itself considered by the writer of the Gk. *Apocalypse of Baruch*. Baruch, on his trip through the heavens, is perplexed to know how the vine which is considered the forbidden tree of the Garden of Eden could now be useful in the Eucharist. The

---

[1]) Cf. *Wisd.* 10:4; II *Enoch* 33:8-35:3; IV *Ezra* 3:8-13; Heb. *Bk. of Noah* (A. Jellinek, *op. cit.*, II, 158).

[2]) R. H. Pfeiffer, *Hist. of N. T. Times* (N. Y.: Harper and Bros., 1949), p. 215.

[3]) The imagery here used is less detailed, but not greatly different in substance from Philo's allegory which makes the flood a storm of passion within the soul.

seer who is guiding him informs him that when the waters of the flood entered paradise,[1]) they destroyed every flower and cast the shoot of the vine outside. After the flood when Noah found it, he prayed forty days for knowledge of what to do with it. The angel Sarasel was sent to command him to plant it:

Its bitterness shall be changed into sweetness, and its curse shall become a blessing, and that which is produced from it shall become the blood of God; and as through it the human race obtained condemnation, so again through Jesus Christ the Immanuel will they receive in Him the upward calling and entry into paradise (III *Bar.* 4:15).

The flood episode furnished the extra-canonical writer with material with which to expound to his audience God's ways of the past. The disinheriting of the Canaanites may be taken as one example. The act is justified by the wickedness of the Canaanites, for whom there was no hope of change. "For they were an accursed race from the beginning" (*Wisd.* 12:11). It is likely that the writer is alluding to the curse of Noah (Gen. 9:25), and if so, it is in marked contrast to those who attempt to extend the curse to all descendants of Ham and to the African people in particular.

God's providence, which manifests itself in guiding sailors in wooden ships, which wood could just as readily have been used to make an idol, earlier manifested itself at the flood:

For even in the beginning, when arrogant giants were perishing, the hope of the world took refuge on a raft, and guided by thy hand left to the world the seed of a new generation. For blessed is the wood by which righteousness comes (*Wisd.* 14:6-7).[2])

In his effort to reconcile divine justice with Israel's affliction, Ezra surveyed Israel's past, admitting sin at every stage, but asking at the end if Babylon's ways are better than those of Zion. The second stage in the apostasy is that which brought the flood:

Nevertheless again in due time thou broughtest the flood upon the earth and upon the inhabitants of the world and destroyed them. And their fate was one and the same; as death overtook Adam, so the Flood over-

---

[1]) Cf. *T. Ps.-Jon.*, Gen. 9:20. Rabbis insisted that the flood did not reach the Garden of Eden: *Gen. R.* 33. 6; *Lev. R.* 31. 10; *Cant. R.* 1. 15, § 4; 4. 1, § 2. The Syrian church fathers also debated the question; see A. Levene, *The Early Syrian Fathers on Genesis* (London: Taylor's Foreign Press, 1951), p. 83.

[2]) The wood in this instance is the ark, and not the cross as some have thought; see A. T. S. Goodrick, *The Bk. of Wisdom* (N. Y.: Macmillan Co., 1913), pp. 292-293.

whelmed these. Nevertheless one of them thou didst spare—Noah with his household and with him all the righteous of his descendants. And it came to pass that when the inhabitants upon the earth began to multiply, and there were born children also and peoples and nations many, that they began to practise ungodliness more than former generations (IV *Ezra* 3:9-12).

Having seen from this detailed survey the impact that the moral interest had upon non-canonical writers in their presentation of the flood, we now consider the several surveys in which that interest is not paramount. The Pseudepigrapha furnishes us four reviews of the flood from four widely different life situations. No writer is interested in the flood as an isolated event. I *Enoch* depicts the flood as an episode of the past in a Jewish apocalyptic survey of history; [1]) *Jubilees* also has some features of apocalyptic, but is chiefly a midrash; the *Sibylline Oracles* are Jewish propaganda under a heathen mask; and the *Bk. of Adam and Eve* is a Christian apocalypse. We shall now attempt to see what effect each of these situations had upon the presentation of the flood.

The composite nature of I *Enoch* is revealed in the several separate handlings of the flood within the book. We have already considered the fall of the angels in this chapter and need not return to that matter here. Other episodes are perhaps best considered in the order in which they are found in the book. In the midst of an account of the prediluvian wickedness seen by Enoch, the angel Uriel was sent to command Noah to hide himself, to tell him that a deluge was coming to destroy the whole world and all in it, and to instruct him that he and his seed might be preserved for all generations of the world (I *Enoch* 10:1-3). The writer then returns to the sins of the Watchers. The use of an angel as an intermediary plays an important role in I *Enoch's* treatment of the flood and is in keeping with the advanced angelology of the book.

The section of I *Enoch* known as "The Parables" (chs. 37-71) covers the flood in the course of the second and third parables. In the second parable (45-57), Enoch is shown the valley of judgment where final punishment is being prepared for the hosts of Azazel. This topic leads into a consideration of an earlier punishment from the Lord of Spirits, here revealed to Enoch as about to come. The chambers of water above the heavens with their masculine waters would be opened,

---

[1]) II *Enoch* 34-35 also includes the flood in an apocalyptic survey of history, but not in a detailed way.

as would the fountains beneath the earth with their feminine waters.[1])
All who dwelt under the ends of the earth would be destroyed after
they recognized their unrighteousness (I *Enoch* 54:7-10). The Head
of Days would then repent, admit that He has destroyed the inhabitants of the earth in vain, and swear by His great name not to repeat
the deluge. He would set a sign in the heaven as a pledge of good
faith "between Me and them forever, so long as heaven is above the
earth" (I *Enoch* 55:2). At this point the writer reverts to the angels of
punishment.

In the third parable (58-69) there is a date of the 500th year, the
14th of the 7th month of the life of Enoch (I *Enoch* 60:1). R. H.
Charles felt that Noah should be read rather than Enoch.[2]) It is quite
true that it would be difficult to fit such a date into the life of Enoch
(cf. Gen. 5:23); however, the section has little else to do with the
flood. The quaking of the heavens, the fate of Leviathan and Behemoth,
and the chambers of the various heavenly forces make up its content.
In the course of the parable the flood is reverted to when Noah saw
that the earth had sunk down and when he went to Enoch to enquire
the meaning. Enoch revealed that, because of the sorceries which
men had learned from the fallen angels, the earth and its inhabitants
would be destroyed. Enoch declared that Noah was pure and guiltless
of reproach concerning the secrets; Noah's name was destined to be
among the holy; he would be preserved. His righteous seed was
destined for kingship and great honors; from it would proceed a
fountain of righteous and holy men without number (I *Enoch* 65:1-12).
Enoch showed Noah angels of punishment who were prepared to
loose the powers of water beneath the earth; however, the Lord
ordered them to hold the waters in check. Following this vision Noah
departed from Enoch (I *Enoch* 66:1-3). The word of the Lord came
to Noah in those days to tell him that his lot was of love and righteousness without blame. He was informed that the angels were making
a wooden building, which when completed would be preserved by
the Lord that from it should come the seed of life to keep the earth
from being without inhabitant (I *Enoch* 67:1-2).[3]) Noah was promised
that his seed would be before the Lord forever and would fill the

---

[1]) Cf. *PRE.* 23 and *J. Ber.* 9. 2. For the Babylonian cosmology back of this
passage see R. H. Charles, *The Bk. of Enoch* (Oxford: U. Press, 1912), p. 107,
and A. Heidel, *The Babylonian Genesis* (Chicago: U. Chicago Press, 1954), 153 pp.
[2]) R. H. Charles, *op. cit.*, p. 113.
[3]) Cf. 89:1 where Noah builds the ark.

earth (I *Enoch* 67:3). At this point the parable reverts to the punishments of angels in pictures that combine deluge and volcanic disturbances. Some features are: "convulsion of waters" (I *Enoch* 67:5); "streams of fire" (I *Enoch* 67:7); when the angels are punished the waters change their temperatures; when the angels ascend the waters become cold (I *Enoch* 67:11); [1]) "those waters will change and become a fire that burns forever" (I *Enoch* 67:13). It is likely that this picture contributes to the "flood of fire" motif of eschatology.

In the section known as the "Dream Visions" (83-90), Enoch recounts how that before his marriage he saw the heaven collapse and fall to earth. The earth in turn was swallowed up in a great abyss. When awakened, he recounted the dream to his grandfather Mahalalel who urged him to pray that a remnant might remain on earth (I *Enoch* 83:1-9). Though the vision is not interpreted, the destruction which he saw is obviously that of the approaching flood. The section concludes with Enoch's prayer to the Lord.

In the second dream the history of the world is related in apocalyptic symbolism in which O.T. patriarchs are animals. Following the fall of the angels and the resulting wickedness and punishment of angels, Noah is introduced as a white bull (I *Enoch* 89:1 f.). One of the angels instructed the white bull; he became a man and built a great vessel.[2]) Three bulls dwelt with him on it and were covered in. Seven water torrents of heaven flowed from a lofty roof; [3]) below the surface fountains were opened; and water, darkness, and mist increased on the "enclosure" into which it had been poured until it overflowed it and stood upon the earth. All the cattle of the enclosure died, as did the elephants, camels, and asses which represent the giants of Scripture. Then the water torrents were removed from the roof, the chasms of the earth were leveled up, and other abysses opened into which the water ran. The vessel settled on earth, and it became light again.[4]) The white bull that became a man came out of the vessel, accompanied by the three bulls: one white, one red, and one black. The white bull departed from them. This is the death of Noah (I *Enoch* 89:1-9). The survey continues in similar symbols to the time of the Messiah.

---

[1]) Cf. Origen, *C. Celsum* v. 52 (*GCS*. 3. 56).
[2]) Cf. 67:1-2 where the angels build it.
[3]) Cf. *Jub*. 5:24.
[4]) Cf. rabbinic debate over whether the planets functioned during the deluge, *Gen. R.* 34. 11; 25. 2; Philo has a cloud cover heaven (*Abr.* 43).

The final account for I *Enoch* is in ch. 106 which begins with the birth of Noah. At birth Noah's body was white as snow and red as a blooming rose, his hair was white as wool, and his eyes beautiful, the opening of which made the whole house lighten up like the sun. He arose in the hands of the midwife and conversed with the Lord of righteousness.[1]) The matter so affrighted his father Lamech that the latter went to his father Methuselah to relate the matter. Methuselah then went to Enoch at the ends of the earth to ask him. Enoch related the story of the angels sinning with women and the birth of the giants, all of which had been revealed to him in advance. He made known that there should be a deluge and great destruction for one year. This one son and his three children would be saved. Methuselah was to make known to Lamech that the son was really his, and that his name should be Noah, for "he shall be left to you, and he and his sons saved from the destruction." [2]) But after that there would still be more unrighteousness. All of this Enoch had read on the heavenly tables. Methuselah then returned and called the name of the child Noah, for he would comfort (נחם) the earth after all the destruction (I *Enoch* 106-107:3).[3])

The midrashic treatment of the flood in the *Bk. of Jubilees* is related under the form of a revelation to Moses by the angel of the presence (*Jub.* 1:27). The general scheme of the book divided history into jubilee periods of forty-nine years each. The role of preacher to the antediluvians is filled by Enoch (*Jub.* 4:22).[4]) Lamech, whose wife (also his second cousin) is named Betenos,[5]) became the father of Noah in the 15th jubilee, the third week (A. M. 701-707). He said,

---

[1]) All children of the prediluvial period are presented as being precocious in *Lev. R.* 5. 1; the description of Noah in the *Gen. Apoc.* II is in general agreement with I *Enoch*. Cf. also D. Barthélemy and J. T. Milik, *op. cit.*, I, 85; J. T. Milik, "The Dead Sea Scrolls Fragment of the Bk. of Enoch," *Biblica*, 32 (1951), 393-400.

[2]) The text assumes an etymology from ינוח. This idea is paralleled in *Sir.* 44: 17, where Noah is a remnant (שארית) left to the earth and in II *Enoch* 35:1: "I shall leave over one just man." The Latin text of I *Enoch* for this passage explains the name from the fact that Noah caused one "to find rest in the ark." This puns on הניח. Cf. Ps.-Philo, *Bib. Ant.* i. 20.

[3]) See L. Ginzberg, *Legends of the Jews* (Phila.: Jewish Pub. Soc., 1909-1955), V, 168. Note the three possible etymologies suggested for "Noah" in I *Enoch* 106:18 and 107:3.

[4]) Cf. I *Enoch* 12:4; 13:3; and 15:1-2. In *Sefer Hayashar* (*EBI.* II, 18) it is Methuselah.

[5]) Cf. *Gen. Apoc.* II. 3.

"This one will comfort me for my trouble and all my work and for the ground which the Lord cursed" (*Jub.* 4:28).[1]

Noah married Emzara (also his second cousin) [2] in the first year of the 5th week of the 25th jubilee (A. M. 1205); Shem was born in the third year of the 5th week; [3] Ham in the fifth; while Japheth was born in the first year of the sixth week (*Jub.* 4:33).

In the midst of the prediluvian wickedness, upon which generation God decreed that His spirit should not abide,[4] Noah found grace before the Lord (*Jub.* 5:5). He had not departed from aught that was ordained for him. God saved his sons for his sake (*Jub.* 5:19).[5]

Noah was commanded to build the ark in the 27th jubilee, the fifth week, and the 5th year, on the new moon of the first month (A. M. 1307).[6] He entered into the ark in the 6th year, the 2nd month on the new moon. The angels brought the animals together.[7] The Lord closed the ark on the 17th evening.[8] Seven flood gates of heaven and seven fountains of the deep were opened.[9] Water poured out forty days and nights. The whole world was full of water, which extended fifteen cubits above the mountains (*Jub.* 5:22-26; cf. Gen. 7:12, 18, 20). Water was on the earth for five months (150 days).[10] On the new

---

[1]) This passage, following Gen. 5:29, attributes to Noah the meaning derived from נחם.

[2]) Tobit 4:12 assumes that Noah married a relative. She is named Naamah in *Gen. R.* 23. 3 and Haikal, daughter of Abaraz, in *Bk. of Adam and Eve* iii. 1.

[3]) Cf. *Jub.* 10:14 where also Shem is made the oldest as the writer interprets אחי יפת הגדול of Gen. 10:21.

[4]) *Jub.* 5:8 seems to take the difficult *yadon* in the sense of allowing men to live on; cf. Philo, *Gig.* 19; *QG.* i. 90.

[5]) See also Ramban (*EBI.* II, 33); but cf. IV *Ezra* 3:11 and I *Clem.* 7: 6 and *Tanhuma B*, Noah 5 where they are righteous men.

[6]) The ten generations cover 1656 years in the MT.; 2642 in the LXX; 2262 in Josephus, *Ant.* 1. 3. 3; and only 1307 in the Samaritan text. See J. E. Steinmueller, *Some Problems of the O.T.* (N. Y.: Bruce Pub. Co., 1936), p. 94. Some rabbinic sources follow the MT.; cf. *Seder Olam*, ch. 1; while the church fathers use the LXX or a variant of it; cf. Julius Africanus, *Chron.* 5 (*PG.* 10. 68); Sulpicius Severus, *Chron.* i. 3 (*CSEL.* 1. 5). Augustine, *Civ. Dei* 15. 20 (*CSEL.* 40. 2. 102), notes the difference in the LXX and MT. and remarks that even if one subtracts the one from the other, it would still be a long period. Ephraem's figure of 2060 years is arrived at from dogmatic assumptions rather than from textual evidence; see D. Gerson, *Die Comm. des Ephraem Syrus im Verhältniss zur jüdischen Exegese* (Breslau: Schletter'schen Buchhandlung, 1868), p. 33.

[7]) This view is repeated in *PRE.* 23; *T. Ps.-Jon.*, Gen. 6:20; *Bk. of Adam and Eve* iii. 8.

[8]) The date is in agreement with MT., Gen. 7:11.

[9]) Cf. I *Enoch* 89:2.

[10]) Cf. Gen. 7:24; 8:3.

moon of the 4th month the sources of the deep and of heaven were closed. On the new moon of the seventh month the mouths of the abysses were opened and the water descended into the deep. On the new moon of the tenth month the mountains were seen.[1]) The ark rested on the top of Lubar,[2]) one of the mountains of Ararat. In the seventh year of the fifth week, the seventeenth day of the second month, the earth was dry (*Jub.* 5:27-31).[3]) On the 27th day Noah opened the ark and brought the creatures forth (*Jub.* 5:32).[4])

On the new moon of the third month Noah built an altar on that mountain, took a kid and made atonement for the guilt of the earth (*Jub.* 6:1-2; cf. 14:20).[5]) The writer further embellishes Gen. 8:20 by specifying that Noah also offered an ox, a goat, a sheep, a kid, salt, a turtledove, and the young of a dove. Oil, wine, and frankincense were sprinkled on to make a goodly savor.[6]) The Lord smelled it and covenanted no more to destroy the earth with a flood; cold and heat, summer and winter, day and night should not cease all the days of the earth (*Jub.* 6:1-4). God set His bow in the clouds as a sign of the covenant (*Jub.* 6:15-16). Man was to increase and multiply and be a blessing on earth.[7]) All things were to fear him (cf. Gen. 9:2). All beasts, winged things, and fish were to be his food, but the blood should not be eaten (cf. Gen. 9:3). The blood of man was to be required at the hand of man and beast, for man was made in God's image (cf. Gen. 9:5-6). Noah and his sons swore that they would not eat any blood (*Jub.* 6:5-10). The angel of the presence who was

---

[1]) The date agrees with the MT., Gen. 8:5.

[2]) Lubar is found in the *Gen. Apoc.* XII. 13; cf. X. 12; Heb. *Bk. of Noah*; and Epiphanius, *Pan. Haer.* 2.1 (*GCS.* 25. 174), the latter of whom locates it between Armenia and Kurdistan. The verse of *Jubilees* is reproduced in Syncellus, i. 147, and Cedrenus, i. 21, cited in R. H. Charles, *The Bk. of Jubilees* (London: A. and C. Black, 1912), notes p. 59.

[3]) In MT. it is the first month in Gen. 8:13, but in v. 14 it is the second month. This writer follows v. 14.

[4]) The date agrees with the MT. This chronology of *Jubilees* makes Noah remain in the ark one year and ten days. Several dates not in the MT. have been supplied by the writer.

[5]) This explanation for the sacrifice is a unique contribution of *Jubilees*. Philo, *QG.* ii. 50, 52, and *PRE.* 23 have Noah to act out of gratitude. Josephus, *Ant.* i. 3. 7, suggests that Noah was afraid God might drown the earth each year and so he besought Him that the earth might not again undergo God's wrath.

[6]) For the relationship of the details of the offering to the Halacha, see Ch. Albeck, *Das Buch der Jubiläen und die Halacha* (Berlin: Hochschule für die Wissenschaft des Judentums, 1930), p. 21.

[7]) The last item is not in MT., Gen. 9:7. A theory of its derivation is given by R. H. Charles, *The Bk. of Jubilees* (London: A. and C. Black, 1902), p. 50.

revealing these things to Moses went ahead to inform him that the prohibition was to be observed continually. The penalty for the offender and his seed would be to be rooted out of the land. The feast of weeks which had previously from creation been celebrated in heaven was to be celebrated once each year to renew the covenant (*Jub.* 6:12-18).[1]) The writer further remarks that Noah and his sons observed it seven jubilees and one week. After his death, his sons did away with it until the days of Abraham, when the observance was revived and kept by Abraham, Isaac, and Jacob. Other observances to be kept were the new moons of the first, fourth, seventh, and tenth months. Each of these commemorated an event connected with the flood: in the first month Noah went into the ark and in it the earth became dry; in the fourth month the depths were closed; in the seventh month the abysses were opened and the water descended into them; and in the tenth month the mountains were seen. The angel insists that these observances had been placed on the heavenly tables with thirteen weeks lapsing between each of them. This made a year of 52 weeks or of 364 days (*Jub.* 6:19-32). The writer of the book is quite specific in connecting this type of year with Noah and also quite concerned lest man change the days of the festivals (*Jub.* 6:37-38).

Noah planted vines on Lubar in the first year of the seventh week. When they produced in the fourth year,[2]) he kept the wine made from them until the new moon of the first month of the fifth year.[3]) At that time he offered a sacrifice of one ox, one ram, seven sheep a year old, and a kid of the goats that he might atone for himself and his sons. Oil, wine, and incense were mingled with the sacrifices. He and his children drank wine with joy.[4]) That evening he lay in his tent drunken. After Ham reported the state of his father, Shem and Japheth took a garment on their shoulders, walked backwards, and covered him. Canaan was cursed to be an "enslaved servant" to his brothers. Shem and Japheth were blessed in what is declared by the writer to

---

[1]) *Jubilees* is unique both in connecting the feast of weeks with the Noah covenant and in dating it to the middle of the third month (*Jub.* 6:16 f.; cf. 15:1; 44:4, 5 where patriarchs keep other festivals; cf. also the law of Lev. 23:15 ff.).

[2]) Cf. the law of Lev. 19:23-25.

[3]) Ephraem Syrus, *Comm. in Gen.* 7:1 (*CSCO.* 72. 50-51), has a lapse of six years before the drunkenness.

[4]) Cf. the ritual of Num. 29:2, 5; Josephus, *Ant.* i. 6. 3, also connects the drunkenness with a sacrifice.

be a prophecy (*Jub.* 8:18). God would dwell in the dwellings of Shem.[1]) Afterwards each of the sons of Noah proceeded to build himself a city (*Jub.* 7:14-19).

In the 28th jubilee (A. M. 1324-1372), Noah began to give commandments to his sons: to observe righteousness, to cover their shame, to bless the creator, to honor father and mother, to love neighbor, and to guard themselves from the sins which brought the flood—fornication, uncleanness, and iniquity (*Jub.* 7:20).[2]) Blood was to be covered and not eaten under any circumstances.[3]) When things were planted, the fruit should not be eaten until the fourth year.[4]) Firstfruits were to be offered to the Lord (*Jub.* 7:35-36; cf. Lev. 19:23-24). A release was to be made in the fifth (seventh?) year (*Jub.* 7:37).

The sons of Noah divided the land. Ham's portion which was located "beyond Gihon towards the south, to the right of the Garden" extended southward to the mountains of fire; westward to the sea of 'Atel; westward to the sea of Ma'uk; northward to Gadir, then along the great sea to Gihon and along Gihon to the Garden of Eden (*Jub.* 8:22-23).[5]) Ham divided that territory putting Cush on the east; Mizraim to the west of him; Put to the west of Mizraim; while Canaan was along the sea, west of them all (*Jub.* 9:1). After the dividing of the land took place in the presence of Noah, each son was bound with an oath not to seize land not his own (*Jub.* 9:14-15).

Canaan, after the overthrow of Babel, saw that territory from Lebanon to the river of Egypt was desirable. Though his father and brothers warned him that this land had been allotted to them and that Noah's curse would be on him, he did not hearken. It was this seizure of land that gave this region the name of the Land of Canaan (*Jub.* 10:29-34). This demonstrates that the *Bk. of Jubilees* does not connect the curse of Noah with the Negro race.

---

[1]) An antecedent is supplied to the pronoun of the MT. of Gen. 9:27. See also *T. Onkelos*; *T. Ps.-Jonathan*; and Justin Martyr, *Dial.* 139, who take the antecedent to be Japheth. It is not in keeping with *Jubilees'* teaching of the separation of the Jew and Gentile (*Jub.* 15:34; 22:16, 20; 30:11) to have Japheth in the tents of Shem.

[2]) Cf. *Gen. R.* 31. 6 where it is idolatry, impurity, and bloodshed.

[3]) Cf. *T. Lev.*, Gk. Frag. 56-57. Though Abraham says he learned the prescription from the Bk. of Noah, the wording echoes Lev. 17:13. Other instruction about blood is found in the *Gen. Apoc.* XI; see N. Avigad and Y. Yadin, *op. cit.*, p. 20.

[4]) See *infra*, p. 98, note to *T. Ps.-Jon.*, Gen. 9:20.

[5]) This is perhaps the land of Africa; see R. H. Charles, *op. cit.*, p. 73.

Prior to Noah's death the evil demons (whose fathers were the Watchers) began to bother the sons of Noah to make them err.[1]) He prayed to God that the same sort of grace that had saved them from the flood should now deliver his descendants. The Lord gave orders that the demons should be bound, but Mastema, the chief, begged that a tenth be left to him in freedom, and his request was granted (*Jub.* 10:1-9). One of the angels was commanded to teach Noah medicine and the value of herbs to heal diseases. Noah gave his writings to Shem, died, and was buried on Mt. Lubar in Ararat. He had lived 950 years (19 jubilees, 2 weeks, and 5 years). He had excelled the children of men in righteousness, except for Enoch who was perfect (*Jub.* 10:11-17).[2])

The significance of this material from *Jubilees* is that it demonstrates the manner in which the writer has embellished the flood narrative for the purpose of tracing certain of the Jewish festivals and practices to the patriarchs. Festivals, according to him, begin with Noah. Exact dates have been supplied for each event of the flood in the effort to validate a religious calendar for which the writer is doing propaganda. An effort is made to demonstrate that Noah acts in keeping with the ritual prescriptions of the Law and that he is the transmitter of esoteric knowledge (*Jub.* 10:14; 12:27; 21:10). Elements of the story that do not fit his purpose, such as the sending out of the dove, have been omitted. Theological interpretations have been added: angels assemble the animals for the ark; Noah's post-flood sacrifice is an atonement; his drunkenness is in connection with a sacrifice; and God is to dwell in the tents of Shem.

The Jewish Sibyl,[3]) who claims to be the daughter-in-law of Noah (*Or. Sib.* iii. 818-828), in the course of tracing out six races of the world, which seem to be in imitation of Hesiod's ages, depicts the flood in the fifth race.[4]) Amidst the wickedness of the age, Noah was the single man just, faithful, and attentive to all good works (*Or. Sib.* i. 148-149).[5]) When commanded to preach repentance to all people, he was told that they would not heed (*Or. Sib.* i. 151-154). He was

---

[1]) Cf. the same material in the Heb. *Bk. of Noah.*

[2]) Cf. Philo's emphasis (*Cong.* 90) upon Noah as the first man called righteous in Scripture.

[3]) For an account of the Sibyls, see Lactantius, *Div. Inst.*, i. 6 (*CSEL.* 19. 18-25). The present book is a composite work with materials of various dates.

[4]) An English translation is found in M. S. Terry, *The Sibylline Oracles* (N.Y.: Hunt and Eaton, 1890), pp. 37-47.

[5]) Cf. iii. 824, "the only man who found favor."

further commanded to build an indestructible house from the "non-imbibing root" (*Or. Sib.* i. 156).[1])

The Sibyl furnishes a lengthy sermon of Noah's in which he chided the people for unbelief and wicked works, especially murder. He reminded them that God sees all and should be adored. He warned of the impending flood (*Or. Sib.* i. 177-201). Noah's countrymen turned up their noses and called Noah mad (*Or. Sib.* i. 202-204). Noah became more specific about their sins: lack of reverence, tyranny, lying, adultery, and slander. He then described the destruction and terror which would accompany the flood (*Or. Sib.* i. 204-233).

Noah was instructed to take his family and all the beasts which God commanded into the house. To the animals God had imparted a "prompt and willing mind to enter in." God fitted the key to the lid (*Or. Sib.* i. 236-252). The sun was obscured; thunder and wind rolled as streams were unloosed from heaven and from the earth's recesses. The ark ("the divine house") floated, tossed by many a furious wave and swept by blasts of wind. The world was covered over and drowned (*Or. Sib.* i. 260-272). After a time the lid of the ark, which was joined with skillful stays, was lifted by Noah.[2]) Death was all around (*Or. Sib.* i. 275-279). Noah sent forth the dove to see if the world was yet solid, but she returned. The second time after resting on humid ground, she brought back an olive branch, "the sign of tidings great."[3]) Then Noah sent forth a black winged bird who reached land and stayed there, and by this sign Noah knew that land was near (*Or. Sib.* i. 286-305).[4]) The ark landed on Mt. Ararat which is on the Phrygian mainland (*Or. Sib.* i. 309-310).[5]) Noah was commanded to come forth with his family and to render justice until judgment comes to all (*Or. Sib.* i. 317-323). Noah, the most just of all men, the eighth member of the party, was the last to leave the ark.[6]) He had been on the

---

[1]) ἐν ῥίζῃσιν ἀδιψήτοισι; cf. iii. 825 where the term is "hewn wood (ὑλοτόμῳ ἐνὶ οἴμῳ)."

[2]) For a similar artistic representation of the ark, see *infra*, pp. 161-162.

[3]) The biblical order of the birds is reversed. *The Gilgamesh Epic* has the dove sent out first; see A. Heidel, *The Gilgamesh Epic* (Chicago: University Press, 1954), pp. 251-252.

[4]) An effort to illustrate the purpose of sending forth the raven "to sight land," on the basis of certain sea customs is found in H. Heras, "The Crow of Noe," *CBQ.*, X (Ap., 1948), 131-139.

[5]) Cf. the rejection of Phrygia in favor of Parthia by Julius Africanus, *Chron.* 4 (*PG*. 10. 68); for a location in Armenia, see Josephus, *Ant.* i. 3. 5-6.

[6]) In another fragmentary passage, Noah is alluded to as the sole fugitive, *Or. Sib.* vii. 10.

water 202 days.[1]) The sixth race of men, which was a golden period, began. Later when wickedness again became rampant, another flood would have destroyed the Titans, had not Saboath promised not again to bring a deluge on malevolent mankind (*Or. Sib.* i. 330-375). Later events are dated by the Sibyl in generations from the flood (*Or. Sib.* iii. 109).

In another of her pictures of the times of the end, the Sibyl threatens:

And God shall judge all with war and sword, and with fire and cata-
clysms of rain (*Or. Sib.* iii. 689 f.).

This picture is relevant in the discussion of the "flood of fire." Certain sources seem to reflect that the flood of fire was to come before the flood of water. It is to be noticed that the fire is placed before water by the Sibyl.[2])

The material from the *Sibylline Oracles* shows us the way an un-known Jew would present the flood to a heathen audience in pleading for belief in monotheism, attempting to pretend that the heathen Sibyl described the main outlines of the event.

In the *Bk. of Adam and Eve*, also known as the *Cave of Treasures*,[3]) we have a recitation of history for the purpose of attempting to connect the experiences of the first Adam with the second Adam. Many embellishments not present in the earlier pseudepigraphical writings have made their appearance.

Adam before his death,[4]) informing Seth that a flood would come in which only eight would be saved, charged that his body be taken into the ark and buried in the middle of the earth after the flood (ii. 8). Gold, incense, and myrrh, which would later be found and offered by the magi, should also be buried.[5])

Additional warnings of the approaching flood were made by Jared and Enoch. Jared, when Noah was 360 years old, again charged that Adam's body should be taken into the ark and later be buried by

---

[1]) This date is not in agreement with MT., LXX, or any other source included in this study.

[2]) Cf. *Or. Sib.* ii. 244; 308; 355; "the river of fire," iii. 85; iv. 160 f.; Philo, *Mos.* ii. 263, mentions repeated destructions in which fire and water alternate. Josephus, *Ant.* i. 2. 3, puts fire before water. Some rabbis also spoke of a flood of fire; see *Mekilta, Amalek* iii. 14.

[3]) Translations are to be found in S. C. Malan, *The Bk. of Adam and Eve* (London: Williams and Norgate, 1882), 255 pp.; and P. Riessler, *Altjüdisches Schrifttum ausserhalb der Bibel* (Augsburg: Benno Filser, 1928), pp. 942-1013.

[4]) Cf. the warning in *T. Adam* iii. 15.

[5]) Cf. *Bk. of Adam and Eve* iv. 14.

Shem. He informed Noah that he would be the one "that shall be left" (ii. 21).[1]) Enoch before his translation repeated the prediction of approaching ruin (ii. 22).

Noah from his youth up, observing the increase of wickedness, held his soul in fasting. He was obedient to his parents when with them, and obedient to God when away from them. He did not transgress against God in one evil thing. After Noah had continued in chastity and obedience to God for 500 years, God commanded him to take a wife.[2]) He chose Haikal, daughter of Abaraz, a descendant of Enos.[3]) His three sons, Shem, Ham, and Japheth (in this order) [4]) were born during the first one hundred years the ark was being constructed (iii. 1, 3). The book insists that the LXXII interpreters tell us that these sons married daughters of Methuselah (iii. 3). [5])

The instructions about the ark specified that it should be built of "wood that will not rot" [6]) in the lowland of Eden, in the presence of the children of Cain as an additional warning to them. The trees were to come from the Holy Mountain. The dimensions of the ark in this book correspond with the MT. It proceeds to detail out that there should be one door above, and three stories, each ten cubits

---

[1]) Noah as the one left over, assuming an etymology from הנוח, is also found in I *Enoch* 106:18; II *Enoch* 35:1; *Sir.* 44:16-18; and *Wisd.* 14:6.

[2]) Noah's refraining from marriage until he reached the age of 500 is mentioned in *Num. R.* 14. 12; *Tanhuma Yashan B'reshith* 39 (*EBI.* I, 181); cf. *Sefer Hayashar Noah* (*EBI.* II, 17); Ephraem Syrus, *Comm. in Gen.* 6:1 (*CSCO.* 72. 43); Aphraates, *Hom.* 13. 4 (*TU.* III. 3. 200); cf. S. Funk, *Die haggadischen Elemente in den Homilien des Aphraates* (Wien: Selbstverlag des Verfassers, 1891), p. 26; L. Ginzberg, *Die Haggada bei den Kirchenvätern* (Berlin: S. Calvary and Co., 1900), pp. 74-75.

[3]) The name does not correspond to that given in any other source studied. Cf. *Jub.* 4:33; *Gen. R.* 23. 3; *EBI.* II, 18.

[4]) *Jub.* 4:33; Ps.-Clem., *Recog.* i. 30 (*PG.* 1. 1224); Cyprian, *Ep.* 63. 3 (*CSEL.* 3. 2. 702); Augustine, *Civ. Dei* 16. 3 (*CSEL.* 40. 2. 129); Aphraates, *Hom.* 13. 4 (*TU.* III. 3. 200); and *PRE.* 8 give Shem as the oldest son; cf. Radak (*EBI.* II, 6).

[5]) *Sefer Hayashar* gives Eliakim, son of Methuselah, as their father (*EBI.* II, 31). Aphraates, *Hom.* 13. 4 (*TU.* III. 3. 20) tells of Noah's carefully admonishing his sons not to marry daughters of Cain. Noah's flesh revolted against the daughters of Cain; see Ephraem Syrus, *Nisibene Hymns* 1. 4 (*NPNF.* ser. ii. 13. 167). Hippolytus, *Arabic Frag. to Pent.*, Gen. 6:18 (*GCS.* 1. 2. 87) supplies a name for each wife and has Ham's wife announce the approach of the flood. The wives play a role in Jerome's argument for asceticism, *Adv. Jovin.* i. 5 (*PL.* 23. 226), and for monogamy, *Ep.* 123. 11 (*CSEL.* 56. 85). On the other hand, Aphraates, *Hom.* 13. 4 (*TU.* III. 3. 201), argues that the sons married only at the time of the entrance into the ark.

[6]) Syrian church fathers said, "Gopher is a very stout wood. Some say it is acacia wood. Mar Abba and Gabriel of Katar say that teak is gopher," A. Levene, *op. cit.*, pp. 81-82.

high.¹) The first story was for "lions, beasts, animals, and ostriches."
The second story was for birds and creeping things; while the third
was for Noah and his family.²) The ark should have wells,³) lined
with lead where drinking water should be drawn, and storehouses for
corn for Noah and those with him (iii. 2).⁴)

A trumpet of ebony should be made and blown three times a day:
to assemble the workmen, for lunch time, and for quitting time (iii. 2).
Lest Noah's sons be tempted by the Cainites,⁵) they stayed on the

---

¹) This is a unique but obvious deduction from the thirty cubits.

²) The division of floor levels is in agreement with Hippolytus, *Arabic Frag.
to Pent.*, Gen. 6:18 (*GCS*. 1. 2. 87); the Arabic ms. cited by J. G. Frazer, *Folklore
in the O.T.* (London: Macmillan, 1919), I, 145-146; and *PRE*. 23. Other arrange-
ments are given in *Gen. R.* 31. 11; *T. B. Sanh.* 108b; Philo, *QG.* ii. 38; Origen,
Hom. in Gen. ii. 1 (*GCS*. 29. 25); cf. *Num. Hom.* xxi. 2 (*GCS*. 30. 201).

³) Wells are also mentioned by Hippolytus, *Arabic Frag. to Pent.* i, Gen. 6:18
(*GCS*. 1. 2. 87); cf. "protected cisterns," *PRE*. 23; *T. Ps.-Jon.*, Gen. 6:14. Some
early Syrian fathers thought the water was secured from outside the ark as needed;
see A. Levene, *op. cit.*, p. 82. Levene has evidently overlooked *PRE*. and *T.
Ps.-Jon.* when he says there is no reference in rabbinic literature to the water
supply, *ibid.*, p. 185.

⁴) Storerooms for food are mentioned in *PRE*. 23 and *T. Ps.-Jon.*, Gen. 6: 14.

⁵) From the time of Julius Africanus, the church fathers tend to identify the
sons of God with the descendants of Seth. Africanus explains that righteous men
and patriarchs have descended from Seth. The descendants of Cain are named
the seed of men, for they have nothing divine in them (*Chron.* 2 [*PG.* 10. 65]).
Ps.-Clem., *Recog.* i. 29 (*PG.* 1. 1223), calls them "righteous men who had lived the
life of angels." Ephraem Syrus uses the phrases: "Sons of God, saints that sudden-
ly waxed wanton," and "Noah revolted against the daughters of Cain," *Hymns
on the Nativity* 1; *Nisibene Hymns* 1. 4 (*NPNF*. ser. ii. 13. 167, 224); see also E.
Beck, *Ephraems Hymnen über das Paradies* (Rome: Herder, 1951), pp. 5-6. John
Cassian, *Collatio VIII*. 21 (*CSEL*. 13. 2. 237-238), explains that God at creation
had enacted the marriage law later reenacted in Deut. 7:3. Seth's descendants
had always remained separate from the society of the Cainites. This, says he, is
the purpose of the divided genealogy of the lines in Genesis. As long as they
remained unmixed, because of their sanctity, the Sethites were termed "angels of
God" or "sons of God."

Augustine, *Civ. Dei* 15. 22, 23 (*CSEL*. 40. 2. 109-113), says that he could not
dream of thinking that they were angels, not even on the evidence of II Pet.
2:4, for this verse refers, says he, to a fall of angels before the fall of man. That
men can be known as angels he attempts to prove from the use of the word
messenger for John the Baptist and Malachi. "The angels were not creatures
different from men." It is by grace that they are called angels. Other early writers
making this identification include Theodoretus and Aphraates; see also
L. Ginzberg, *Die Haggada bei den Kirchenvätern* (Berlin: S. Calvary and Co.,
1900), pp. 75-76.

A further study of this topic is to be found in D. Poulet, "The Moral Causes
of the Flood," *CBQ.*, IV (Oct., 1942), 293-303.

Holy Mountain and did not work on the ark.[1]) Noah descended day
by day to carry on the work (iii. 3).

During the one hundred years,[2]) Noah did not change his clothes,
nor his staff. Neither his clothes nor his shoes wore out, nor did his
hair grow long nor diminish.[3]) During these years he was a vegetarian.[4])
When asked about the ark he was building, he at God's command
told the enquirers of the flood. But they laughed, committed adultery,
and revelled the more.[5]) They called him a "twaddling old man,"
and insisted that the water would not rise over the mountains (iii. 2).
Noah preached repeatedly: "The flood will come and destroy you, if
you do not repent." [6])

Both Lamech and Methuselah died before the onset of the flood
(iii. 3, 5).[7]) At God's command, the body of Adam was carried from
the Cave of Treasures. The body, en route, expressed its hope of a
resurrection, and was placed on the third story of the ark on the east
side.[8]) Shem took gold, Ham took myrrh, and Japheth took incense

---

[1]) *Gen. R.* 44. 7 has Shem as the builder of the ark.

[2]) That it took 100 yrs. to build the ark is suggested by Origen, *C. ¦Celsum*
iv. 41 (*GCS.* 2. 314); Ps.-Tertullian, *Apol.* I. *adv. Marc.* iii. 3 (*PL.* 2. 1127);
Chrysostom, *In Ep. I Thess.* 4. hom. 8. 2 (*PG.* 62. 442); Augustine, *Civ. Dei* 15.
27 (*CSEL.* 40. 2. 120); *De Catech.* 19. 32 (*PL.* 40. 334); and George Cedrenus,
Compend. Hist. (Bonn, 1838-1839), pp. 20-23. The only dissenting voices are
PRE. 23 where 52 years are suggested and *Sefer Hayashar*, Noah (*EBI.* II, 31),
where 5 years are mentioned.

[3]) This is also found in *Ap. of Paul* 50.

[4]) That all antediluvians were vegetarians is found in: *T. B. Sanh.* 59b; *Gen.
R.* 34. 13; Irenaeus, *Demonst.* 22; Tertullian, *De anima* 38 (*CSEL.* 20. 365);
De Jejunio 4 (*CSEL.* 20. 278); Ps.-Clem., *Hom.* viii. 15 (*GCS.* 42. 127); Jerome,
Adv. Jovin. ii. 15 (*PL.* 23. 319); Theodoretus, see L. Ginzberg, *Die Haggada bei
den Kirchenvätern* (Berlin: S. Calvary and Co. 1900), pp. 83-84.

[5]) In this book it is adultery that causes the flood (iii. 25).

[6]) Noah as a preacher is found in Josephus, *Ant.* i. 3. 1; II Pet. 2: 5; *Gen. R.*
30. 7; *Eccl. R.* 9. 15. § 1; *PRE.* 22; *Or. Sib.* i. 150-233; I *Clem.* 7:6; Theophilus,
ad Autol. iii. 19; *Ap. of Paul* 50; Methodius, *Conv. decem virg.* 10. 3 (*GCS.* 27. 125);
Hippolytus, *Arabic Frag. to Pent.*, Gen. 6:18 (*GCS.* I. 2. 88); Augustine, *De
catech.* 19. 32 (*PL.* 40. 334); Chrysostom, *In Ep. I Thess.* 4, hom. 8. 2 (*PG.* 62.
442).

[7]) In MT. Lamech dies five yrs. before Methuselah. Methuselah dies in the
year of the flood. In LXX Lamech dies 49 years before Methuselah and Methuselah is still alive at the time of the flood; see L. Ginzberg, *The Legends of the Jews*
(Phila.: Jewish Pub. Society, 1955), V, 165.

[8]) This story is also known to Hippolytus, *Arabic Frag. to Pent.*, Gen. 6:18
(*GCS.* 1. 2. 88). The rabbis debated whether the body of Adam was destroyed
by the flood; see *Gen. R.* 28. 3.

out of the cave. These were placed with the body of Adam on Friday at the second hour on the 27th of the month of Gembot (iii. 6).[1]

Noah blew the trumpet three times while standing on top of the ark, and at the same time an angel blew a horn from heaven to assemble the animals.[2] At the third hour on Friday, the animals went into the lower story of the ark; the second story was filled at midday; and Noah and his family came in at the ninth hour. There was one male and female of each of the clean and unclean animals,[3] plus six additional pairs of clean animals. In the ark the women dwelt on the western side of the ark while Noah and his sons were on the eastern side (iii. 8). During the flood the animals were kept quiet by the power of God (iii. 11).[4]

After God shut the door, he commanded the windows of heaven to open. Down came the rain accompanied with wind to make a day of terror. Sun, moon, and stars withheld their light.[5] Fountains of the deep burst open. Seeing the water, the sinful sons of Seth gathered around the ark begging Noah to open, but an angel had sealed the door. An angel sat on the ark to act as captain (iii. 9). The rain continued for forty days and nights (iii. 10).

The sons of Cain were drowned in keeping with Noah's prediction (iii. 9).[6] Water rose to 45 cubits, since the Holy Ghost cubit is equal to

---

[1] See also the Arabic ms. cited by J. G. Frazer, *op. cit.*, I, 146.

[2] Ephraem has God assemble the animals; see L. Ginzberg, *Die Haggada bei den Kirchenvätern* (Berlin: S. Calvary and Co., 1900), pp. 80-81; for the text of Ephraem, see R. M. Tonneau, *S. Eph. Syr. in Gen. et Ex. Comm.* (*CSCO*. 72. 47). An angel collects the animals in *T. Ps.-Jon.*, Gen. 6:20 and *PRE*. 23.

[3] Resh Lakish (*T. B. Sanh*. 108b) and Sulpicius Severus, *Chron.* 1. 3 (*CSEL*. 1. 5) also assume that there were only two unclean animals. The view that there were fourteen clean animals is quite widespread. Tertullian in his argument on monogamy insists that there were two, male and female, of all beasts and "pairs of sevens" of the others, *De monog.* (*CSEL*. 76. 51). Origen, seemingly expressing the view of Apelles, insists that the repetition of the numeral in the text supports him, *C. Celsum* iv. 41 (*GCS*. 2. 314).

The Hebrew *Bk. of Noah* (A. Jellinek, *Bet Ha-Midrasch* III, 158-159); and Victorinus, *De fabrica mundi* 8 (*CSEL*. 49.8), give seven unclean animals. Jerome is quite specific in making the point that there was an "uneven number" of clean animals, *Adv. Jovin.* 2. 15 (*PL*. 23. 320); *Ep.* 123. 11 (*CSEL*. 56. 85); *Ep.* 49 [48]. 19 (*CSEL*. 54. 383).

[4] Philo, *Mos.* ii. 61; *QG*. ii. 27, assumes that the animals became tame from association with man; cf. also "entered in concord into the ark," I *Clem.* 9:4.

[5] Philo, *Abr.* 43, has a cloud cover heaven; R. Johanan insisted that the planets could not be seen, *Gen. R.* 25. 2; 34. 11.

[6] The writer informs us that the whole earth was not yet inhabited, but only the land of the garden where Seth's descendants dwelt and the place of Cain's descendants (iii. 25).

three ordinary cubits, and covered all the high mountains. The ark was brought to the lower side of the Holy Garden, and there the survivors bowed in worship.[1]) After floating 150 days, the ark landed on the mountains of Ararat on the 27th of Tkarnt (iii. 9).

The tops of the mountains were visible on the first day of the eleventh month, but not until forty days later did Noah open the window on the western side of the ark to let the raven go to see if the waters were gone from the earth.[2]) When the raven did not return,[3]) Noah waited a while, and then sent the dove, who found no rest, and returned to Noah. After seven days, a second trip of the dove brought back an olive leaf at evening time. This writer proceeds to allegorize the dove as a figure of the old and new covenants. Her first trip signified the coming of the Christ to find no reception among the Jews. The second trip is the reception of the Gospel by the nations.[4])

The earth was dry in the 607th year of Noah's life, the 2nd day of Barmudeh. The exit from the ark came on Sunday, the 27th of Gembot, which was also the month and day that Noah went into the ark.[5]) Husbands and wives came together again.[6]) Once out of the ark, Noah

---

[1]) Debates over whether the flood reached as high as the garden of Eden are found in rabbinic literature: *Gen. R.* 33. 6; *Lev. R.* 31. 10; *Cant. R.* 1. 15, § 4; 4. 1, § 2; cf. *PRE.* 23. Of the Syrian fathers, Mar Ephrem said it only reached the outer confines of Paradise; see A. Levene, *op. cit.*, p. 83. Cf. D. Gerson, *Die Commentarien des Ephraem Syrus im Verhältniss zur jüdischen Exegese* (Breslau: Schletter'schen Buchhandlung, 1868), p. 12. III *Bar.* 4:10 and *T. Ps.-Jon.*, Gen. 9:20, have the vine float out of Paradise.

[2]) Cf. Origen, *Hom. in Gen.* ii. 1 (*GCS.* 29. 26); Sulpicius Severus, *Chron.* 1. 3 (*CSEL.* 1. 5).

[3]) Philo, *QG.* ii. 36, 39, and certain Christian sources following the misunderstanding of the Hebrew idiom by the LXX (ἐξελθὼν οὐχ ὑπέστρεψεν), repeated by the Vulgate, inferred that the raven never returned to the ark. Chrysostom argues that the "until" of Matt. 1:25 does not imply later sex relations any more than "until" in Genesis implies that the raven later returned: *In Matt.* Hom. v. 3 (*PG.* 57. 58); cf. Augustine, *In Ps.* 102. 16 (*PL.* 37. 1330); *In Ioannis Evang.* Tr. 6. 3 (*PL.* 35. 1426); see also M. V. David, "L'Épisode des oiseaux dans les récits du déluge," *V.T.*, 7 (Ap., 1957), 189-190. It is a common assumption on the part of many that the raven found ample food from the dead bodies: *PRE.* 23; Augustine, *C. Faustum* 12. 20 (*CSEL.* 25. 348); Sulpicius Severus, *Chron.* i. 3 (*CSEL.* 1. 5).

[4]) The dove in Christian literature is more frequently allegorized to represent the Holy Spirit; see *infra*, p. 174. In a midrash, the dove represents Israel who finds no rest in exile and returns to Palestine, *Gen. R.* 33. 6; cf. *Lam. R.* 1. 3. § 29.

[5]) The one year stay in the ark is in agreement with the chronology of the LXX. This book differs from LXX on the date of the drying of the earth and in having the end of the flood come in the 607th yr. of Noah's life.

[6]) This Haggadah was known to Philo (*QG.* ii. 49); some rabbis: *Gen. R.* 31. 12; *J. Taan.* 1. 6 (*EBI.* II, 15. § 49); *T. B. Sanh.* 108b; *PRE.* 23; Rashi (*EBI.*

requested the Lord to show him what sacrifices to offer. Instructed by the Word of the Lord, Noah offered clean animals (iii. 11).[1]) God, having smelled the offering,[2]) made a covenant that there should be no more flood. The bow in the cloud, intended to stir men to fear and repentance, should be a sign that God's anger and the punishment He intended had passed by.[3]) Noah and his sons were blessed and commanded to be fruitful and multiply.[4]) The earth was commanded to produce herbs (iii. 12).

Noah lived 100 years on the mountain. He and his sons built a city named Semanan after the eight people in the ark. Noah took a root of vine, planted it, made wine, and became drunken.[5]) In this state he came in unto his wife unawares.[6])

Ham saw him senseless, laughed, and told his brothers. Shem and Japheth took a coverlet, walked backwards, and covered the pair. Noah's wife informed her husband of Ham's fault on the next day. Noah cursed Ham and made him a servant to his brothers. Shem and Japheth were blessed (iii. 13).

II, 43); and to a large group of church fathers: Origen, *Selecta in Gen.* 53 (*PG.* 12. 105); Julius Africanus, *Chron.* 4 (*PG.* 10. 68); Hippolytus, *Arabic Frag. to Pent.* II, Gen. 7:6 (*GCS.* 1. 2. 88); John of Damascus, *De fide orth.* 4. 24 (*PG.* 94. 1207 C); Hilary, *Tract. myst.* i. 13 (*SC.* 19. 101); see also the Arabic ms. cited by J. G. Frazer, *op. cit.,* I, 146 and L. Ginzberg, *Die Haggada bei den Kirchenvätern*, pp. 81-82.

[1]) Sulpicius Severus, *Chron.* i. 4 (*CSEL.* 1. 5), has Noah to offer birds.

[2]) Certain Christian writers were disturbed by the anthropomorphism involved in God's smelling the savor of the sacrifice as they were also by His repentance. Simon attempts to prove by this and other anthropomorphisms that the God spoken of is not the supreme God; see Ps.-Clem., *Hom.* iii. 39 (*GCS.* 42. 71). This must have been a common argument made by opponents for Ambrose, *De spiritu Sancto* ii. 68 (*PL.* 16. 788), replies that we are not to assume that God is fashioned after bodily form, but that there are spiritual nostrils. Cf. Novatian, *De Trinitate* 6 (*PL.* 3.922); Gregory of Nyssa, *C. Eunomian,* Bk. II (*NPNF.* ser. ii. 5. 274). Ps.-Melito, *The Key,* Frag. 9 (*ANF.* 8. 760), allegorizes the phrase to imply God's delight in the prayers and works of the saints.

[3]) For additional references to the rainbow, see Victorinus, *Comm. Ap.* 4. 3 (*CSEL.* 49. 48); Ephraem, *Nisibene Hymns* 1. 2 (*NPNF.* ser. ii. 13. 167), sings of the bow and the cross as God's two great signs. Ps.-Tertullian, *Ap.* I, *Sodoma* 1 (*PL.* 2.1101 B), poetically comments on the colors of the bow.

[4]) Passing allusions to the fact of blessing are to be found in *Tobit* 4:12; *Jub.* 19:27; and Ps.-Clem., *Recog.* i. 30 (*PG.* 1. 1224).

[5]) To Lactantius, *Div. inst.* ii. 13 (*CSEL.* 19. 161), the entire affair made Noah the inventor of wine rather than Bacchus. The claim for Bacchus was only another example of how the Greeks had falsified in their claims to antiquity. Other references to Noah's planting are found in *Jub.* 7:1-9; Josephus, *Ant.* i. 6. 3; and *Gen. Apoc.* XII. 13.

[6]) That Noah's drunkenness was an affair with his wife was taught by some rabbis, *Gen. R.* 36. 4; cf. "self indulgence culminated in lust," Jerome, *Ep.* 22. 8 (*CSEL.* 54. 155).

Noah lived on 350 more years after he came out of the ark; meantime he had married again and begotten seven other children.[1]) Prior to his death, he charged Shem to bring the body of Adam out of the ark and to bury it in the middle of the earth in the presence of Melchizedek. The writer declares that this spot is the place where God "will work salvation for the whole world" (iii. 13). The ark had been closed with a padlock (iii. 18) since the time of the flood with no one permitted to touch it except Noah. He had kept a lamp lighted morning and evening before the body of Adam (iii. 14). Noah divided the earth among his descendants and then died on Wednesday, the 2nd of Gembot, on the mountain where the ark was. He had attained an age of 950 years (iii. 15).

This survey of material from the *Book of Adam and Eve* demonstrates that this writer treats the flood out of a background where the Christological interpretation of the O.T. has thoroughly penetrated. At the same time, his writing reflects considerable influence of haggadic materials. The typological exegesis, so characteristic of other Christian treatment of the O.T., only reveals itself in the interpretation of the dove.

We have seen in this section something of the great variety of presentations of the flood to be found in Apocrypha and Pseudepigrapha. The exegesis exhibits homiletical exhortation, Scripture paraphrase, midrashic exegesis, apocalyptic symbolism, and allegory. Whether the material be Jewish or Christian, the narrative is condensed or embellished, as the case may be, in keeping with the requirements of the atmosphere that produced the exegete.

---

[1]) The MT. does not include the phrase with Noah "he begat sons and daughters" as it does for other patriarchs. That Noah married again or had other children is unique to this source. Cf. the stress in other Christian writings that from the three sons the world was repopulated, Augustine, *In Ps.* 68. 1 (*PL*. 36. 840); *Civ. Dei* 15. 26 (*CSEL*. 40. 2. 118).

CHAPTER THREE

THE FLOOD IN HELLENISTIC-JEWISH WRITERS

Each of the three figures to be considered in this chapter: Philo, Pseudo-Philo, and Josephus, represents a different degree of penetration of the Greek spirit into Judaism. The consequences are that each offers a different solution to flood problems.

A. Philo of Alexandria

In Philo we encounter a loyal Jew into whom the Greek spirit has penetrated to the maximum. Philo is trained in philosophy and uses the language of mystery, but he chooses to present the bulk of his ideas in connection with Scripture passages. Back of it all is a spirit of exhortation which would instruct one on how to live the religious life.[1]

Philo relates the flood "both as a marvel and as a means of edification." [2] Three levels are observable in his material: the historical event of the past, the lessons to be drawn from it, and the allegories which may be attached to it.[3] The fact that a particular passage was interpreted in one way did not at all preclude the possibility of its also having a second meaning.[4] Repeatedly when citing a passage he says, "The literal meaning is clear," and makes no further comment.[5] For some passages, however, he suggests that the entire passage is to be taken allegorically; [6] while for still others no allegory is offered.[7]

It is extremely difficult to segregate the various levels, but we shall attempt to consider the first two together and save the allegorical for a separate section. It is obvious, however, that the literal often slips off into allegory. There are also numerous cases where the passage

---

[1] Samuel Sandmel, "Philo's Environment and Philo's Exegesis," *JBR.*, XXII (Oct., 1954), 251.

[2] *Mos.* ii. 59.

[3] Cf. R. Marcus, *Philo*, "QG., Intro." (Loeb Series), p. ix.

[4] H. A. Wolfson, *Philo* (Cambridge: Harvard U. Press, 1948), I, 126-127. Philo compares the two meanings to body and soul, both of which need attention, *Mig.* 89-94.

[5] E.g., *QG.* ii. 25, etc.

[6] E.g., *QG.* ii. 36, 37; *Det.* 167. Philo suggests that the story of the creation of woman (Gen. 2:21) is a myth, *LA.* ii. 19.

[7] *QG.* ii. 67.

is merely quoted with no literal explanation attempted. To make anything like a complete flood story, these episodes must be included in the literal. It is well to keep in mind that Philo comments upon the Greek rather than upon the Hebrew text. However, even when we compare his biblical quotations with the LXX, they show some interesting variants. It is not unusual for him to offer two or more alternative explanations to the same passage.

For our purpose, the several treatises which take their titles, from the flood material [1]) prove rather disappointing. In most cases in these books Philo has merely used texts as his point of departure. His conception of the flood even must be drawn from the passages scattered here and there where he uses it as an illustration of some other point. The most complete treatments are to be found in *De Abrahamo*, *De Vita Mosis*, *Quod Deus immutabilis sit*, and finally in even greater detail in *Quaestiones et Solutiones in Genesin*.

A glance at the index to scriptural passages which is included as an appendix to this study will reveal that Philo has quoted or referred to a considerable majority of the verses in the flood material. Even a casual reading of all the pertinent discussion will demonstrate that Philo has wrestled with the major problems about the flood that have bothered men through the centuries.

Since there are repetitions in Philo's flood material and since he has not presented his thoughts verse by verse, we have chosen to follow a general logical order, rather than the pedantic method of attempting to go verse by verse. Though no such system is observable in Philo, the modern mind finds it practically impossible to grasp his thought without using a system. We trust that we shall not do complete violence to him in supplying the lack.

1. *The Literal Noah.*

Philo understood the בני־האלהים who took wives of whom they chose, to be angels of God.[2]) Insisting that we are not to consider this story a myth, he asserts that souls, demons, and angels are but different names for the same object. Moses called them angels, but the philosophers call them demons. We are not to doubt that, though imperceptible to the senses, they do hover in the air, and that it is filled with them.[3]) While some angels remained in the service of God, others

---

[1]) *Gig.*, *Agr.*, *Plant.*, *Ebr.*, and *Sob.*
[2]) *Gig.* 6; Codex Alex. reads ἄγγελοι in this passage of Gen.; cf. P. Katz, *Philo's Bible* (Cambridge: U. Press, 1950), pp. 20-21.   [3]) *Gig.* 6-9.

descended into the bodies of men, to become more wicked than the generation of the flood.[1]) It should be noticed, however, that Philo can also assert that "sons of God" is a name which Moses uses for "good and excellent men." [2])

Philo solves the problem of angels having sex by his suggestion that angels, for the purpose, were able to imitate the forms of men.[3]) This could not take place until after God's spirit had departed.[4]) For Philo the giants were the progeny of the angels and women.[5]) Relying on the order of mention of events in Scripture, Philo insists that a rapid increase in population took place after Noah and his sons were born. He insists that when rarity appears, such as the justice of Noah, its opposite (injustice) always is found in abundance.[6])

Upon Philo's presuppositions, there can be no change in God; hence he must struggle with the idea that God is said to repent. This he does in several ways. First he asserts that only the careless inquirer can suppose that God really repents. This is a sin more serious than that of the generation of the flood.[7]) He renders Gen. 6:6, "God was concerned when reflecting that He had made man on the earth." [8]) Philo understood by this that God merely considered the fact that He had made man a mixture of body and soul and that even the heavenly man is merely a corpse bearer.[9]) Man, made with freedom of choice and having turned to evil, may justly be charged with guilt.[10]) Philo at other times considers the passage to say that God was "angry" that he had made man [11]) or that they had become what they were through God's wrath. [12]) Since God is also by definition without anger—for wrath is a source of misdeeds, but the reasoning faculty is the source of right actions [13])—Philo has engulfed himself in a prob-

---

[1]) *Gig.* 12-13.

[2]) *QG.* i. 92.

[3]) *QG.* i. 92. Philo's assertion is repeated in Ps.-Clem., *Hom.* viii. 12 (*GCS.* 42. 126).

[4]) This is Philo's interpretation of Gen. 6:4, μετ᾽ ἐκεῖνο (after that), *Immut.* 1-2.

[5]) *QG.* i. 92; *Immut.* 1; cf. *Gig.* 58.

[6]) *Gig.* 1.

[7]) *Immut.* 21.

[8]) Philo's quotation differs from the LXX and the Armenian O.T.; cf. R. Marcus (Loeb Series), *QG.* i. 93, note v; cf. *QG.* ii. 54 for a discussion of God's reflection.

[9]) *QG.* i. 93; cf. *Immut.* 33.

[10]) *Immut.* 48.

[11]) *QG.* i. 95; cf. LXX; *Immut.* 51.

[12]) *Immut.* 70-72, cf. Loeb editor's note.   [13]) *Immut.* 72.

lem which he makes several efforts at solving. It may be that an
elementary lesson is taught in which God accommodates himself to
our feeble nature.[1]) Elsewhere he explains that Moses, by exaggerating,
wished to say that the deeds of the generation were such as to provoke
to anger one who is naturally without anger.[2])

In considering the statements that the earth was corrupted, filled
with injustice,[3]) and all flesh had corrupted his way,[4]) Philo deals at
length with the problem that σάρξ (flesh) is feminine while αὐτός
(his) is masculine. He concludes that God is the antecedent of αὐτός;
hence that it is the way that leads to the Eternal that is corrupted.[5])
He enlarges upon the wickedness of the generation by saying that
men were engaged in rivalries for the first place in premeditated sins,
leaving nothing undone to excel in a guilty life. Every nation, country,
city, household, and private individual was filled with evil practices.[6])
God then said that the time of all mankind had come against Him for
the earth was filled with violence, indicating that all agreed in iniquity.[7])

God declared that His spirit could not καταμένειν (abide) on these
because they were flesh.[8]) Man's life span was set at 120 years, which
length Moses reached.[9]) Philo, however, elsewhere admits that this
may not be the limit of human life, since men lived longer in later
generations. He admits that it may only be the time the men who
were later to perish in the flood were given for repentance.[10])

Philo found three reasons why the beasts were included in the
decree of destruction: (1) When a king dies in battle, his force is
usually struck down with him, and in this case, man is the king of the
animals. (2) When the head of the body is removed, the rest of the
body dies. Here man is the head.[11]) (3) The beasts were made for man's
service, and without him they were no longer of value.[12])

---

[1]) *Immut.* 52. [2]) *QG.* i. 95. [3]) *QG.* i. 98.
[4]) *QG.* i. 99.
[5]) *Immut.* 140-143.
[6]) *Abr.* 40.
[7]) *QG.* i. 100.
[8]) *Gig.* 19; *QG.* i. 90.
[9]) *Gig.* 55-57. The rabbis also connect the 120 yrs. with Moses, though in
different ways, *Gen. R.* 26. 6; *T. B. Hullin* 139b. Lactantius, *Div. inst.* ii. 13
(*CSEL.* 19. 160), comments on the 120 years: "that the length of life might not
again be a cause of mediating evils [God] gradually diminished the age of man
by each successive generation, and placed a limit at 120 years, which it might
not be permitted to exceed."
[10]) *QG.* i. 91; cf. *Wisd.* 12:20.
[11]) *QG.* ii. 9, 56.
[12]) *QG.* i. 94; ii. 9; cf. *Gen. R.* 28. 6 and *T. B. Sanh.* 108a.

The survivor of the flood, Noah, son of Lamech,[1]) was the tenth generation from Adam.[2]) He was named "Noah" because he brought rest from the work of hands and from the ground which God had cursed.[3]) Philo also attempts to set forth the word δίκαιος (righteous), which really stands in the text as an adjective modifying Noah, as though it were intended for an etymology.[4])

Philo comments that Noah is the first man called "just" in Scripture.[5]) That this righteousness was quite important for him is seen in the fact that he regularly introduces a comment with such phrases as: "the man who proved righteous,"[6]) "righteous Noah,"[7]) "Noah was just," [8]) or "the righteous man." [9])

Philo further praises Noah by asserting that he was of excellent nature from birth.[10]) In addition he had acquired all virtues;[11]) he had committed no deliberate wrong;[12]) and he was of special holiness.[13]) In a generation in which the earth was corrupt and filled with iniquity, only Noah was grateful to God.[14]) Philo assures us that Moses particularly intended to extol his virtues in the order of ascending importance in the phrases of Gen. 6:9: "just, perfect in his generation, well-pleasing to God."[15]) Because of his just and excellent character he was worthy of two rewards, one of which was to survive the flood, while the second was to be the beginner of a new generation and to have the animals entrusted to his care.[16])

Despite all these praises, however, Philo is well acquainted with the idea of a comparative righteousness based on the phrase "in his generation." Noah was the best of his contemporaries,[17]) and all the

---

[1]) *Post.* 48. [2]) *QG.* i. 87.
[3]) *Det.* 121; *QG.* i. 87.
[4]) *QG.* i. 87; ii. 45; *Abr.* 27; *LA.* iii. 77; *Det.* 121. Origen, *Hom. in Gen.* ii. 3 (*GCS.* 29. 31), and Ambrose, *De Noe* i. 2; cf. *De paradiso* iii. 19 (*CSEL.* 32. 1. 413, 277), seem to have borrowed the idea from Philo.
[5]) *Cong.* 90.
[6]) *Det.* 170.
[7]) *Post.* 48, 173, 174; *Mig.* 125; *Conf.* 105; *Gig.* 3, 5; *Mut.* 139.
[8]) *Heres* 260.
[9]) *QG.* ii. 33, 34.
[10]) *LA.* iii. 77; cf. *Gen. R.* 30. 8: "unchanged from beginning to end."
[11]) *Abr.* 34; *Praem.* 22-23.
[12]) *Mos.* ii. 59.
[13]) *Virt.* 201.
[14]) *QG.* i. 96; cf. *Immut.* 122.
[15]) *Abr.* 31 ff.; *Immut.* 117.
[16]) *Abr.* 46; *Mos.* ii. 59-60; *QG.* i. 96; *Praem.* 23. Noah as the beginner of a new race is a concept which is frequent in the church fathers.
[17]) *Abr.* 36, 47; cf. *Gen. R.* 30. 9.

myriads of the generations of the unjust are not his equal in value,[1]) but Abraham begins his progress at the highest point Noah reached,[2]) while Moses is still greater.[3])

Philo equates Noah with the Greek flood figure, Deucalion. Such an equation of Greek mythical, heathen figures with O.T. characters is almost unique for Philo's writings.[4])

The grace which Noah found before God [5]) is not to be understood in the sense that Noah obtained grace, for all creatures are recipients of divine grace. More likely the idea is that he was thought worthy of grace. But Philo hesitates to ascribe so high a thing to Noah as to say that he was "worthy," [6]) so he concludes that Noah discovered that all things are a grace of God.[7]) This favor, as has been implied, was to be allowed to be the τέλος (end) of one generation, to have the animals entrusted to him, and to be the ἀρχή (first) of another generation.[8])

When Philo turns from the hero of the flood to the ark, he operates with the measurements 300 by 50 by 30 cubits taken from Scripture. The ark was finished to a cubit above, coming together gradually in the manner of a mound.[9]) The large size was required in order to accommodate all the animals.[10]) Squared beams were used,[11]) and the interior was divided into nests.[12]) Elsewhere Philo used οἰκήματα (rooms) without repeating the word as he does in the above passage;[13]) however, his allegory on the passage is dependent on the reading "nests." The ark had four floor levels[14]) and was covered with tar inside and outside.[15])

Noah, knowing that God was gracious, looked for better times

---

[1]) *Praem.* 23.
[2]) *Post.* 175.
[3]) *Immut.* 109.
[4]) *Praem.* 23; cf. note by editor in Loeb series. Historical figures are sometimes used, for Terah is said to be Socrates, *Som.* i. 58.
[5]) *QG.* i. 96; *Immut.* 70, 74, 86.
[6]) *Immut.* 106.
[7]) *Immut.* 107.
[8]) *QG.* i. 96; cf. *Praem.* 22.
[9]) *QG.* ii. 5; cf. note by editor of Loeb series.
[10]) *QG.* ii. 5; cf. *Mos.* ii. 59-61.
[11]) *QG.* ii. 2.
[12]) *QG.* ii. 3. The text would presuppose νοσσιάς; however LXX mss. do not repeat νοσσιάς as Philo does; see note, p. 70, Loeb edition.
[13]) *Mos.* ii. 60.
[14]) *Mos.* ii. 60; cf. Josephus, *infra*, p. 78.
[15]) *QG.* ii. 4.

ahead, and preserved seed along with himself—a male and female of creatures of land and air.[1]) For this purpose, the animals became tame and followed him into the ark as a flock follows its leader.[2]) Since in the effort to preserve each genus of animal,[3]) some of all sorts were in the ark, the whole collection was a sort of miniature of earth.[4]) When the collection was completed, the ark was carefully closed from without, lest the water come through any part in the storm-tossed year it experienced.[5])

The seven days which elapsed after the entrance into the ark provided men of the generation one more opportunity to repent. The fact that the animals were already in the ark re-emphasized Noah's preaching that the flood was approaching. God's mercy in its abundance is revealed in this added time. Repentance of a few days releases from many years of sin. The seven day period also reminds one of the seven days of creation. Since God both creates and destroys, the ungrateful should note the correspondence and repent.[6])

As the rain began, the waters increased, lifted up the ark, and bore it upon the water.[7]) The great deep rose to unprecedented heights, coming up into seas, and making tides which flooded islands and continents. Rivers and streams also added their waters.[8]) A great cloud covered the whole heaven.[9]) A great rainstorm from heaven with thunder, lightning, and wind added its water. The highest mountains were covered; all parts of the earth sank beneath the water. The air also was made away with except a small part belonging to the moon.[10]) Philo is quite specific that the flood went fifteen cubits over the highest mountains and still higher over others.[11]) However when he, in another place, says that it almost flowed out beyond the Pillars of Heracles and the Great Sea,[12]) he reveals his limited conception of the size of the world.

With such a flood, crops and animals perished, while only the house

---

[1]) *Mos.* ii. 60-61.
[2]) *Mos.* ii. 61.
[3]) *QG.* ii. 12.
[4]) *Mos.* ii. 62.
[5]) *QG.* ii. 19.
[6]) *QG.* ii. 13.
[7]) Philo's text differs from the LXX; see editor's note, *QG.* ii. 20.
[8]) *Abr.* 42.
[9]) *Abr.* 43.
[10]) *Abr.* 43-45; *Virt.* 201.
[11]) *QG.* ii. 21.
[12]) *QG.* ii. 28.

of one just man was preserved; [1]) but we are not to understand that this blotting out of all growth of vegetation (thusly he renders the Heb. יקום) included roots, or seeds, or other things below the surface, for the passage says "upon the surface" of the earth.[2])

In his chronology of the flood, Philo departs both from the MT. and from the LXX. He has the flood begin in the seventh month (against MT. and LXX which have "second"), the twenty-seventh day (as LXX). His chronology is preserved only in *Quaestiones et Solutiones in Genesin* which has been transmitted to us in Armenian. His beginning month corresponds with that of the Armenian O.T., but the fact that his major argument demands the seventh month precludes its being merely a scribal harmonization. The fact that Philo asserts that the seventh month may under other conditions be called the first makes it obvious that he started his count at Tishri. The flood came at the vernal equinox, which made it an even more severe punishment since everything was giving birth or was in bloom.[3]) The day also happens to correspond, according to Philo, with Noah's birthday.[4])

Following the forty days of rain, there comes a period of 150 days when the fountains of the deep flowed only enough to keep the water level up.[5]) This was a five month period. Philo seems at first not entirely certain whether to take the 150 days of Gen. 8:3 as simultaneous with the period of Gen. 7:24 which he does not discuss in detail, or to consider it as an additional period. A little later he becomes specific, making the two figures separate periods, and explains that the water rose 150 days, then took an additional 150 days to decrease. This of course creates a chronological impossibility in his total system, for when two forty day periods and then three seven day periods are added, one goes quite beyond one year. However, Philo wants the increase of the flood to equal its waning exactly.[6])

In this chronological system, the tops of the mountains are seen in the tenth month, the first day of the month. After forty days, Noah opened the window of the ark.[7]) Philo is perfectly capable of changing horses in the middle of the stream, and this he does when he comes to

---

[1]) *Abr.* 45-46.
[2]) *QG.* ii. 15.
[3]) *QG.* ii. 17, 45, 47.
[4]) *QG.* ii. 33.
[5]) *QG.* ii. 29.
[6]) *QG.* ii. 33.
[7]) *QG.* ii. 32, 33.

4

the date (Gen. 8:4) upon which the ark landed on Mt. Ararat. Here
the MT. and LXX have the seventh month. Philo has to calculate this
date, not from his previous starting point of the year, but rather from
the beginning of the flood, or from Nisan rather than from Tishri. He
asserts that this landing on the 27th day took place at the fall equinox,[1]) though anyone can see that between Nisan and Tishri there are
really only five months. This forces him to count the beginning and
ending portions of months as full months.

The command to go forth from the ark comes in the seventh
month, the twenty-seventh day, of the 601st year of Noah's life.[2])
Philo wants us to understand that this is both the first and the seventh
month.[3]) He uses the phrases "seventh in nature, but first in time"
and "seventh in time, but first in nature." [4]) The juggling is for the
purpose of having the flood last exactly one calendar year.[5]) Thus
Philo equates the month of Gen. 8:13 when the covering of the ark
is removed, with that of Gen. 8:14, though MT. and LXX separate
the two events by a month and twenty-seven days. The flood, then,
both began and ended on the vernal equinox,[6]) which also, as we have
already seen, was Noah's birthday.[7])

Since for Philo God is the self-existent one (Tὸ Ὄν), He had and
needed no name except for man's benefit that man might invoke Him
in prayer.[8]) Nevertheless, Philo did not hesitate to attribute names
and personifications to God's powers. The chiefs of these were the
creative or beneficent power which is called Θεός and the regal power
called Κύριος. Since a ruler must punish, the latter of these may be
thought of as a punitive power through which destruction comes.[9])

In his exegesis of flood material, Philo notes that both of these
names occur together in Gen. 7:5 because, though it was a time of
judgment which demanded that Κύριος occur first, it was also a time
of mercy in that some were spared.[10]) After the flood, in the time of
regeneration, God displayed His beneficent aspect, therefore Noah

---

[1]) *QG.* ii. 31, 33, 47.
[2]) MT. and LXX have the second month and the twenty-seventh day.
[3]) *QG.* ii. 45.
[4]) *QG.* ii. 47.
[5]) *QG.* ii. 46, 47.
[6]) *QG.* ii. 47.
[7]) *QG.* ii. 33.
[8]) *Abr.* 51.
[9]) *Gig.* 45-47; *QG.* ii. 16; *Heres* 166; *Som.* i. 163.
[10]) *QG.* ii. 16. LXX differs from MT.

sacrifices to Θεός.[1]) However, it is Κύριος Θεός who receives it,[2]) and from this we should learn that God is inclined to us with both his powers.[3]) Later in the narrative, Shem, while being blessed, is considered worthy of honor from both powers, but has a double grace from the beneficent power in that Θεός is repeated in Philo's text.[4])

The effort to form a direct connection between Philo's powers and the *middot* of the rabbis [5]) seems vulnerable on three scores: first the rabbis deal with אלהים and יהוה while Philo deals with the Greek terms, Θεός and Κύριος, which the LXX had used to translate the Hebrew terms. Second, the significance attached to the names is precisely the reverse to that of the rabbis. Rabbis used אלהים for justice and יהוה for mercy.[6]) Third, even more significant is the fact that for the rabbis God had a name. For Philo it is only the powers of God, not God himself, that are designated by the variant names.[7])

Reverting to the point at which we were before the chronology and the names of the powers were considered, we note that while the flood was on, God is said to have remembered Noah. We are to understand that this means He remembered the whole family, for they are included along with their head.[8]) The phenomenon that the beasts are mentioned between man and cattle in Gen. 8:1 occurs that the treatment may illustrate the saying, "He drove the base ones in the middle." Their place also serves to tame them through their association with the other two; and furthermore, Scripture was about to bless them along with the others by mentioning the going down of the flood.[9])

God next brings the πνεῦμα over the earth, but we should not understand this to be "wind." Philo would have had this problem whether dealing with Greek or Hebrew since πνεῦμα and רוח both may mean either "spirit" or "wind." Philo remarks, however, that wind would only stir up the water, so we learn that it was the

---

[1]) *QG.* ii. 51; cf. Gen. 8:20.
[2]) MT. reads יהוה.
[3]) *QG.* ii. 53.
[4]) *QG.* ii. 75.
[5]) H. A. Wolfson, *Philo* (Cambridge: Harvard U. Press, 1948), I, 224-225.
[6]) *Gen. R.* 33. 3; cf. G. F. Moore, *Judaism* (Cambridge: Harvard U. Press, 1930), III, note 123.
[7]) For a survey of further debate over names, see S. Sandmel, *Philo's Place in Judaism* (Cincinnati: H. U. C. Press, 1956), pp. 21-22, 180; J. Drummond, *Philo Judaeus* (London: Williams and Norgate, 1888), II, 84-86.
[8]) *QG.* ii. 26.
[9]) *QG.* ii. 27.

spirit of God which made things secure which passed over the earth.[1])
The drying up of the flood was in part due to the heat of the sun and
in part due to its receding at God's command, each part into the
places from whence it came.[2])

Noah waits forty days after the ark grounds before opening the
window of the ark. These days correspond to the forty days of rain.[3])
The raven is sent forth as a sort of "heralding and fulfilling" creature.
People observe its flight because it caws as though indicating something hidden.[4]) Following the failure of the raven to return, Noah
sends the dove to see if the earth is "dried of water." However, to
Philo, the order of words in this phrase makes it certain that the
phrase is entirely allegorical.[5]) The dove is sent "from himself" which
indicates that the dove as a clean creature was a fellow inhabitant
with Noah.[6]) Finding no resting place for its feet,[7]) it returns to Noah,
and he stretches out his hand to bring it to himself.[8]) After holding
back another seven days he again sends out the dove [9]) which returns
at evening with an olive leaf, a dry branch, in its mouth,[10]) and Noah
knows that the water has ceased from off the earth.[11]) After seven more
days the dove is sent forth a third time and does not return.[12])

Noah opens the covering of the ark and discovers the renewed
earth is quite like it had been when originally created.[13]) The trees,
following the flood, had sprouted and borne fruit in one day just as
plants were produced in one day at creation.[14])

Noah remains in the ark until commanded to go out, because
righteousness is reverent. As he entered by command, so he leaves
by command. With him go the living creatures.[15]) He had not only
won his own safety, but became the inaugurator of a second cycle.[16])

---

[1]) *QG.* ii. 28.   [2]) *Mos.* ii. 63.
[3]) *QG.* ii. 33.
[4]) *QG.* ii. 35.
[5]) *QG.* ii. 37.
[6]) *QG.* ii. 38. Philo's text is nearer the MT. than to the LXX which has "after
him," meaning after the raven. See note in Loeb edition.
[7]) *QG.* ii. 39.
[8]) *QG.* ii. 40.
[9]) *QG.* ii. 41.
[10]) *QG.* ii. 42.
[11]) *QG.* ii. 43.
[12]) *QG.* ii. 44.
[13]) *Mos.* ii. 64.
[14]) *QG.* ii. 47.
[15]) *QG.* ii. 48. Philo abbreviates the MT. which has "birds, beasts and reptiles."
[16]) *Mos.* ii. 65.

From the fact that the wives are mentioned with their mother-in-law when they go into the ark, Gen. 7:7, but with their husbands when they go out, Philo, as does the Midrash, deduces that there was no sexual intercourse in the ark.[1]) The argument could be based on the order of words in the LXX which harmonizes the order of Gen. 8:16 with Gen. 8:18. The MT. has the wife of Noah mentioned before the sons in v. 16, but following them in v. 18, even as it does in Gen. 7:7.

Though Noah had not been commanded to do so, he builds an altar without delay and offers clean beasts and birds to show his gratitude.[2]) The Lord God reflects and promises not to curse the earth again because of the deeds of men for the thought of man is resolutely turned toward evils from his youth.[3]) Though there may be many future floods, they will not inundate the whole earth.[4]) Never again will God smite all living flesh as He had done.[5]) How could He fail to destroy them should the same cause arise again? Arguing from the exact wording of the passage, Philo concludes that all mankind will not again be destroyed, but only the greater part of those who commit undesirable wrongs. Philo, in further considering God's repentance, makes a distinction between a passage intended for "truth" and one designed for "teaching." In this case he understands "reflecting" to indicate God's sureness of purpose, of which purpose Philo does not feel man is capable. God need not curse the earth again, for the one curse already in operation since Adam has sufficient evil in it to handle the situation.[6]) God proceeds to promise the permanent recurrence of the annual seasons that the animals may be secure in their suitable climates.[7]) Philo seems to have understood that God, in making this covenant, made it to stand on Noah.[8])

The blessing of God after the flood when He said, "Increase and multiply and fill the earth and dominate it," [9]) is the same blessing granted to the man of Gen. 1 and indicates that God considers the

[1]) *QG.* ii. 49; *Gen. R.* 31. 12; 34. 7.
[2]) *QG.* ii. 50, 52. Philo considers all the episode to convey "a deeper meaning."
[3]) *QG.* ii. 54.
[4]) *QG.* ii. 63.
[5]) *QG.* ii. 54.
[6]) *QG.* ii. 54, 63.
[7]) *QG.* ii. 55.
[8]) *Som.* ii. 224; cf. editor's note, Loeb series.
[9]) *QG.* ii. 56. Philo is quite specific that the wording of the text quotes the spoken blessing. The reading agrees with LXX in harmonizing the wording of Gen. 9:1 with 1:28 as does Augustine, *De nuptis* ii. [9] 21 (*CSEL.* 42. 273).

beginning of a second genesis of man of equal honor and kingship with the one made in His image. Philo has slightly abbreviated the remainder of the spoken blessing.[1]

All reptiles are given Noah for food, by which we are to know that reptiles are of two sorts: poisonous and tame. Poisonous reptiles are those that crawl on the belly, while tame ones have legs above their feet.[2] Animal flesh, like herbs of fodder, is given man to eat.[3] Philo admits that some think this enjoins the eating of meat, but he thinks it means that it is necessary to eat herbs and feels that this implies that other types of food may be, but are not commanded to be, eaten. However he admits that the passage may be intended to be allegorized.[4]

Eating of flesh in the blood of its life is prohibited to Noah's descendants,[5] for blood is the substance of the sense-perceptive soul. Philo has three souls: the first is the divine spirit which is the substance of the rational soul; the second is sense-perceptive; while the third type is the nutritive. Mind and reflection are not in the flesh. We are to understand by the wording of the expression in Genesis that the soul is one thing and the blood another. The real substance of the soul is spirit, but it is carried along and mixed together with the blood. This Philo seems to derive from the fact that there are both blood and breath in the arteries.[6]

Philo smooths out some of the awkwardness of Gen. 9:5 by having God declare that He will "require your blood of your souls of all living creatures, and from the hand of man of his brother." He understands that both beasts and man prey on others, but men are the more dangerous of the two. The preyers are called "brothers" either from ancient kinship, or because it speaks of family strife, or thirdly because it enjoins blood revenge. Philo favors the last and warns that God is an overseer of those who are slain by men. Those then who despise the carrying out of justice are to beware.[7]

In commenting upon "The one who sheds blood of a man in return for his blood he shall be shed," [8] Philo wants us to know that

---

[1] *QG.* ii. 56; cf. editor's note, Loeb series.   [2] *QG.* ii. 57.
[3] Philo follows the LXX. The MT. has "herbs of grass."
[4] *QG.* ii. 58.
[5] Philo is quoting the LXX.
[6] *QG.* ii. 59.
[7] *QG.* ii. 60; cf. *T. Onkelos*; *T. Ps.-Jon.*, Gen. 9:6.
[8] Philo follows the LXX which is less intelligible than the MT.; cf. R. Marcus in the Loeb series, *QG.* ii. 61.

this awkward passage is not in error, but the murderer is to be shed like blood. Since the passage says "in the image of God" rather than "in His image" we are to understand that man is in the image of the *Logos* rather than of the most high God. We are further to know that God avenges virtuous and decent men because of this kinship.[1]

The two above mentioned items are the only ones which Philo connects with the flood which overlap the "Noah laws" of the rabbinic oral law.[2] Wolfson has attempted to show that Philo has a series of natural laws, not all connected with the flood, which overlap, to an extent, the Noah laws: (1) Belief that the place of the created is lower than the creator and a belief in providence. Compare this with the rabbinic prohibition of worship of idols. (2) Courts of justice. (3) Prohibition of murder. (4) Prohibition of adultery. (5) Prohibition of hybridization, which is in some rabbinic lists.[3] There is, however, a fundamental difference between Philo's concept of law and that of the oral law of the rabbis. For Philo, the patriarchs observe the laws of nature. The Law of Moses, an enacted law, is merely a copy of those things which the patriarchs did. The patriarchs are the norm. The rabbis, on the other hand, set up a norm and then date back the observance of the laws prior to their enactment to make the patriarchs conform.[4]

Philo has certain objections to those who think the bow of the promise is the rainbow. The chief of these is his feeling that this "bow" must be of special nature that has previously been non-existent. He is well aware of the relationship of sun, clouds, and the rainbow, and the fact that the last neither appears on a completely cloudy day nor at night. The bow indicates that in the laxness and force of earthly things, they will not be loosened to the point of complete breaking. The bow is not a weapon but is merely the instrument of the real weapon which is the arrow. It is, then, the invisible power of God which is in the air; which power does not permit the clouds to turn entirely to water so that the flood comes again.[5]

---

[1] *QG.* ii. 62.
[2] *T. B. Sanh.* 56b.
[3] H. A. Wolfson, *Philo* (Cambridge: Harvard U. Press, 1948), II, 184-187.
[4] S. Sandmel, *Philo's Place in Judaism* (Cincinnati: H. U. C. Press, 1956), pp. 107-108.
[5] *QG.* ii. 64. The early Syrian church fathers solve the problem of the prior existence of the rainbow by saying that the prediluvial mist made it invisible; see A. Levene, *op. cit.*, p. 195.

We are to learn by Noah's husbandry of earth,[1]) that agriculture here begins again as it did with the first man. At that time the earth's appearing out of the water was a sort of recovering from a flood. Noah is then the beginning of seed, agriculture, and other forms of life.[2])

Philo wonders where Noah got the vine, and concludes that since the earth dried in the spring, plants may have sprung up and were gathered by him. The choice of the vine was due to the fact that God furnished the staples of life so that no man should claim credit for them. The vine, however, is a luxury and God allows man to claim credit for it.[3]) From the phrase "drank of the wine" we are to understand that Noah drank only a portion of the wine. Philo is embarrassed by the thought of Noah's drunkenness and wants us to understand that Noah did not drink to excess. He contrasts the type of drunkenness which is drinking to excess and the drunkenness which is merely partaking of wine which the wise man does.[4]) He elsewhere speaks of a lapse into which Noah had involuntarily fallen.[5])

It is to the praise of Noah that his nakedness is concealed by the screen of his house.[6]) Philo agrees with the LXX on Gen. 9:21 in reading "house" where MT. has "tent." [7])

Ham's fault is the casting of shame upon his father by holding up to laughter and scorn some lapse of his.[8]) Philo, like others, has to wrestle with the problem of why Canaan is cursed when no previous crime of his is mentioned.[9]) He prepares for his solution by saying that only the generation of Ham is given in Gen. 9:18 because Noah is soon to speak about Canaan.[10]) However, when he gets to the actual episode, he notes that Canaan's name is missing and that only Ham is specified. Thus Moses convicts both Ham and Canaan of acting in common in the act of folly.[11]) In one place he has Canaan do the

---

[1]) The text agrees with LXX; *QG.* ii. 66.

[2]) *QG.* ii. 66.

[3]) *QG.* ii. 67.

[4]) *QG.* ii. 68.

[5]) *Virt.* 202.

[6]) *QG.* ii. 69; cf. *LA.* ii. 60 ff.

[7]) Cf. also on Gen. 9:25 and 9:27; Edwin Hatch, *Essays in Biblical Greek* (Oxford: Clarendon Press, 1889), pp. 152-153; H. B. Swete, *Intro. to the O.T. in Greek* (Cambridge: U. Press, 1902), p. 374.

[8]) *Virt.* 202; cf. *Sob.* 32.

[9]) *Sob.* 31.   [10]) *QG.* ii. 65.

[11]) *QG.* ii. 70; others who make both guilty include Origen, *Selecta in Gen.* 61 (*PG.* 12. 108); the Syrian fathers; see A. Levene, *op. cit.*, p. 84; and Abrabanel (*EBI.* II, 69).

reporting.[1]) In another place he remarks that Ham, being saddened by what befell his son, in a sense, suffered punishment.[2]) In still another place he speaks as though Ham were actually cursed.[3])

The folly of Ham is even more obvious when we learn that he told "both" brothers of Noah's condition. From the word "outside" which is in the text, we are to understand that he also made it known to others, both men and women alike.[4])

While he considerably abbreviates the biblical verse, Philo makes known to us that Shem and Japheth cover their father with a garment.[5]) Noah then sobers up.[6])

Philo notes that some who have investigated the matter think that Japheth is the oldest son of Noah, Ham the second, and Shem the youngest. As far as he is concerned, one can think what he pleases on the matter. He then proceeds to his allegory based on the sons.[7]) Elsewhere he has given us to understand that Scripture allegorizes entirely when it calls Ham the youngest son.[8])

Noah utters his predictions about his sons under divine possession; hence he is to be considered a prophet as had earlier been indicated by his being called just.[9]) Philo considered many of the patriarchs prophets. When Noah says "Blessed be the Lord God, God of Shem," he indicates Shem's honor from both the beneficent and destructive powers of God, but there is a double portion of the beneficent power since "God" occurs twice.[10]) God is to enlarge Japheth and it is more

---

[1]) *LA*. ii. 62.
[2]) *QG*. ii. 77.
[3]) *Virt*. 202.
[4]) *QG*. ii. 71.
[5]) *QG*. ii. 72.
[6]) *QG*. ii. 73.
[7]) *QG*. ii. 79.
[8]) *QG*. ii. 74.
[9]) *Heres* 260; *QG*. i. 87. The view that Noah's blessing is a prediction concerning his son's descendants, set forth in *Jubilees* 8:18, cf. *Seder Olam* 21 (*EBI*. II, 3), is fairly common in the church fathers; see Justin M., *Dial*. 139. To Theophilus, *Ad Autolycum* iii. 19, it is the foretelling of the coming of the flood that made Noah a prophet. Origen, *C. Celsum* vii. 7 (*GCS*. 3. 159), is less specific about the basis on which he considers Noah a prophet, but Augustine, *Civ. Dei* 18. 38 (*CSEL*. 40. 2. 328), supplied a second reason when he suggested that the building of the ark and the deliverance from the flood was a typological prophecy of what happened later in the church. See also Cyril of Jer., *Catech*. 16. 27 (*PG*. 33. 957A), who included Noah in his list of righteous men and prophets.
[10]) *QG*. ii. 75; *Sob*. 58. Philo seems to consider "Shem" as a dative and thus arrives at his meaning: "Let the Lord be blessed by Shem"; cf. note in Loeb edition.

literal to suppose He is to dwell in the "house" of Shem. Philo, however, is not certain whether to take Japheth or the Lord as the antecedent of the pronoun in Gen. 9:27.[1]

Noah, having become the father of a new race,[2] finally died three
hundred and fifty years after the flood.[3]

This extensive survey reveals that the literal Noah of Philo is a
creation of the currents of Philo's religious background, used by
Philo to expound the virtues he admired. This background had its
philosophical presuppositions, an example of which is its definition
of God, which create some of the problems Philo has attempted to
solve in his treatment of the flood narrative. The Septuagint version
furnishes the text of which Philo gives exegesis; however, there are
a few examples which have been noted where Philo's opinions show
similarities to rabbinic traditions in such matters as that the 120 years
prior to the flood are to be connected with Moses; that the beasts were
destroyed because they were worthless with man gone; that Noah's
righteousness was of a relative nature, a concept based on the phrase,
"in his generation"; and that significance is to be attached to the
alternation of the divine name. In each of these, significant differences
from the rabbis could be pointed out. Philo has developed them in his
own way.

2. *The Allegorical Noah*

In order to understand Philo's allegory on Noah and the flood, one
must keep in mind Philo's presuppositions. Like the rabbis, he
assumed that there is nothing superfluous in Scripture. Grammatical
difficulties and redundancies indicate hidden allegory. Not only is
there the written law given at Sinai, but some individuals were living
embodiment of the law before it was given. In fact, they lived according to nature, and the law from Sinai is the codification of what they
were. Man is a mixture of soul and body. The goal of his striving—
salvation—is to free himself from the fetters of the body which he
must do by a process of mystic knowledge. Noah and the other
patriarchs, in addition to being living men, are types of souls [4]
which represent stages in the advance of the soul toward that mystic
vision.

---

[1] *Sob.* 59-68; *QG.* ii. 76.
[2] *Abr.* 56.
[3] *QG.* ii. 78.
[4] *Abr.* 47.

The patriarchs fall into two triads. The preliminary one is made up of Enos, Enoch, and Noah; while the more advanced group are Abraham, Isaac, and Jacob. Enos represents hope, Enoch is repentance, but Noah is justice. However, his name means "rest," and for that reason he is the limited tranquillity which one may attain short of the ultimate goal. In the struggle for victory over the passions, this first triad is comparable to the studies of children.[1]) Further progress would take one to the second and higher triad of Abraham, Isaac, and Jacob, whose struggles to overcome the passions are comparable to an athlete who despises bodily training and fosters robustness of soul in his struggles for victory.[2]) These latter individuals are symbols of the virtues: teaching, nature, and practice.[3])

Noah then is a preliminary stage in the advance of any soul which has an insatiable desire to be filled with things beautiful. Noah started at the high point of knowledge reached by Seth; Abraham began where Noah ended; while Moses began at Abraham's high point and went still higher to please Him who is pure being.[4]) When one has advanced to the level of Moses he lives in accordance with nature itself.[5])

It is obvious that Philo has not presented a consistent and straightforward allegory that can be traced through the entire flood narrative. It is difficult to follow him when he insists that Noah was of noble character from birth and righteous before the flood,[6]) but then underwent a flood of passion from which he barely escaped. It is hard to see how the deluge can be a symbol of spiritual dissolution and turmoil in the soul and elsewhere be a cleansing of the soul. How can the mind go into the ark when the ark is the body? Is it not already there? It seems a lack of consistency to have Noah escape from the body to higher things and then fall back into a foolish and deranged condition represented in his nakedness. If, however, Philo considers Scripture to be without chronological sequence this problem is

---

[1]) *Abr.* 48.
[2]) *Abr.* 48; cf. S. Sandmel, "Philo's Environment and Philo's Exegesis," *JBR.*, XXII (1954), 251-252; *Philo's Place in Judaism* (Cincinnati: H. U. C. Press, 1956), pp. 100-102; "Philo and His Pupils: An Imaginary Dialogue," *Judaism: A Quarterly J. of Jewish Life and Thought*, IV (Winter, 1955), 52-53.
[3]) *Abr.* 53-54.
[4]) *Post.* 174; *Immut.* 109.
[5]) S. Sandmel, *Philo's Place in Judaism* (Cincinnati: H. U. C. Press, 1956), pp. 100-102.
[6]) *Det.* 170; *LA.* iii. 77.

alleviated. The lapse of Noah becomes a second presentation of the same general idea seen in the flood. Another difficulty is experienced when virtue is represented both by Noah and the dove. To make the passions either male or female, depending on who possesses them, is quite strained.

There are blanks in Philo's scheme which we greatly regret. The link between the multitude of evils in the world and the crisis in the life of the individual righteous man, we miss. It would have helped a lot had Philo been specific about what the man comes forth to as he comes out of the ark.

The details of the allegory are minute, repetitious, and farfetched. Philo's message, nevertheless, can be briefly told. The goals for which men spend their efforts—fame, display, and pleasure—minister only to the body and its lusts and are not worthwhile. The real man cannot at this present time entirely separate himself from his passions, but he can keep them under control, even as Noah was the king over the animals in the ark. He must make use of his body until the flood of passion has dried up and he has expelled the last residue of darkness from his soul, then he can come forth. We assume that it must be to immortality, though Philo is not specific about it in his discussion of this material.

We now proceed to the specific details of the allegory. Moses has reminded us of the multitude of men on the earth immediately after he spoke of the birth of Noah to teach us that while the unjust are many in the earth, the righteous are only few.[1] The unjust produce only "daughters"—nerveless and emasculated passions [2]—in contrast to Noah who, following masculine reason, begets males.[3]

For Philo, angels, demons, and souls are merely different names for the same thing. That there are good angels, he admits; but in this case "angels of God" are wicked souls in fellowship with darkness [4] who woo sensual pleasures ("daughters of men"): pleasures of sight, hearing, palate, belly, sex, or still others.[5]

By the union of the unjust and sensual pleasures, vices are born; for the family of the evil are vices.[6] Since for Philo, the spirit of God

---

[1] *Gig.* 1-3.
[2] *Immut.* 3.
[3] *Gig.* 4-5.
[4] *Immut.* 1-3.
[5] *Gig.* 17-18.
[6] *Immut.* 3-4.

represents that wisdom, intelligence, and pure knowledge that every
man shares,[1]) such a union could not take place until after God's
spirit had departed.[2]) Here Philo is insisting that Scripture has followed
a strict chronological order.[3]) Naturally he must consider why God's
spirit—wisdom—does not always abide in man. He admits that even
the reprobate may have a sudden fleeting glimpse of the excellent,
but he has not the strength to grasp it and keep it for his own.[4])
Only those persons who have stripped themselves of mere opinion and
all created things and come to God naked can experience pure knowledge.[5]) The chief cause of ignorance is the flesh.[6]) The soul must be
free of the flesh and body to hear things divine.[7]) Family cares wither
the flower of wisdom before it blooms.[8]) The nature of the flesh is
also alien to wisdom as long as it is familiar with desire.[9]) Furthermore,
to have many ends in life particularly contributes to impermanence
of wisdom.[10]) In all of these ways Philo stresses that our fleshly nature
thwarts the growth of wisdom. For him, it was only Moses who had
God's spirit continuously.[11])

By the episode of the giants, Moses wishes to show us that some
men are earth-born, some heaven-born, and some God-born. The
heaven-born are votaries of arts and lovers of learning, since it is the
mind that pursues learning. The men of God are priests and prophets
who have risen above the sphere of sense perception and registered
in the commonwealth of ideas.[12]) Earth-born men, pleasure bent, have
turned the mind into the inert nature of the flesh.[13])

The 120 years of Gen. 6:3 is the subject of a long discourse in
which seven cryptic ways of attaining the number are set forth.[14])
The details of these are hardly pertinent here. Philo does not seem
to have carried out his promise of explaining the mystery of this
number.[15])

---

[1]) *QG.* i. 90; *Gig.* 23.
[2]) *Immut.* 1, 3; cf. Gen. 6:4.
[3]) Cf. Gen. 6:3, 4.
[4]) *Gig.* 20.
[5]) *Gig.* 53.
[6]) *Gig.* 28-29.
[7]) *Gig.* 31.
[8]) *Gig.* 29-30.
[9]) *QG.* i. 90.
[10]) *Gig.* 53.
[11]) *Gig.* 54-55.
[12]) *Gig.* 60-61.
[13]) *Gig.* 60, 65.
[14]) *QG.* i. 91.   [15]) *Gig.* 57.

The ten generations from Adam to Noah and from Noah to Abraham are not to be understood as any set number of years.[1]) Instead, these mark the first and second enlargements of Seth. Seth, unlike Abel who has relinquished the mortal and has gone to a better existence, will never relinquish the race of men. Philo would have us mark the advance to improvement made by the soul that has a desire to be filled with things that are beautiful.[2]) Ten in this case is the perfect number that represents that justice in the soul which is the perfect and true end of our life's actions.[3])

Lamech, son of Seth (in contrast to Lamech, a descendant of Cain, who is a type of lawlessness made low by sickness and infirmities brought on by passions), to Philo means "low estate." Lamech is made low by the exercise of hardy strength to keep himself in check, which effort, like the day of atonement, signifies the putting away of boasting and self-conceit. Being low in such a way is an imploring for pardon.[4]) It is this Lamech who is the father of righteous Noah.[5])

Noah is a sort of cognomen of justice.[6]) Philo obtained his notion that Noah could either be called "rest" or "just" by treating the latter word, which is an adjective in Gen. 6:9, as though it were in apposition.[7]) Justice, chief among the virtues,[8]) gives rest from that earthly nature by whose curse the body is afflicted with sickness.[9]) Justice creates rest in place of toil since it is indifferent to objects on the borderline between vice and virtue such as wealth, fame, official posts, etc., and at the same time it abolishes the grief of actions we do entirely of our own motion. Justice especially delivers from the wickedness that has taken up abode in the soul of the unwise like a disease, as we learn from the phrase: "the earth which God cursed."[10])

Noah, as righteous, illustrates the fact that when righteousness has for some soul given birth to a male progeny in the shape of righteous reasoning, from that soul all painful things are henceforth banished. Righteousness gives rest and is the safeguard against the

---

[1]) *Cong.* 90; *Post.* 173.
[2]) *Post.* 174.
[3]) *Cong.* 90.
[4]) *Post.* 48.
[5]) *Post.* 46-48.
[6]) *QG.* i. 87.
[7]) *Abr.* 27; *LA.* iii. 77; *Det.* 121.
[8]) *Abr.* 27.
[9]) *QG.* i. 87.
[10]) *Det.* 122-123.

wickedness which is in the soul of the unwise.[1]) Noah is the man who
has expelled from his soul the untamed and frantic passions and beast-
like vices.[2])

"Rest," the opposite of unnatural movements that cause turmoil,
confusion, and war, is to be sought by those who value nobility of
conduct.[3]) We are given to understand, however, that in Noah's
own case there was no cessation of evils, but rather an intensification
in the disasters and innovations of the flood.[4])

Philo insists that the phrase "works of our hands," in its figurative
sense, does not describe God as the author of evil, but describes our
own undertakings and the spontaneous movement of our minds to
what is wrong.[5])

Rather than giving a list of Noah's descendants, Moses gives his
genealogy in a list of virtues, for virtue is a generation of souls.[6])
The offspring of a proper mind are the virtues described in the text; he
was just, perfect, and well-pleasing to God. The last of these is the
definition of supreme happiness.[7]) "Perfect" implies that he acquired
all virtues.[8])

"Man" standing in apposition to "just" implies that the unjust, a
beast in human form, is really no man; while the righteous alone is a
man.[9]) Noah acquired all the virtues and continued to exercise them
all as opportunity allowed,[10]) but despite his three special virtues—just,
perfect, and well-pleasing to God—he was good, not absolutely, but
only in comparison with the men of the time.[11]) For this reason he
will win only a second prize, while those absolutely perfect will get
the first prize.[12]) Since he had done no fair deed when he is said to be
righteous, he is to be considered of excellent nature from birth.[13]) That
he found favor implies that he discovered that all things are a grace
of God—a free gift—which He bestows on those who stand next to
Him.[14]) In finding favor with God, Noah is to be contrasted with

[1]) *Det.* 121-123; cf. Ambrose, *De Noe* i. 2 (*CSEL.* 32. 413).
[2]) *Abr.* 32.
[3]) *Abr.* 27. [4]) *QG.* i. 87.
[5]) *Det.* 122.
[6]) *Abr.* 31; *QG.* i. 97; cf. *Gen. R.* 30. 6.
[7]) *Immut.* 118.
[8]) *Abr.* 34.
[9]) *Abr.* 33.
[10]) *Abr.* 34-35.
[11]) *Abr.* 36; cf. *infra*, p. 133, n. 5.
[12]) *Abr.* 38.
[13]) *LA.* iii. 77. [14]) *LA.* iii. 78.

Joseph who served "pleasure" and who when cast into the jail of the passions finds favor in the eyes of the chief jailor—the concentration of all vices. Philo considers this to be the greatest of all ills.[1]

The earth is said to be corrupted immediately after the recital of Noah's virtues because when the immortal element takes its rise in the soul, the mortal is forthwith corrupted.[2] In this experience, not one part of the soul, which is composed of mind, spirit, and appetites,[3] is left uncorrupted.[4] Moses made no mistake in using the masculine pronoun in the expression "his way," for the passage means that the perfect way of the Eternal and Indestructible—the way that leads to God—has been corrupted. This way by which one attains to recognition of God is wisdom.[5] Philo argues at length that the antecedent of the pronoun is God rather than "flesh." "Flesh" represents "man" and the way is corrupted through desires and pleasures of the flesh. Since flesh is the seat of desires and passions, the Lord has well said it corrupted His way.[6]

God decides to punish "man," which really means the mind, along with the creeping and flying creatures. These latter are possibly Θῦμος and ἐπιθυμία of the soul.[7] These beasts are sense perception which must perish, since it no longer has virtue when the mind is perverted.[8] When the soul is deluged by streams of passion, the earthly parts of the body must die with it. Every sense dies when it perceives unjustly.[9]

Philo uses two figures to explain the significance of the ark. The laden ark is a counterpart of the world which is perishing, since it contains all sorts of creatures; but it also shows the principle and the proportions of the human body.[10] The ark is the body or vessel which contains the soul.[11]

According to Philo, the body, except for "pot-bellied" people, has quadrangular form, even as the ark had quadrangular beams.[12] The

---

[1] *Immut.* 111 ff.
[2] *Immut.* 122-123.
[3] *Conf.* 21.
[4] *Conf.* 25.
[5] *Immut.* 140-143.
[6] *QG.* i. 99.
[7] *Conf.* 24; cf. the note of the editor in the Loeb series.
[8] *QG.* i. 94.
[9] *QG.* ii. 9.
[10] *QG.* ii. 7; cf. Ambrose, *Hexaemeron* vi. 9. 72 (*CSEL.* 32. 258-259); Augustine, *Civ. Dei* 15. 26 (*CSEL.* 40. 2. 116-117).
[11] *Det.* 170.
[12] *QG.* ii. 2.

nests of the ark correspond to the orifices of the body, for they are where sounds, smells, and tastes nestle. Likewise, the brain, lungs, etc., have their nests.[1]) The tar inside and outside the ark holds it together even as the body is of various parts united inside and outside. By way of contrast, the ark in the temple is of much more value since it is overlaid with gold and is a likeness of the intelligible world and remains in its place. During the flood, Noah's ark is carried here and there as a type of corruptibility.[2])

Even the details of construction of the ark also correspond to the body.[3]) The dimensions of the ark are not to be taken as a quantity of cubits, but as the accurate proportions of the body. The length of three hundred cubits is six times fifty, even as a properly proportioned man's height is six times his chest width; five times the width of his side (fifty cubits high equals five times ten); and the width is five-thirds of the thickness. The finishing of the ark to a cubit above is comparable to the head with the mind in it. Each of these three figures is subjected by Philo to further breakdowns in intricate mathematics.[4])

The door in the side of the ark is an euphemism for the anus through which the excreta are removed.[5]) The three stories of the ark represent the organs for food consumption which are one above another in the body.[6])

Coating the ark with asphalt represents a stage in Noah's development when he had not yet arrived at a place where he was able to behold existences as they are, through the soul alone. He strengthens the impressions of which the body is the medium and finds it as a source of strength. But later, realizing that "asphalt" can never give real safety, he comes forth to exercise his understanding, free from the body, for the apprehension of truth.[7]) By way of contrast Moses who is further advanced, is never contented with the "asphalt" which serves the body and weeps when put into the ark as a babe, yearning for the nature that knows no body.[8])

---

1) *QG*. ii. 3.
2) *QG*. ii. 4.
3) *QG*. ii. 1; cf. Ambrose, *De Noe* vi. 13-14 (*CSEL*. 32. 422-423).
4) *QG*. ii. 5; cf. *infra*, p. 163.
5) *QG*. ii. 6; cf. Ambrose, *De Offic.* i. 78 (*PL*. 16. 50), who also assumes that garbage was thrown out at the door.
6) *QG*. ii. 7.
7) *Conf.* 104-105.
8) *Conf.* 106; cf. note of editor of Loeb series, p. 67.

Noah, in one section of the *De Migratione Abrahami*, represents the righteous mind in the soul which survives when so many parts of the soul are swallowed up by the flood and which can eventually bring healing to the soul; but in the remainder of the same section, he is the righteous man in the race out of which came the patriarchs.[1]

The wild animals in the ark represent the body obliged to make room for the savage and untamed pests of passion and vices.[2] Since man's nature is made up of contraries, it is necessary that the irrational parts of the soul be saved as seed bearing principles of non-holy things.[3] These are lethal and poisonous in the case of the wicked man, but are transformed into domestic animals in the case of the righteous man; hence they are mentioned between man and cattle in Gen. 8:1.[4] The seven clean beasts, male and female, represent the seven elements of the irrational side of man—seeing, hearing, smelling, tasting, touching, speaking, and begetting—which purged and under the control of the "reasoning faculty" are clean,[5] while in the worthless man they are exposed to punishment and are polluted. To have these under control is the unfailing mark of the wise man.[6] They are to be considered male when in action, but as female when in restraint or in passivity.[7] The clean reptiles, in contract, represent joy, reflection, remorse, constraint, and caution. To possess these is to be truly living.[8]

The command to enter the ark with one's household implies that when God saves the mind, He saves the whole household with it. As fares the mind, so fares the household.[9] The closing of the ark outside of him represents the skin of the body which prevents cold and heat from having power to harm one.[10]

The deluge itself, an event in the life of the righteous man,[11] an upheaval within the soul, is the symbol of spiritual dissolution.[12] As Philo put it, a deluge comes when from the mind wrongdoings burst

---

[1] *Mig.* 124-125.
[2] *Plant.* 43.
[3] *QG.* ii. 12.
[4] *QG.* ii. 27.
[5] *Det.* 168-173; *QG.* ii. 12.
[6] *Det.* 171.
[7] *Det.* 170-172.
[8] *QG.* ii. 57.
[9] *QG.* ii. 11.
[10] *QG.* ii. 19.
[11] *QG.* ii. 45; *Conf.* 23 ff.
[12] *QG.* ii. 15.

in on the soul as in a cataract.[1]) The "man" whose thoughts are only
evil continually is the mind. In this affair not one part of the soul is
left uncorrupted.[2]) There is a flood when streams of the mind are
opened by folly, madness, insatiable desire, wrongdoing, senselessness,
recklessness, and impiety, and when the fountains of the body are
opened by sensual pleasure, desire, drunkenness, gourmandism, and
licentiousness with kin and sisters, and by incurable vices.[3]) It is a
punishment—a letting loose of sin in such a torrent of iniquity that
there is nothing to hinder those who seek opportunities to take
pleasure in it. All parts of the soul cooperate in sin. From the mind
(heaven) fall torrents of absolute wickedness,[4]) while from the body,
or sense perception (earth),[5]) flow streams of each passion. The
cataracts are luxuriousness, intemperance, lewd habits, and empty
desires.[6]) These meet in the soul causing wild commotion.[7]) The high
mountains which were covered fifteen cubits represent the five senses
which have a fixed position in the top of our head, each considered
as threefold.[8]) These are destroyed by the sudden onrush of never
ending vices and evils. The blotting out of all vegetation is the casting
off from the mind of all sensible and corporeal things—arrogance and
pride—by which it is stained.[9]) Philo remarks that these are blotted
out from the Lord's memory and from the divine narrative.[10]) Moving
flesh died, for the flesh moves the sensual pleasures and is moved by
sensual pleasures. These movements cause the destruction of souls.[11])
"All on the dry land died," implies that the soul when not mixed
with wisdom, justice, and piety, and other fine virtues dries up like
an aged tree and dies when it is given over to the flood of the body.[12])

Elsewhere Philo makes the flood a cleansing of the soul from its
unutterable wrongdoings by washing away and purging out its
defilements.[13]) As the ark was borne upon the waters, so the body

---

[1]) *Fug.* 192.
[2]) *Conf.* 24-25.
[3]) *QG.* ii. 18; Ambrose, *De Noe* ix. 30 (*CSEL.* 32. 432), repeats the idea that
the flood represents the passions.
[4]) *Conf.* 23.
[5]) *QG.* ii. 18.
[6]) *QG.* ii. 25.
[7]) *Conf.* 23-25; *Fug.* 191-192.
[8]) *QG.* ii. 21.
[9]) *QG.* ii. 15.
[10]) *QG.* ii. 24.
[11]) *QG.* ii. 22.
[12]) Gen. 7:22; *QG.* ii. 23.
[13]) *Det.* 170; cf. Ambrose, *De Offic.* iii. 108 (*PL.* 16. 185).

must be storm-tossed by necessities, overcoming hunger, thirst, cold, and heat, by which it is perturbed.[1]) When we wish to cast off from the mind sensible and corporeal things by which it is stained, it is inundated.[2])

In this presentation of the theme, Noah and those in the ark alone remained, for when the mind cuts off all immoderateness of the passions, it alone is left in the body, now pure of all passions, but not yet able to become entirely incorporeal.[3])

When Philo continues his allegory of the flood as a deluge within the soul, he informs us that to stop the sources of the flood, it was necessary for the word of the divine physician to enter the soul to heal it of its illness and to keep back both streams that were causing the trouble.[4]) The form of speaking, "water dried from the earth" instead of "earth dried of water," indicates allegory to Philo. The water (Gen. 8:7) indicates the immeasurableness of the passions which corrupt the soul while it is stuffed with them. After it dries up, however, the soul is saved since they can no longer injure it.[5]) The drying up is a drying up of ignorance.[6])

The window of the ark which Noah opens is the senses which permit sense perceptible things to enter the mind and through which it reaches out to seize them.[7])

The raven is a symbol of evil [8]) which, swift to meet all things in the world, brings night and darkness upon the soul. This evil leads to the destruction of all who would seize it. Noah, therefore, is expelling beyond the borders whatever residue of darkness there is in the mind that might lead to folly.[9]) The raven does not return, for unrighteousness considers that being merry with its relative, the flood, is more desirable than the good works of the virtuous man.[10])

The dove, a symbol of virtue, a matter of humaneness and socia-

---

[1]) *QG*. ii. 20.
[2]) *QG*. ii. 15.
[3]) *QG*. ii. 25.
[4]) *QG*. ii. 29.
[5]) *QG*. ii. 37.
[6]) *QG*. ii. 49; cf. E. R. Goodenough, *Jewish Symbols in the Greco-Roman Period* (N. Y.: Pantheon Books, 1958), VIII, 160-164.
[7]) *QG*. ii. 34.
[8]) *QG*. ii. 35, 39; cf. Jerome, *Ep.* 69. 6 (*CSEL.* 54. 690): "the foul bird of wickedness"; and Ambrose, *De myst.* 11 (*CSEL.* 73. 93): "the figure of sin which goes forth."
[9]) *QG*. ii. 35.
[10]) *QG*. ii. 36.

bility, an inspector and messenger of affairs,[1]) is a means by which the virtuous man may learn whence to know how that he may be careful of injurious things.[2]) When sent forth, virtue could not find any spot in the soul worthy of it amid the streams of passion, so it returned to the ark.[3]) There were none at this time who were receiving discipline.[4])

However, we are not to suppose that in sending virtue forth, the wise man really separates himself from it. Rather it is as the sun sends forth a ray without being diminished of light.

It would seem that Philo has shifted horses when he has virtue stretching forth its hand in word and deed, opening the whole mind and unfolding it, as a means of taking the dove back into the ark.[5]) Previously and afterwards in Philo's allegory, it is not Noah that is virtue, but the dove.

The second return of the dove has several symbols: the return itself is a symbol of repentance; the evening is a symbol of the end of the affair; while the olive leaf is a sign of the beginning of repentance that may result in change. That it is a dry olive branch which is in the mouth indicates that virtue bears seeds of wisdom and justice in its speech which it shares with outsiders.[6]) On the third trip, virtue remains abroad as the common good of all who wish to take the outpouring of wisdom.[7])

The covering of the ark symbolizes pleasure which closely guards and preserves and sustains the body. The mind, smitten by heavenly pleasure, removes that which covers it that it may be able to bring sense perception to naked and incorporeal natures.[8])

The men and women go forth together from the ark, having practiced abstinence in the ark, for when the soul (man) is about to wash off and cleanse its sins, the mind should join its sovereign thoughts.

The mind is the father and the thoughts are its sons. The females are those things which belong to sense; but after the cleansing, the females (sense) may associate with the males and become manly by receiving from them seed, and may then come to perceive things with wisdom, prudence, justice, and

---

[1]) QG. ii. 38-40.
[2]) QG. ii. 38.
[3]) QG. ii. 39.
[4]) QG. ii. 42.
[5]) QG. ii. 40.
[6]) QG. ii. 42.
[7]) QG. ii. 44.
[8]) QG. ii. 46.

courage. A second treatment of the same idea makes known that when confusion comes on the mind like a flood, it is impossible to conceive, sow, or give birth to anything good, but when all is dried up, it produces virtues and excellent things.[1]

The clean beasts and birds offered up by Noah are the senses and the mind of the wise man, since thoughts rove in the mind of the wise man. These make a fitting offering to the Father.[2]

The making of the covenant with Noah really means that Noah is the pedestal of the covenant; that God has given Noah to himself; or that justice and God's covenant are identical. This conclusion is really reached by a play on ὁ δίκαιος, which for Philo is Noah, and upon τὸ δίκαιον which for him is the covenant.[3] The whole affair seems to indicate progress from perpetual turmoil towards virtue.[4]

As we turn to the allegory on various details of the covenant made after the flood, we learn that seed is the beginning, while harvest is the end. Each looks to the other and both are the causes of salvation. Cold indicates fear and heat anger. The fruits of spring are virtues that bring good to the mind, while the fruits of summer bring corporeal and external good to souls. Day is lucid reason and night is shadowy folly.[5]

God desires that the souls of intelligent men increase in greatness and fill the mind with their forms, leaving no part empty and void for their follies. He desires that they rule the earthly body and its senses and strike terror into evil that is untamed. He desires that they rule the birds, which represent those who are filled with vain and empty arrogance, and reptiles, which represent poisonous passions. Fish are those men who welcome a moist and fluid life rather than a continent one.[6]

The clean reptiles that shall be for food to Noah represent the passions of joy, reflection, and constraint, as against the unclean reptiles which represent sensuous passions. These joys are the causes of life for him who has them.[7] The giving of herbs of fodder may imply that irrational creatures are given over and made obedient to man just as he tends herbs.[8]

---

[1] *QG.* ii. 49.   [2] *QG.* ii. 52.
[3] See note in Loeb edition, V, 544; cf. *QG.* ii. 10.
[4] *Som.* ii. 225.
[5] *QG.* ii. 55.
[6] *QG.* ii. 56.
[7] *QG.* ii. 57.
[8] *QG.* ii. 58.

The requiring of blood from beasts and brothers implies that God does not overlook the purity of the soul; hence he drives off the thoughts and words which, when expressed, are heard and which bring misfortune.[1] The phrase which states that man's blood shall be shed in return for blood he shed implies that the cruel and laboring soul is tossed about and overwhelmed by its intemperate way of life.[2]

The promise that there will not again be such a destruction implies that the divine grace adorns in some respects and that one should do what he can to achieve vigor in body and to correct his life.[3]

Next we shall consider Philo's allegory on the postdiluvial episodes of Noah's life. Noah's "tilling" of the soil becomes for Philo a sort of soul culture which plants virtues and reaps a happy life.[4] Back of this argument is his distinction between working the earth as Cain did and the skilled trade of tilling it as Noah did.[5] The earth which is worked represents the body.[6] The wise man, "the husbandman mind," cuts away the shoots of passions and vices, leaving only such as would furnish a fence for the soul.[7] Such is the function of the study of logic and rhetoric.[8] He also attempts by continence and moderation to bring the fruitbearing growth to full fruition and seeks to attain immortality.[9]

Great stress is placed by Philo on ἤρξατο ("began") to be a husbandman. Though a good beginning is a thing half done, we must go on from right beginnings to right endings if profit is to be gained.[10] Noah was able to master only the elements of the science of husbandry, but not able to reach the furthest limits of full knowledge. The argument is based on the silence of Scripture about the end.[11]

At great length Philo argues the question whether or not a wise man will get drunk and concludes that he may without losing any of his virtue.[12] In the treatise *de Ebrietate*, though it was doubtless intended as a discussion of Gen. 9, he hardly gets around to Noah at

---

[1] *QG.* ii. 60.
[2] *QG.* ii. 61.
[3] *QG.* ii. 63.
[4] *Agr.* 25.
[5] *Agr.* 21-25; *Plant.* 140; cf. *QG.* i. 59-60.
[6] *QG.* ii. 66.
[7] *Det.* 105.
[8] *Agr.* 13-15.
[9] *Det.* 110-111; *QG.* ii. 66.
[10] *Agr.* 124 ff.
[11] *Agr.* 181.
[12] *Plant.* 172-174.

all. Drunkenness is a symbol of foolish talking, insensibility, and greediness.[1]) But when Philo considers the sequel to Noah's drunkenness, he has three types of nakedness. One is to remain void of either virtue or vice.[2]) A second sort is that of the soul when it escapes from the body as from a tomb, stripping itself of sense pleasures and passions. Philo considers this a great blessing.[3]) But the third, the nakedness of Noah, represents an involuntary deprivation of virtue when the soul becomes foolish and deranged.[4]) Knowledge obtained by good instruction and training would be the cure for this type.[5]) The fact that this nakedness was in the house reveals that the wise man does not run riot when he commits sin as does the wicked man. Canaan proceeds to carry out the planned deed when he reported it abroad. Shem and Japheth act differently when they cover over the sad change in the soul.[6]) It is a great evil not to conceal the sins of the mind and of sense-perception.[7]) Their going backward implies that the wise mind looks ahead, protecting the soul from blows that might come from any side.[8])

To sober up is to repent of sin and recover as from an illness.[9]) The sober mind possesses clear-sightedness in the soul[10]) and is able to comprehend the nature of things past, present, or future.[11])

In the allegory on the sons of Noah and on the curses and blessings which Noah spoke, the fact that Ham is at times mentioned in the middle of the three, but in Gen. 9:24 is called the youngest, is ample evidence to Philo to indicate an allegory. The boys represent secondary goods in nature: the good, the bad, and the indifferent.[12]) Ham is the youngest son because he suggests the temperament that loves rebelliousness and defiance.[13]) Elsewhere he says that wickedness is not able to receive aged teaching; hence it is called "youngest."[14]) Wicked-

---

[1]) *Ebr.* 4.
[2]) *LA.* ii. 64.
[3]) *QG.* ii. 69; cf. *LA.* ii. 54 ff.
[4]) *LA.* ii. 60.
[5]) *QG.* ii. 69.
[6]) *LA.* ii. 62.
[7]) *Fug.* 192.
[8]) *QG.* ii. 72.
[9]) *LA.* ii. 60.
[10]) *Sob.* 4.
[11]) *QG.* ii. 73.
[12]) *QG.* i. 88; ii. 71, 79; cf. Ambrose, *De Noe* ii. 3 (*CSEL.* 32. 4 14).
[13]) *Sob.* 6.
[14]) *QG.* ii. 74.

ness is placed between the other two that they may crush it. Shem's name is placed first in some instances to indicate that bad is only potentially present. When it becomes an actual act, then Shem takes the last place, leaving the first to one more powerful.[1]

Arguing on the basis that Scripture says "Ham was the father of Canaan" rather than saying "Canaan was the son of Ham," Philo asserts that kinship of the flesh is not involved, but rather it is kinship of thought with thought, for Canaan is far from kinship with virtue.[2] These are really characters rather than men.[3] Ham in Hebrew means "heat," a sign of vice in the soul, while Canaan is "merchant," or "mediator," or "tossing." [4] Ham is vice in its quiescent state while Canaan is vice in the active state. The two represent a single object—wickedness. Since rest comes before motion, it can be called the parent.[5] One can only punish the active state; [6] hence we punish the result of our reasonings, while the reasonings themselves go scot-free.[7]

Canaan is made the slave of the others that he may learn a better life, or if he clings to his evil, that they may chastise him.[8]

Shem represents generic "good," at which meaning Philo seems to arrive by equating "name" (שם) with a thing of good.[9] As the wise man, he has a double honor: that common one which all the world has and that of being loved of God in that he receives the special grace of having Scripture say "God of Shem."[10] In return for his special grace, Shem should bless and praise God.[11]

The blessing on Japheth (Gen. 9:27) implies an enlargement of health, keenness of perception, beauty, power, wealth, glory, nobility, friends, and offices. Lest these bodily and external things bring harm, Noah prays that he dwell in the house of the wise man of which Shem

---

[1] *QG.* ii. 79.
[2] *QG.* ii. 65. Origen argues at length that the statement "Ham is the father of Canaan" is not to give genealogy, but his characteristics, *Selecta in Gen.* 32-33 (*PG.* 12. 108). Cf. L. Ginzberg, *op. cit.*, p. 84. See also Basil, *De spiritu sancto* 20 (*PG.* 32. 161 B); Ibn Ezra and Sforno (*EBI.* II, 65).
[3] *QG.* ii. 77.
[4] *Sob.* 44, 45, 48; *QG.* ii. 77.
[5] *Sob.* 47.
[6] *Sob.* 44, 46.
[7] *Sob.* 48.
[8] *Sob.* 69.
[9] *Sob.* 52.
[10] *Sob.* 53; *QG.* ii. 75.
[11] *Sob.* 58.

is the symbol, and that he set his way straight by what he sees.[1]) Thus Japheth comes to have the good of the soul.[2])

To summarize, it is in Philo's allegorical Noah and the flood that the *Sitz im Leben* of Philo's exegesis becomes most obvious. It is here that he is the farthest removed from the other treatments included in this study. Philo has found an arbitrary existential value in the flood episode. Under the form of a narrative of the past, it depicts occurrences that may happen in the present day experience of any person.[3]) This value is not a unified thing. The flood may either be an overwhelming of evils or it may be a cleansing of the soul; but either way, the narrative displays contemporary religious values which Philo wishes to sell to his readers.

B. Pseudo-Philo

Some justification is needed for treating Pseudo-Philo in a section of Hellenistic Jewish writings. In reality the book is a pseudepigraphon, probably written in Hebrew by a Palestinian Jew shortly after the destruction of the temple in A.D. 70.[4]) The writer, choosing the style of the Bk. of Chronicles as his model, intends to supplement existing narratives, for the purpose of infusing a more religious tone into them.[5]) Since the book, though it is now preserved in Latin, was at one stage of its history in Greek, and since it has been preserved under the name of Philo, it seems not amiss to treat it here in order that the contrast with the real Philo may be the more obvious.

The material out of the writer's survey of history from creation to the death of Saul which falls within the scope of this study is to be found in the first five chapters. The writer is particularly concerned with the danger of lapse into idolatry and of union with the Gentiles, though these items do not come specifically into the flood section.

The writer informs us that in the 182nd year of his life, Lamech begot a son and called his name Noah, saying, "This child will give

---

[1]) *QG*. ii. 76; *Sob*. 61.

[2]) *Sob*. 68.

[3]) Cf. S. Sandmel, "Philo and His Pupils: An Imaginary Dialogue," *Judaism*, IV (Winter, 1955), 47-57.

[4]) M. R. James, tr., *The Biblical Antiquities of Philo* (London: SPCK., 1917), p. 7. The date is dependent on a speech of Moses (19. 7) where he points to a destruction on the 17th of the 4th month, which is to be compared with *M. Ta'anit* 4. 6. The fall of Jerusalem was associated with the 17th day of the 4th month (*Tammuz*); cf. M. R. James, *op. cit.*, p. 30.

[5]) *Ibid.*, pp. 33-34.

rest to us and to the earth from those who are therein, upon whom (or in the day when) a visitation shall be made of the iniquity of their evil deeds." [1]) After three hundred years, Noah begot Shem, Ham, and Japheth.[2])

When men had multiplied, beautiful daughters were born to them. The sons of God saw that they were exceedingly fair and took wives from them. God said, "My spirit shall not judge among these men forever, because they are flesh; but their years shall be 120 years." The thoughts of the men were upon iniquity all of their days. God said, "I will blot out man and all things that have budded upon the earth, for it repenteth me that I have made him." [3])

Noah found grace and mercy before the Lord. Noah was a righteous man, undefiled in his generation. God told him to make an ark of cedar wood, 300 cubits long, 60 cubits broad, and 30 cubits high. God promised to make a covenant with him to destroy the dwellers on the earth.[4]) He was to take his sons and the wives of the four into the ark. He was also to take of the clean beasts and fowls, by sevens— male and female—but of the unclean, he was to take by twos. Noah obeyed and entered the ark. After seven days the flood came. The depths, the great springs of water, and the windows of heaven were opened so that there was rain for forty days and forty nights.[5])

It was on the 1652nd (1656) year from the time that God made heaven and earth. The flood continued for 140 days. Only those in the ark remained alive. God remembered Noah and made the water abate. In the 90th day, when God dried the earth, He commanded Noah to go out of the ark and to grow and multiply in the earth. Noah brought all from the ark, built an altar, and offered of cattle and clean fowls. It was accepted of the Lord for a savor of rest.[6])

God promised not to curse again the earth for man's sake, "for the guise of man's heart hath left off from his youth." [7]) When the inhabitants of earth sin, they are to be judged by famine, sword, fire, or pestilence, and there shall be earthquakes so that they be scattered to uninhabited places. In all the days, seedtime and harvest, cold and heat, summer and autumn, day and night shall not cease. However,

---

[1]) *The Biblical Antiquities of Philo* i. 20.
[2]) *Ibid.*, i. 22.
[3]) *Ibid.*, iii. 1-3; the book assumes that *yadon* is to be traced to דין.
[4]) This is a unique idea. For other purposes of the covenant, see *Gen. R.* 31. 12.
[5]) Ps.-Philo, *Bib. Ant.* iii. 4-5.
[6]) *Ibid.*, iii. 6-8. In *Jub.* 5:23 the flood comes in A.M. 1308.
[7]) *Ibid.*, iii. 9.

the writer proceeds to comment, when the years are fulfilled, then light will cease, darkness will be quenched; and God will quicken the dead and raise up from the earth them that sleep; and Hell shall pay his debt of destruction and give back that which was committed unto him that it may be rendered to every man according to his works. God will judge between soul and flesh. There shall be another earth and another heaven, even an everlasting habitation.[1]

God told Noah of his covenant with him and his sons. He would not again spoil the earth with a flood. God further instructed that everything that moves should be to Noah and his descendants for meat; but the blood of the soul they should not eat. Everyone shedding man's blood should have his blood shed, for man was made in the image of God. Noah and his sons were to grow and multiply and fill the earth. The bow in the cloud was to be a memorial of the covenant "between me and you and all the dwellers upon the earth." [2]

Further along in the book, it is promised that if the feast of tabernacles is kept God will remember the earth with rain, even as God spake after the flood of the earth. The nights will also yield dew. God had ordained the years after He visited the city of men and showed Noah the place of birth and the color of the serpent. He also showed him the ways of paradise.[3] Noah was commanded concerning the salvation of the souls of men whom God would not forsake if they walked in His ways. The earth would be fruitful; there would be rain. Men would corrupt their ways, and God would forsake them, but not forever. In the last days they would know that it was for their corrupt ways that their seed was forsaken.[4]

The writer of this book is particularly interested in giving the names of various descendants of Noah and their numbers. The whole total comes to be 914,000 during 350 years that Noah lived after the flood. He died at the age of 950 years.[5] The book says nothing about the blessings or curses of Noah on a son.

This survey reveals that Pseudo-Philo's treatment of the flood has little in common with the exegesis of the genuine Philo or with the rabbis. Nothing of allegory or Haggadah is here to be seen. A fairly

---

[1]) Ps.-Philo, *Bib. Ant.* iii. 9-10.
[2]) *Ibid.*, iii. 11.
[3]) *Ibid.*, xiii. 7-9; see M. R. James, *op. cit.*, p. 115.
[4]) Ps.-Philo, *Bib. Ant.* xiii. 10.
[5]) *Ibid.*, v. 8.

literal and straightforward presentation of biblical history with very little comment, but nevertheless with some distinctive elements, is offered. That the "rest" implied in Noah's name is the relieving of the earth of its wicked inhabitants is not found elsewhere in the literature surveyed. It is also likely that there is intended to be a connection between "savor of rest" in the post-flood sacrifices and Noah's name. The age given for Noah at the birth of his sons is not in agreement with MT., the versions, or the rabbis, and is unique. Other items in the chronology are peculiar. It is difficult to see how the writer calculated.

It is not until we come to the post-flood blessing that the *Sitz* of the writer really begins to come to light. It was an atmosphere in which eschatology with resurrection, the final judgment, hell, and the new heaven and earth played a prominent role.

C. JOSEPHUS

In Josephus we have a Palestinian Jewish soldier who claims a priestly and philosophic education, but who learned Greek late in life, and who required the help of friends to correct his syntax. He surveys Jewish history to instruct his heathen readers and to inspire them with respect for Jewish antiquity.[1] His account of the flood is to be found in Bk. i, chapters 3-4 of his *Antiquities*.

According to Josephus, Adam prior to his death prophesied a violent destruction of the universe, once by fire and once by a mighty flood. His descendants erected pillars of stone and of brick on which they inscribed their learning that it might survive either calamity.[2]

The posterity of Seth became perverted and began to show a double degree of wickedness. Angels of God companioned with women and begot sons that were unjust, despisers of good.[3] Their strength enabled them to do acts that resemble those of ones the Grecians call giants. Noah, who was the tenth from Adam and who was the son of Lamech, attempted to persuade them to do better, but

---

[1] *Ant.* xvi. 6. 8.
[2] *Ant.* i. 2. 3; that former generations wrote on a rock is stated in *Jub.* 8:3; II *Enoch* 33:12; see S. Rappaport, *Agada und Exegesis bei Flavius Josephus* (Wien: Alex. Kohut Memorial Foundation, 1920), p. 91; *Bk. of Adam and Eve* 49.3-50:1. The flood of fire is known in rabbinic literature: *Mekilta, Amalek* 3. 14; *Bahodesh* 5. 55 f.; *Gen. R.* 49. 9; 39. 6; *Lev. R.* 10. 1.
[3] *Ant.* i. 3. 1; cf. LXX.

they would not listen. Lest they should kill him and his family, he departed out of the land.[1])

God loved Noah for his righteousness, but He condemned the wicked. He limited their years to 120 years and turned the dry land into sea.[2]) Josephus must not mean that all human life was forever limited to 120 years, for later he knows of men living longer than that.[3]) It was suggested to Noah that he build an ark four stories high, 300 cubits long, 50 broad, and 30 high.[4]) Into it went provisions, the male and female of all living creatures, "and others by sevens." The ark had firm walls and a roof so that it could not be destroyed by the violence of the waters.[5])

The flood came in the second month of the 600th year of Noah's life,[6]) on the 27th day, which was 2262 years from Adam. Josephus notes that those living in this early age accurately kept account of the births and deaths of illustrious men. Noah was born when Lamech was 188 years old, and he lived 950 years.[7])

The rain lasted for forty days until the water was 15 cubits higher than the earth. At the end of 150 days it just began to abate (the 17th day of the 7th month). The ark came to rest on a mountain in Armenia.[8]) Noah opened the ark, remained in it for some time, then sent out a raven which, finding no place to land, returned to Noah.[9]) Seven days later he sent a dove which returned covered with mud, bringing an olive branch.[10]) After seven days more he sent the living

---

[1]) Josephus, *Ant.* i. 3. 1. For Noah as a preacher, see II Pet. 2:5; I Pet. 3:20; *Or. Sib.* i. 175 ff.; that Noah migrated out of the land is a legend not known to the rabbis. In rabbinic thought Noah did not separate himself from his generation, but went on warning them during the 120 years; see C. Kaplan, "The Flood in the Bk. of Enoch and Rabbinics," *JSOR.*, 15 (1931), 22-24 and S. Rappaport, *Agada und Exegese bei Flavius Josephus* (Wien: Alex. Kohut Memorial Foundation, 1930), p. 94, n. 55.

[2]) Josephus, *Ant.* i. 3. 2.

[3]) *Ibid.*, i. 6. 5.

[4]) Josephus uses λάρναξ which is used by classical authors for Deucalion's ark rather than κιβωτός which was used by the LXX for Noah's ark. Philo, *Mos.* ii. 60, also has four stories in the ark, but Scripture has only three.

[5]) Josephus, *Ant.* i. 3. 2.

[6]) Josephus gives this month the Gk. name of *Dius* as well as its Hebrew name which he calls *Marsuan*.

[7]) Josephus, *Ant.* i. 3. 4.

[8]) Cf. the Vulgate: "the ark rested upon the mountains of Armenia"; Chrysostom, *In Ep. I Thess.* c. 4, hom. 8. 2 (*PG.* 62. 442); and *T. Ps.-Jon.*, Gen. 8:4.

[9]) Josephus, *Ant.* i. 3. 5.

[10]) Josephus condenses the biblical account to only one trip.

creatures out of the ark. He sacrificed and feasted with his companions. The Armenians call the place ἀποβατήριον ("the place of descent"). The remains of the ark have been saved in the place, says Josephus, and are shown until this day.[1])

The flood is mentioned in the histories of Berosus the Chaldaean. Berosus says that the ark is in Armenia in the mountain of the Cordyaeans. People take away the bitumen to use as amulets. Hieronymus the Egyptian, Mnaseas, and others tell of it. Nicholas of Damascus in his 96th book tells of a great mountain in Armenia (above Minyas) called *Baris* on which people who fled at the time of the flood were saved. An ark carried one man ashore there. The timbers were a great while preserved. It is guessed by Josephus that this might be the man of whom Moses wrote.[2])

Noah was afraid God might drown the earth each year; hence he sacrificed and besought God that nature go on in an orderly way, that it might not again undergo God's wrath, and that men might attain the length of days they had attained before.[3]) God loved Noah for his righteousness and granted entire success to his prayers. God stated that it was man's great wickedness that forced him to send the flood; however in time to come he would not require such great punishments; hence Noah need not be afraid when it rained. Man should refrain from shedding man's blood and should punish those who shed it. God permitted man to use other living creatures at his pleasure—man is the lord of them all—but their blood he should not eat.[4]) The sign that God had left off His anger is the bow (which means the rainbow).[5])

Noah, after the flood, set about to cultivate the ground.[6]) When his vines brought fruit, he offered sacrifice,[7]) feasted, became drunken, and fell asleep, lying naked. His youngest son came laughing to tell the others. They proceeded to cover him. Noah invoked a blessing for these other sons. He did not curse Ham by reason of his nearness in blood, but instead cursed his posterity. When the rest of the posterity escaped that curse, God inflicted it on the children of Canaan.

---

[1]) Josephus, *Ant.* i. 3. 5.
[2]) *Ibid.*, i. 3. 6.
[3]) Cf. S. Rappaport, *Agada und Exegeses bei Flavius Josephus* (Wien: Alex. Kohut Memorial Foundation, 1930), p. 11.
[4]) Cf. J. Weill, *Oeuvres complètes de Flavius Josèphe* (Paris: Ernest Leroux, 1900), p. 24, n. 2.
[5]) Josephus, *Ant.* i. 3. 7-8.
[6]) *Ibid.*, i. 6. 3.
[7]) That Noah's fault is in connection with a sacrifice is also known to *Jub.* 7:4 f.

Noah lived 350 years after the flood, which made him 950 years old. The ancients were beloved of God, and their food was more fitting for prolongation of life. Because of their virtue, God afforded them longer time which they used in astronomical and geometrical discoveries. Josephus asserts that Manetho, Berosus, Mochus, Hestiaeus, and Hieronymus support the claim of long lives for the ancients; while Hesiod, Hecataeus, Hellanicus, Acusilaus, Ephorus, and Nicolas all say that the ancients lived a thousand years, but each may look upon these matters as he thinks fit.[1]

Canaan, the fourth son of Ham, inhabited the country now called Judea and called it from his own name. Amanthus inhabited Amathe, and so on. Of the cities of seven of Canaan's sons, we know nothing, for the Hebrews overthrew their cities.[2]

Josephus promises more, but does not seem to have carried out his promise. He does state in the *War* that had the Romans not punished the reprobates of Judea, they would have been swept away with some calamity like the flood.[3]

This survey reveals that Josephus' treatment of the flood is a simple paraphrase of Greek Scripture. He is interested in the letter of the Bible rather than the spirit behind the letter. He presents a statement of fact without stopping to draw moral lessons from it. He embellishes the biblical story with materials he has drawn from the Pseudepigrapha and from folklore. He parallels Philo in ascribing four stories to the ark. He sets up a chronology. He is interested in confirming biblical data by an appeal to the histories of other people. He tends to give place names that his readers would know. He shows his inherent rationalism when he allows each to form his own opinion about the validity of the tradition ascribing extremely long lives to ancient people. He condenses Scripture when he has only one journey of the dove.

This chapter has disclosed that Hellenistic Jewish writers interpreted the flood, each out of his own background and for his own purpose. Ps.-Philo and Josephus are interested in it chiefly as an event of the past which forms a part of their chronicle. Philo is interested in its moral and allegorical implications. Ps.-Philo represents the minimum of penetration of Hellenistic influence, perhaps

---

[1] *Ibid.*, i. 3. 9.
[2] *Ibid.*, i. 6. 2.
[3] Josephus, *B.J.* v. 13. 6.

limited to a linguistic influence stemming from its having been pre-served at one stage in Greek. While Josephus shows only minimal contact with rabbinic materials in the flood episodes, the influences of the Greek spirit is also marginal. Philo, on the other hand, has thoroughly imbibed Greek ideas and presents the flood in keeping with them.

CHAPTER FOUR

THE FLOOD IN THE EARLY VERSIONS

A. THE GREEK VERSIONS

1. *The Septuagint.*

The translation of the flood section in the LXX is of particular importance for this study in view of the fact that it is this version upon which Philo, Josephus, and the church fathers comment. The prologue to *Sirach* informs us that material translated from Hebrew into other languages often has a different meaning from that which it originally conveyed. The Greek version is no exception. Perhaps made for the use of the Alexandrian community in the third century B.C.,[1]) this version offers the understanding of flood linguistic problems held in that atmosphere.

Tendencies of translators observable elsewhere in the Bible manifest themselves in the flood section. First, we see evidences of "translation Greek" in the use of non-Greek expressions that are traceable to the endeavor to render word for word : [2])

a. Gen. 5 : 29 ; 8 : 15 ; 9 : 8 : Pleonastic use of λέγων to render לאמר.

b. Gen. 6 : 4 : "Men of fame" (οἱ ἄνθρωποι οἱ ὀνομαστοί) for אנשי השם.

c. Gen. 6 : 12 : "All flesh" (πᾶσα σάρξ) for כל־בשר ; cf. Gen. 6 : 17, 19 ; 7 : 15, 16, 21 ; 8 : 17, 21 ; 9 : 11, 15, 16, 17.[3])

d. Gen. 6 : 17 ; cf. 9 : 11 : "Flood of waters" (κατακλυσμὸς ὕδωρ) for המבול מים.

e. Gen. 6 : 20 : "Birds of wings" (ὄρνεα τῶν πετεινῶν) would seem to be a literal rendering of צפור כל־כנף, though the MT. does not have this phrase. However in the rendering of Gen. 7 : 14, where it does occur, the semitism is omitted.

f. Gen. 6 : 20 ; 7 : 2, 9 : Nouns are repeated to express distribu-

---

[1]) H. B. Swete, *Intro. to the O.T. in Greek* (Cambridge: U. Press, 1902), p. 21. For other discussions of the problems of LXX origin, see D. W. Thomas, "Textual Criticism of the O.T." in H. H. Rowley, *The O.T. and Modern Study* (Oxford: Clarendon Press, 1952), pp. 248-259; B. J. Roberts, *O.T. Texts and Versions* (Cardiff: U. of Wales Press, 1951), pp. 101-187.

[2]) H. B. Swete, *op. cit.*, p. 323.

[3]) *Ibid.*, p. 307.

tion : [1]) "two of all" (δύο δύο) ; cf. Gen. 7 :2, 3 : "seven of all" (ἑπτὰ ἑπτά). The idiom recurs in Gen. 7 :2 concerning unclean beasts where it is not found in MT.

g. Gen. 7 :19 : There is a doubling of the emphatic adverb "exceedingly" (σφόδρα σφοδρῶς) for מאד מאד.[2])

h. Gen. 7 :4 : A subterfuge is used to indicate the *hiphʿil* : "I bring rain" (ἐπάγω ὑετόν).

i. Gen. 8 :3 : The translators misunderstood the idioms for continuous action : "The water abated" (ἐνεδίδου καὶ ἠλαττονοῦτο τὸ ὕδωρ).

j. Gen. 8 :5 : "The water continued abating" (πορευόμενον ἠλαττονοῦτο) for הלוך וחסור.

k. Gen. 8 :7 : "And he went out and did not return" (ἐξελθὼν οὐχ ὑπέστρεψεν) for ויצא יצוא ושוב.

l. Gen. 8 :12 : "Did not return to him any more" (οὐ προσέθετο τοῦ ἐπιστρέψαι) for לא־יספה שוב.

m. Gen. 8 :21 : "I will never again curse" (Οὐ προσθήσω ἔτι τοῦ καταράσασθαι) for לא אסף לקלל ; "I will never again smite" (οὐ προσθήσω οὖν ἔτι πατάξαι) for לא־אסף עוד להכות.

n. Gen. 9 :3 : "Green plant" (λάχανον χόρτου) for ירק עשב.

o. Gen. 9 :11 : The causal use of ἀπό rendering מן ; cf. Ps. 76:7.[3])

p. Gen. 9 :12 : "Sign which I give" (διδόναι) for נתן. "Soul of life" (ψυχὴ ζώσης) for נפש חיה.

q. Gen. 9 :14 : "When I bring clouds" (συννεφεῖν με νεφέλας) in imitation of the MT. cognate accusative בענני ענן.

Certain differences between the Hebrew and the Greek must reflect either a different underlying text or an effort on the part of the translators at interpretation :

1. Changes in the harmonization of recurring phrases :

a. Gen. 6 :20 : "From all the creeping things which creep" renders "From all creeping things of earth" to harmonize with Gen. 7 :14.

b. Gen. 6 :20 : "Male and female shall they be" is added to

---

[1]) *Ibid.*, p. 307.

[2]) *Ibid.*

[3]) See J. H. Moulton, *A Grammar of N. T. Greek*, ed. W. F. Howard (Edinburgh: T. and T. Clark, 1919), II, 461.

harmonize with Gen. 6 : 19 ; 7 : 2 ; and 7 : 9, ignoring the variant Hebrew איש ואשתו and זכר ונקבה.

c. Gen. 7 : 17 : Adds "forty nights" to harmonize with v. 4 and v. 12.

d. Gen. 8 : 1 : Adds "and all the birds and all creeping things" to become as inclusive a list as Gen. 7 : 14.

e. Gen. 9 : 1, 7 : The imperatives of the blessing are rendered as futures to harmonize with Gen. 8 : 17 where the same roots in a like context are imperfects.

2. In several passages there is considerable expansion of the MT. perhaps with a desire to clear up what is ambiguous : [1])

a. Gen. 6 : 19 : The repetitious "and from every living thing, from all flesh two, a pair from all . . ." is expanded into "and from all beasts of burden, and from all creeping things and from all wild beasts and from all flesh, a pair (δύο δύο) from all."

b. Gen. 6 : 20 : Adds "with you, male and female" following "to be kept alive."

c. Gen. 7 : 3 : Expands (where MT. seems lacking) "birds of heavens seven pairs, male and female" into "all the clean birds of the heavens seven pairs (ἑπτὰ ἑπτά) male and female and of all the unclean birds a pair (δύο δύο)."

d. Gen. 7 : 20 : Mountains are made "high."[2])

e. Gen. 8 : 7 : Noah sends out the raven "to see if the waters were cut off."

f. Gen. 8 : 13 : Adds τὸ ὕδωρ ἀπό, after the covering of the ark is removed.

g. Gen. 8 : 21 : "On account of man" becomes "on account of the works of man."

h. Gen. 9 : 1 : Adds to the series "and rule over it" (κατακυριεύσατε) to make this passage a parallel to Gen. 1 : 28.

i. Gen. 9 : 22 : Adds "coming out" (ἐξελθών).[3])

3. There are minor abbreviations :

a. Gen. 7 : 22 : "Breath of the spirit of life" is improved to "breath of life."

---

[1]) H. B. Swete, *op. cit.*, p. 325.

[2]) This reading is considered preferable to that of MT. by John Skinner, *A Critical and Exegetical Commentary on Genesis* (Edinburgh: T. and T. Clark, 1951), p. 165.

[3]) This addition is considered an improvement by Skinner, *op. cit.*, p. 183.

b. Gen. 8:17 : "Breed abundantly on the earth and be fruitful and multiply on earth" becomes "increase and multiply."

c. Gen. 9:5 : Omits the third "from the hand of."[1])

4. Statements are made more sweeping than in the MT. :

a. Gen. 7:23 : "Upon the earth" becomes "upon all the earth."

b. Gen. 8:9: "Upon the face of all the earth" becomes "upon all the face of all the earth."

5. There are changes of person :

a. Gen. 9:6 : In the blessing after the flood where God speaks, the third person is changed to the first : "I made."

b. Gen. 9:16 : "Between God and man" becomes "between me and all living flesh."

6. Prepositions are rendered as conjunctions :

a. Gen. 6:13 : "And the earth" for "with the earth."

b. Gen. 8:17 : "And all flesh" for "from all flesh."

7. Changes of the Divine Name :

a. Adonoi :
   1. Κύριος ὁ Θεός : Gen. 5:29 ; 6:3, 5, 8 ; 7:1, 5 ; and 8:21 (twice).
   2. ὁ Θεός : Gen. 6:6, 7 ; 7:16 ; 8:20.

b. Elohim :
   1. Κύριος ὁ Θεός : Gen. 6:12, 22 ; 8:15 ; 9:12.
   2. ὁ Θεός : Gen. 6:2, 4, 9, 11, 13 ; 7:9, 16 ; 8:1 (twice) ; 9:1, 8, 17, 27.
   3. Rendered by the pronoun, ἐμός : Gen. 9:16.

Either the scribes had a Hebrew text which greatly varied from the MT. in the divine name or they found no reason to avoid variety. The latter would seem more likely. A moment's glance will also reveal that their usage does not at all correspond to the alleged sources in the Pentateuch, J and E.

8. Changes in Chronology :

The years of the patriarchs prior to the flood equal a total of 2242 in the LXX in contrast to 1656 in the MT. and only 1307 in the Samaritan text.[2]) Differences in the Greek text on matters of

[1]) See J. Skinner, op. cit., pp. 170 f.
[2]) J. Skinner, op. cit., p. 134.

numbers are not unusual. Lamech was 188 years old at the birth of Noah and lived 565 years afterward to make a total of 753 years. The MT. gives 182, 595, and 777 years respectively for these, while the Samaritan text has 53, 600, and 653.[1]) The flood begins on the 27th day of the second month (Gen. 7 :11) rather than the 17th as in the MT., and rests on the mountains on the 27th of the 7th month (Gen. 8 :4). The mountains are seen in the eleventh month (Gen. 8 :5) rather than the tenth. The result is that in the Greek Bible Noah remains in the ark twelve full months instead of ten days more than twelve months, as in the MT.

9. Other pertinent passages :

a. Gen. 5 :29 : The play on Noah's name is rendered "give us rest" (διαναπαύειν) which seems dependent on the root נוח rather than נחם of the MT.

b. Gen. 6 :2 : The בני־האלהים are "angels of God" (ἄγγελοι τοῦ θεοῦ) in Codex Alexandrinus,[2]) but in v. 4 υἱοὶ τοῦ θεοῦ occurs which would be a literal rendering of the MT. Other mss. have υἱοί in both instances.

c. Gen. 6 :3 : By the addition of the demonstrative adjective and the change of the collective "his days" to plural, it is made clear that it is the prediluvian men in whom God's spirit will not dwell,[3]) because "they" are flesh, and it is "their days" that are limited to 120 years, rather than there being a limitation on the life-span in general.

d. Gen. 6 :3 : The obscure ידון is rendered καταμένειν ("dwell" or "remain") in which rendering it is followed by the English versions.[4])

e. Gen. 6 :4 : The נפלים are "giants" (γίγαντες). It is specified that these are offspring of the unions of v. 2.

f. Gen. 6 :5 : "All which he purposes in his heart" (πᾶς τις διανοεῖται ἐν τῇ καρδίᾳ) renders כל־יצר מחשבת לבו. This reveals

---

[1]) Gen. 5:28, 30, and 31. Codex Alex. has 187 and 782 for the first two of these figures.

[2]) H. B. Swete, op. cit., p. 329. This confusion of reading is reflected in Julius Africanus, Chron. ii. (PG. 10. 65); Augustine, Civ. Dei 15. 23 (CSEL. 40. 2. 112-113); and John Cassian, Collatio VIII. 21 (CSEL. 13. 2. 238).

[3]) The use of the plural for the collective אדם is also seen in 6:1, 2, 4, and 5a. 5b, however, uses the singular and the plural is not resumed until 8:21a; then 21b reverts to the singular.

[4]) The translators must have read ילון or ידור.

a combination of διάνοια and καρδία which are each elsewhere used to render לב.[1])

g. Gen. 6:6-7: Interested in avoiding the anthropomorphisms, the translators have God to be "provoked" (θυμοῦσθαι), instead of "repenting" that he made man (Gen. 6:7). He "reflected" (ἐνθυμεῖσθαι) and "bethinks himself" (διανοεῖσθαι, Gen. 6:6).[2])

h. Gen. 6:9: "Noah is well pleasing to God" (εὐαρεστεῖν) for את־האלהים התהלך־נח. The LXX in Genesis frequently, so renders the phrase; cf. 5:22, 24; 17:1; 24:40; 48:15.

i. Gen. 6:14 and elsewhere: For "ark" the LXX used κιβωτός which elsewhere also renders ארון and משכן. On the other hand, Moses' ark is designated by θίβις. The MT. has תבה for both Moses and Noah.

j. Gen. 6:14: קנים becomes νοσσιαί which clearly means "nests." In this rendering the LXX is followed by the English versions.

k. Gen. 6:14: "Squared wood," i.e. "of boards" (ξύλα τετράγωνα) which latter word occurs of cities laid out in a square, Rev. 21:16,[3]) reveals that either a different text is followed or the translators did not know what the Hebrew phrase עצי גפר meant.[4])

l. Gen. 6:16: The צהר (A.V. renders "window"; R.S.V. "roof") is a "gathering together" (ἐπισυνάγων), which hardly seems to fit the required sense. We note that the Greek, like the Hebrew, uses a different word, θυρίς, in Gen. 8:6 when Noah looks out of the ark.

m. Gen. 6:18: διαθήκη renders ברית.

n. Gen. 7:7: "Because of the water" (διὰ τὸ ὕδωρ) for מפני מי המבול is probably the understanding of the translators rather than "through" which a later legend would demand.

o. Gen. 7:11; 8:2: "Windows" (καταρράκται) for ארבת is also to be found in IV K. 7:19 and Mal. 3:10. In other contexts the word renders five Hebrew words, none of which have a connection with windows.

p. Gen. 7:12: ὑετός ("rain") renders גשם.

q. Gen. 8:4: Αραρατ is merely transliterated.

---

[1]) Edwin Hatch, *Essays in Biblical Greek* (Oxford: Clarendon Press, 1889), p. 104.

[2]) H. B. Swete, *op. cit.*, p. 327.

[3]) W. F. Arndt and F. W. Gingrich, *A Greek-English Lexicon of the New Testament* (Chicago: U. of Chicago Press, 1957), p. 821.

[4]) The Vulgate translates the phrase *lignis laevigatis* which is "planed wood."

r. Gen. 8 : 8 : "After him" (ὀπίσω αὐτοῦ) renders אחריו rather than
    מאתו.

s. Gen. 8 : 21 : "The mind is always upon evil" (ἔγκειται ἡ διάνοια
    . . . ἐπιμελῶς ἐπὶ τὰ πονηρά) for יצר לב האדם רע. Neither ἔγκεισθαι
    nor ἐπιμελῶς are elsewhere used in LXX to render יצר.[1])

t. Gen. 9 : 6 : "In place of his blood he shall be poured out" (ἀντὶ
    τοῦ αἵματος αὐτοῦ ἐκχυθήσεται) for באדם דמו ישפך.

u. Gen. 9 : 20 : "Began" (ἄρχειν) renders ויחל.

v. Gen. 9 : 20 : "Farmer" (ἄνθρωπος γεωργός) for איש האדמה
    occurs only here.

w. Gen. 9 : 21 ; cf. 9 : 27 : "In his house" (ἐν τῷ οἴκῳ αὐτοῦ). In Genesis
    οἶκος regularly renders בית except here and v. 27. On the other
    hand σκηνή, cf. Gen. 18 : 1, etc., would be nearer the MT., אהלה.

x. Gen. 9 : 24 : "Younger" (νεώτερος) renders הקטן.

y. Gen. 9 : 25 : "Household servant" (παῖς οἰκέτης) renders עבד
    עבדים. The Hebrew expression is a superlative. The translators
    may imply that this is the lowest type of servant.

2. *Aquila.*

In the first half of the second century, near A.D. 130, a slavishly
literal translation was made for Greek speaking Jews by one who in
the tradition is Aquila the proselyte. Actually little is known about
him. The translation was popular among Jews and gained some
respect among Christians, being mentioned by several writers
following Irenaeus.[2])

Only fragments of Aquila's work have survived. These do not
contain the flood sections, but certain phrases may be gleaned from
Field's collection of remains of Origen's *Hexapla*, of which they
formed a part.[3])

Aquila's desire for extreme literalness is to be seen in some of his
choices :

a. Gen. 6 : 3 (2) : οἱ υἱοὶ τῶν θεῶν renders בני־האלהים, in which
    choice he agrees with LXX, except in the plural phrase θεοί.[4])

---

[1]) Edwin Hatch, *op. cit.*, pp. 152-153.

[2]) B. J. Roberts, *op. cit.*, pp. 120-121.

[3]) F. Field, *Origenis Hexaplorum quae supersunt, sive Veterum Interpretetum
Graecorum in totum Vetus Testamentum* (Oxford: Clarendon Press, 1925), 2 vols.

[4]) While Jerome, *Heb. Quaest. in Gen.* 6:2 (*PL.* 23. 996), explains that Aquila
means angels, Augustine, *Civ. Dei* xv. 23 (*CSEL.* 40. 2. 112-113), attempts
to explain the choice from the phrase from the Psalms: "Ye are Gods and all
of you sons of the Most High."

b. Gen. 6 : 10 (9) : Noah "walks with God" (σὺν τῷ θεῷ περιεπάτει) for את האלהים התהלך.

c. Gen. 8 : 21 : God speaks "to his heart" (καὶ εἶπε κύριος πρὸς καρδίαν αὐτοῦ) for ויאמר יהוה אל לבו.

d. Gen. 8 : 22 : "and day and night" (καὶ ἡμέρα καὶ νύξ) for ויום ולילה.

e. Gen. 9 : 4 : "In his soul is his blood" (ἐν ψυχῇ αὐτοῦ αἷμα αὐτοῦ) for בנפשו דמו.

Many of his changes need reflect only a difference of opinion in the choice of words and can be paralleled in the LXX in other contexts :

a. Gen. 6 : 7 (6) : μετεμελήθη for נחם, cf. Gen. 6 : 8 (7), occurs in Prov. 5 : 11.

b. Gen. 6 : 14 (13) : τέλος ("end") for קץ is frequent in LXX.

c. Gen. 6 : 15 (14) : ἀλοιφή for כפר is found in Job 33 : 24, but the verb form from this root, ἀλοιφᾶν, apparently meaning "to smear" is an *hapax* with Aquila.[1]

d. Gen. 6 : 17 (16) : ἄνοιγμα ("door") for פתח is found in III K. 14 : 6.

e. Gen. 7 : 11 : θυρίδες ("windows") for ארבת occurs in Is. 24 : 18.

f. Gen. 8 : 1 : παρήγαγεν ("to go away") for ויעבר instead of ἐπήγαγεν of LXX is an improvement.

g. Gen. 8 : 2 (1) : ἐστάλησαν for וישכו is not paralleled in LXX.

h. Gen. 8 : 2 : ἐνεφράγησαν ("close") for ויסכרו is found in Ps. 62 (63) : 12.

i. Gen. 8 : 13 : κάλυμμα ("covering") for מכסה is seen in Ex. 26 : 14 ; Num. 3 : 25 ; 4 : 8, 10, 12, 14, 25.

j. Gen. 9 : 5 : πάντων τῶν ζώων for כל־חיה is frequent in LXX.

k. Gen. 9 : 22, 23 : ἡ ἀσχημοσύνη for את ערות is frequently used in LXX for the private parts or as a euphemism for the sex act.

Among the other more important interpretations of Aquila, we notice that he has assumed that the נפלים (Gen. 6 : 5 (4)) receive their name from נפל ("to fall"); hence he chose a root, ἐπιπίπτοντες, which conveys this idea. The same motive determines the choice of δυνατοί for גבורים ("strong" or "mighty ones" ; Gen. 6 : 5 (4)). The צהר (Gen. 6 : 17 (16)) is a μεσημβρινός which in its other occurrences (I Esd. 9 : 41 ; Job 5 : 14 ; Ps. 90 (91) : 6 ; Is. 16 : 3) means "noon-

---

[1] J. Reider, "Prolegomena to a Gk.-Heb. and Heb.-Gk. Index to Aquila," *JQR.*, VII N. S. (1917), 307.

day." Evidently Aquila understood it to be some sort of opening. συνθήκη (Gen. 6 :19 (18)) is chosen for ברית as the LXX did in IV K. 17 :15, though it elsewhere used διαθήκη.[1]) גשם (rainstorm) becomes ὄμβρος (Gen. 7 :12). ὄμβρος in the LXX renders שעיר (Deut. 32 :2), which in the context must mean "light shower."

3. *Theodotian*

Between A.D. 180 and 190, Theodotian, an Ebionite Christian of Pontus or Ephesus, produced a translation which is a free rendering of the Hebrew. It was considered of first rate importance by early Christians. Some today would regard the work as a revision of the LXX.[2]) The translation has not survived. We are again dependent upon Field's *Hexapla* [3]) for the few remains of the flood section.

Theodotian literally rendered בני־האלהים (Gen. 6 :3 (2)) "sons of God." The נפלים he took to be the "giants" (οἱ γίγαντες), Gen. 6 :5 (4). פתח becomes θύρα, "door" (Gen. 6 :17 (16)) as it is frequently rendered in the LXX.

Like Aquila, he literally renders "the Lord spake to his heart" (πρὸς τὴν καρδίαν αὐτοῦ, Gen. 8 :21). He further agrees with Aquila in choosing ἡ ἀσχημοσύνη for את ערות (Gen. 9 :22, 23).

The flood fragments do not preserve an example of Theodotian's rendering of ברית, but since he elsewhere used διαθήκη (IV K. 11 :4 ; Job 31 :1 ; Ps. 49 (50) :5 ; etc.), we can assume the same here.

The one additional preserved verse from Theodotian, Gen. 8 :1, agrees with the LXX in rendering וישכו by καὶ ἐκόπασε.

4. *Symmachus*

The tradition differs over whether Symmachus was an Ebionite or a Samaritan who became a proselyte to Judaism. The translation, produced between A.D. 193 and 211, while faithful to the Hebrew, displays an elegant Greek style.[4]) He seems to have made use of the prior work of Aquila.)[5] Only fragments are extant. The flood material is from Field.[6])

---

[1]) The relation of these words to each other is considered by W. Barclay, *A N. T. Wordbook* (London: SCM. Press, 1956), pp. 30-32.

[2]) B. J. Roberts, *op. cit.*, pp. 123-126.

[3]) F. Field, *op. cit.*, I, 22-28.

[4]) B. J. Roberts, *op. cit.*, p. 126.

[5]) H. B. Swete, *op. cit.*, pp. 50-53.

[6]) F. Field, *op. cit.*, I, 22-28.

With Symmachus we move still further in the direction of interpretation. עצבון becomes for Symmachus "misery" (κακοπαθείας) not only in Gen. 5 :29, but also in Gen. 3 :18 (17). The בני־האלהים are οἱ υἱοὶ τῶν δυναστευόντων (Gen. 6 :3 (2)), "those who exercise lordship" ; however, since the root occurs in references to divine and human lords, we cannot be sure how Symmachus took it. God's spirit will not "judge" (κρίνειν) men always (Gen. 6 :4 (3)). Evidently Symmachus took ידון to come from דין. The נפלים become "powerful ones," βίαιοι, which in LXX renders five words, but not נפלים or גברים. Symmachus has evidently chosen βίαιοι because of its correspondence to גברים and then equated נפלים to it. עלה־זית טרף becomes θαλλὸς ἐλαίας κάρφος, "a shoot of olive branch" (Gen. 8 :11). קץ becomes πέρας (Gen. 6 :14 (13)) which the LXX uses in Amos 8 :2.

Symmachus agrees with Theodotian in the choice of θύρα in Gen. 6 :17 (16).

He agrees with Aquila in the use of συνθήκη (Gen. 6 :19 (18)) ; ζῷα (Gen. 6 :20 (19)) ; θυρίς (Gen. 7 :11) ; κάλυμμα (Gen. 8 :13); and καὶ ἡμέρα καὶ νύξ (Gen. 8 :22).

He agrees with both Aquila and Theodotian in the rendering of the "shame" (ἀσχημοσύνη) of Noah (Gen. 9 :23).

Symmachus' choice of ἀποστρέφειν to render נחם (Gen. 6 :7 (6)) seems inappropriate unless he has equated נחם with סור or שוב for which the LXX uses ἀποστρέφειν. This rendering would not show the hesitancy of others to say that God changes. However, when he has Noah "follow after God" (τῷ θεῷ ἐπηκολούθησεν) one would wonder if he is not avoiding anthropomorphism. The LXX renders the *hiph'il* of הלך by ἐπακολουθεῖν only in Is. 55 :3.

Symmachus specifies that the ark is to have a second and third story. He strangely chooses ἱλαστήριον to render תבה. ἱλαστήριον is a means of expiation, cf. Rom. 3 :25, and in the LXX designates the lid of the ark of the covenant, "mercy seat" (Ex. 25 :16). The קנים are καλιαῖ (Gen. 6 :15 (14)), which in some contexts are wooden sheds, but in others, bird nests. The צהר is διαφανής, "transparent" (Gen. 6 :17 (16)), evidently understood to be some sort of opening. גשם becomes χειμών, "rainy weather" (Gen. 7 :12).

Symmachus well grasps the Hebrew idiom when he has God to speak "to himself" (πρὸς ἑαυτόν) for אל־לבו (Gen. 8 :22 (21)), but shows a literal interest in "through all time of earth" (διὰ πάντων τῶν χρόνων τῆς γῆς) for עד כל־ימי הארץ (Gen. 8 :22). But Sym machus seems to have missed the idiom when he renders Gen. 9:2 κατὰ πάντων τῶν θηρίων τῆς γῆς, equating על with κατά and the genitive which ordinarily means "against." Likewise Gen. 9:4, οὗ σὺν ψυχῇ αἷμα αὐτοῦ for בנפשו דמו is strained.

In summary, it should be said that the Greek versions represent a definite step in the direction of interpretation: eliminating obscurities, avoiding anthropomorphisms that were offensive to its Greek speaking reader, and at times rendering a different text from the present MT. The varying degrees of literalness seen in the different efforts meet the demands of the communities for which they were intended.

B. The Aramaic Versions

1. *Targum of Onkelos*

The *Targum of Onkelos*, while perhaps of Palestinian origin, was edited and came to its official final form in Babylon by the fifth century A.D. It may, however, be based on works as early as the third century A.D. The identity of Onkelos for whom the work is named is disputed, with some insisting that he is identical with Aquila who is the Greek translator.[1]

In the flood section the regular grammatical and theological features of this translation occur. ית, unnatural to Aramaic, is inserted to correspond to the accusative particle את. Where God is said to do something, in the Targum to avoid anthropomorphism, it is His מימר which does it: God repents in His מימר (Gen. 6:6, 7); in His מימר He covers the ark (Gen. 7:16); He speaks in His מימר (Gen. 8:21); and the covenant is between God's מימר and men (Gen. 9:12, 13, 15, 16, 17).[2] The divine name is uniformly rendered יוי regardless of the Hebrew original.

There are numerous awkward constructions as a result of literally following the Hebrew: "flood of waters" (Gen. 7:6); the distributive repetition of the numeral (Gen. 7:3, 9, etc.); the "all creeping things that creep" and "all birds—even all flying things" are duplicated (Gen. 7:14); the infinitive construction is rendered אזלין ותיבין (Gen. 8:3); cf. אזלין וחסרין (Gen. 8:5); "all who had breath of spirit of life" is redundant even as in Hebrew (Gen. 7:22);

---

[1] B. J. Roberts, *op. cit.*, pp. 204-207.
[2] K. Koehler, "Memra," *J. E.*, VIII, 464-465.

compare נפיק מיפק ותאיב (Gen. 8 : 7) ; the emphatic repetition of the adverb (מאד מאד) is reproduced, לחדא לחדא (Gen. 7 : 19).

Onkelos in the flood sections does not omit any verse or phrase in the MT. The notable interpretations differing from the MT. by chapter and verse are as follows :

Chapter 6.

v. 2. "The great men" or "princes" (רברביא) for בני־האלהים.

v. 3. "This evil generation shall not endure (יתקים) before me forever because they are flesh and their works are evil." The latter phrase is not represented in the MT. The Targum is quite definite in interpreting the 120 years to be given to that generation and then adds "if they repent."

v. 4. The נפלים are "mighty men" (גבריא) which word is also used for the offspring of women and the great ones in v. 3.

vv. 6, 7. נחם is rendered by תוב "repent."

v. 6. God said he would break (למתבר) their strength as he pleased.

v. 8. חן is rendered רחמין "pity."

v. 9. Noah walks in the "fear" (בדחלתא) of the Lord.

v. 12. All flesh of man has corrupted his way. MT. has merely "all flesh."

v. 13. The earth is filled with violence "on account of their evil works." MT. : "on their account."

v. 14. The ark is תבותא, which is also used for Moses' ark, Ex. 2 : 3, 5.
עצי־גפר is rendered "cedar wood" (אעין דקדרוס). "Nests" (קנים) are "dwellings" or "compartments" (מדורין).

v. 16. The צהר is a "light" (נהור) ; cf. 7 : 11 ; 8 : 6. The "stories" are מדורין. This word was used for rendering קנים in v. 14.

v. 17. The "flood" is טופנא which corresponds to Hebrew צוף. MT. uses מבול in this section for the flood.

v. 18. ברית is rendered קים which may mean "covenant."[1])

Chapter 7.

v. 2. The Targum continues to use "male and female" in vv. 2 and 3, though the Hebrew in v. 2 uses איש ואשתו.

---

[1]) See M. Jastrow, A Dictionary of the Targumim, the Talmud Babli and Yerushalmi, and the Midrashic Literature (N. Y.: Pardes Pub. House, 1950), p. 1359.

v. 11.   Cf. 8 : 2. ארבת is rendered by כווא ("window") which in the Targum also renders חלון (Gen. 8 : 6).

Chapter 8.

v. 4.   קרדו for Ararat, which seems to be a district of Cordyene,[1]) conforms to the tendency to supply better known geographical names.[2])

v. 11.   טרף is literally rendered תביר "to break."

v. 17.   "Multiply and replenish" are rendered as third pl. imperfects, as is true in Hebrew, rather than the imperatives that one would expect.

v. 21.   "And the Lord received with pleasure their burnt offering" (וקביל ייי ברעוא ית קורבניה). Notice the avoidance of anthropomorphism. The circumlocution out of reverence for God also teaches His otherness.[3])

        On account of the "guilt (חובא) of man" for "on account of man."

Chapter 9.

v. 5.   The Targum sets forth the idea that blood revenge is to be taken by the slain man's brother (מיד גבר דישוד ית דמא דאחוהי אתבע ית נפשא דאנשא).

v. 6.   "He who sheds man's blood with witnesses, at the word of the judges his blood shall be shed."

v. 25.   Canaan becomes a "servant of work" (עבד פלח) to his brothers. Cf. v. 20 where פלח applies to Noah.

v. 27.   It is the "Shekina" that is to dwell in the dwellings of Shem. [4])

---

[1]) M. Jastrow, *op. cit.*, p. 1412, identifies Mt. Kardu with a district of Cordyene. It was here in the Kurdish mountains that Berossus had the ark to land in his account of the flood; see Josephus, *Ant.* i. 3. 6. Hippolytus, *Arabic Frag. to Pent.* Gen. 8:1 (*GCS*. 1. 91), comments: "As to Mt. Kardu, it is in the east, in the land of the sons of Raban, and the Orientals call it Mt. Godash; the Arabians and Persians call it Ararat" (cf. *ANF.* V, 198). Ephraem Syrus also located the landing of the ark on Mt. Kardu; see A. Dillmann, *Genesis* (Edinburgh: T. and T. Clark, 1897), I, 283, n. 2.

[2]) B. J. Roberts, *op. cit.*, p. 206.

[3]) M. Kadushin, *The Rabbinic Mind* (N. Y.: Jewish Theol. Seminary, 1952), p. 334.

[4]) Cf. Rashi to Gen. 9:27.

2. *The Targum of Pseudo-Jonathan*

The *Targum of Pseudo-Jonathan* represents a mixture of an early version of the *Targum of Onkelos* and the older Palestinian Targum to the Pentateuch. It is characterized by a great deal more Haggadah than the *Targum of Onkelos*. Legend-like stories for edification are included. The doctrine of the future life and a well-developed angelology are set forth. This Targum reached its present form in the seventh century A.D. [1]

The general remarks already made about the literalness, grammatical, and theological peculiarities of the *Targum of Onkelos* also apply to the *Targum of Pseudo-Jonathan* in the flood narrative, except that לחדא is not repeated in Gen. 9:19. מבול is rendered טובענא. Names of the months are supplied: the second is *Marḥeshwan* (7:11; 8:14); the seventh is *Nisan* (8:4); the tenth is *Tammuz* (8:5); the first is *Tishri* (Gen. 8:13).

Noticeable variants from the MT. by chapter and verse are as follows:

Chapter 5.

v. 29.   Noah will comfort from our work "which does not prosper." The Lord cursed the ground "on account of the guilt of the sons of men."

Chapter 6.

v. 1.   The "sons of women" (בני נשא) for אדם; cf. Gen. 7:10; 9:5; אדם is rendered by אינשא in 8:20 and 9:6.

v. 2.   "The sons of the great ones" (בני רברביא) for the "sons of God."
"The daughters of men were fair, with painted eyelids, rouge, and were walking about nude, which led the sons of the great ones to conceive impure thoughts." [2]

v. 3.   God says that every evil generation which will arise in the future will not be judged (יתדנון) according to the order of the generation of the flood which shall be destroyed and exterminated from the midst of the earth. Have I not imparted my Holy Spirit to them that they may do good works? And behold their works are wicked. I give them

---

[1] B. J. Roberts, *op. cit.*, p. 202.
[2] Cf. *PRE.* 22.

a prolongment of 120 years that they may work repentance and not perish.

v. 4.   "*Shamhaza'i* and *'Uzi'el* who were fallen (נפלים) from heaven, were on the earth in those days." There seems to be no connection between the offspring of the women and these, but those born of women and the great ones are nevertheless called "heroes" (גברין).

v. 6.   תוב is equated to נחם; cf. v. 7.

And God passes "judgment" (ואידיין) upon them במימריה.

v. 8.   Adds, Noah "who was righteous" found favor.

v. 9.   Noah was perfect "in good works" in his generation. Noah walks "in the fear of the Lord" (בדחלתא).

v. 11.   The world was corrupted "on account of the inhabitants who went astray from the order which the Lord had established."

v. 12.   "Each and every one" corrupts his way.

v. 13.   The earth is filled with violence from "their evil works."

v. 14.   The ark is "cedar wood" (קיסין קדרונין).

קנים is rendered "compartments" (קולין). There are 150 of these on the left side and 36 along its width. There are 10 storerooms for food in the middle. There are 5 protected cisterns on both the left and right sides.[1]) If any over-all dimensions for the ship were given, they are now missing. There is no verse 15.

v. 16.   Noah is to go to the Pishon and take a "sparkling gem" (יוחרא for צהר) which is to be fixed one cubit up in the ark to give light.

"Stories" (מדורין) are supplied as in Onkelos.

v. 17.   טובענא renders מבול.

v. 20.   The animals were collected and brought by the angel to preserve them.

Chapter 7.

v. 2.   No note is taken of the change from "male and female" (דכר ונוקבא) where MT. reads איש ואשתו ("man and his wife").

v. 4.   God promises seven days to see if they repent. If they do not repent, after seven days, the waters will come and destroy the bodies of man and beast.

---

[1]) The same description is found in *PRE*. 23.

v. 11.   The second month is *Marḥeshwan* for hitherto men were numbering the months from *Tishri* which is the beginning of the year at the completion of the world.

When the fountains were opened, the giants (בני גובריא) were gathering there and shutting them up, so God opened the windows (חרכין; cf. Gen. 8 : 6, כווין) of heaven.

v. 14.   All birds, all which flies (כל צפור כל דפרח).

v. 16.   The door is closed "before him" (באנפיה); MT. has בעדו.

v. 23.   For כל־היקום we read "All the bodies of men and beasts perish from man unto . . ." and the series ends "birds which fly in the air of the heavens."

Chapter 8.

v. 1.   God brings "a wind (רוח) of mercy" over the earth.

v. 2.   חרכין ("latticed window") renders ארבת.

v. 4.   The ark rests in the month of *Nisan* on the "mountains of *Kadron*, which is the name of one peak in *Kardenayya* and the name of one peak is *Armeneya* and there was builded the city of Armenia in the east."

v. 5.   The tenth month is *Tammuz* and in *Tammuz* the heads of the mountains are seen.

v. 11.   The dove has a freshly plucked olive leaf (טרפא דזיתא לקיט) in her mouth which she got from the Mt. of Olives (טור מישחא).

v. 13.   On the first day of the year, the month of *Tishri*, the water had abated.

v. 14.   In *Marḥeshwan* the ground was dry.

v. 17.   The verbs for multiplying are imperfects as they are in MT. and Onkelos.

v. 20.   Noah builds an altar. The altar which Adam built in the time when he was banished from Eden and on which he offered burnt offerings and on which Cain and Abel offered their offerings was destroyed when the flood descended. Noah rebuilt it and offered four of all the clean beasts upon that altar.[1]

v. 21.   The Lord receives with pleasure (ברעוא) his offering. Notice the softening of the anthropomorphism. The earth is not to be destroyed on account of the guilt of בני אנשא.

---

[1] Cf. *PRE.* 23.

v. 22. "All the days of the earth there will be sowing in the autumnal equinox (*tekufat Tishri*) and reaping in the vernal equinox (*tekufat Nisan*) and cold in the winter solstice (*tekufat Tebet*) and heat in the summer solstice (*tekufat Tammuz*)."

Chapter 9.

v. 4. But flesh which is torn from the living flesh while his life is in him or torn from the slaughtered beast before all the breath is gone out, ye shall not eat.

v. 5. "I will require that he be put to death on account of it." "From the hand of the man who sheds the blood of his brother I will require the life of the man."

v. 6. "By witnesses shall the judges declare him liable to the death penalty, and he who sheds blood without witnesses, the Lord of the world shall in the future render him retribution in the day of the great judgment."

v. 14. When God brings "glorious" (יקרא) clouds. The cognate accusative is dropped.
"And the bow is seen in the time that the sun is not covered by the clouds." [1]

v. 17. "Between My מימר and between the 'word' (מימר) of all flesh."

v. 20. "And he found a vine which the river had brought away from the garden of Eden and he planted it in a vineyard and it blossomed in a day and ripened and he gathered them." [2]

v. 24. Noah learned by revelation in a dream what had been done to him by his son who was inferior in worth since he caused him not to beget a fourth son. [3]

v. 25. "Cursed be Canaan," since he is a "fourth son," a "serving servant" (עביד משעבד) shall he be.

v. 26. "Blessed be the God of Shem, for his works are righteous and because Canaan shall be a servant to him."

---

[1] Cf. Josephus, *Ant.* i. 3. 8; *PRE.* 23; Radak and Ibn Ezra (*EBI.* II, 62).
[2] Cf. III *Bar.* 4:10; *PRE.* 23. Some sources think the tree of knowledge of good and evil was the vine; see *Apoc. Abr.* 23.5. *Jub.* 7:1-2 has a lapse of four years between the planting and the producing. The wine was kept until the first of the fifth year. Ephraem Syrus, *Comm. in Gen.* 7:1 (*CSCO.* 72. 50-51), has a lapse of six years.
[3] Cf. *Gen. R.* 36. 7.

v. 27.   May the Lord beautify (ישפר) the borders (תחומיה) of
          Japheth and may his sons be proselytes and dwell in the
          school (מדרשא) of Shem."

3. *The Jerusalem Targum*

The *Jerusalem Targum* II and III which is also known as the *Fragmentary Targum* is perhaps older than that of Pseudo-Jonathan. Some
think it was made up only of variants and marginal glosses of
an independent Targum, of an early version of Onkelos, or of
Pseudo-Jonathan. Extant manuscripts are late, but there may be in
it elements of Halakah which go back to an early date. [1]

Only a few elements (Gen. 6 :3, 6, 8, 11 ; 7 :11, 16 ; 8 :1, 10, 22 ;
and 9 :20) from the flood narratives survive in this collection.

Chapter 6.

v. 3.   The *Memra* of God said the generations of the future shall
          not be judged (יתדונון) as the generation of the flood which
          is to be consumed and blotted out. God's spirit is given
          men because they are flesh and do good works, but their
          works are evil. They are given 120 years that they repent
          and not perish.

v. 6.   There is regret (תהי) before the Lord in His מימר that He
          made man, and He spoke and argued (אמר ואדין) with His
          heart.

v. 8.   Noah finds favor (חן) and mercy (וחסד).

v. 11.   The earth is filled with violence (חומסין) and fraud (גוזלין).

Chapter 7.

v. 11.   The windows (חרכי) of heaven were opened.

v. 16.   The *Memra* of God was merciful (חם) upon him.

Chapter 8.

v. 1.   God remembered in His mercies the good which was with
          Noah and He made to pass over a wind of mercies.

v. 10.   Adds "And he began to number."

v. 22.   Has no notable variant.

Chapter 9.

v. 20.   "And Noah began to be a righteous man and planted" is
          added.

---

[1] B. J. Roberts, *op. cit.*, pp. 201-204.

We have in this section demonstrated that the flood of the Targums is a creation of Scripture paraphrase, reproducing rabbinic tradition concerning the meaning of the text. Haggadic expansions reveal the rabbinic *Sitz* out of which it came. The biblical exegesis evident in both the Greek and Aramaic versions of the flood are clear reflections of the communities which produced them.

CHAPTER FIVE

EARLY CHRISTIAN INTERPRETATIONS
OF THE FLOOD

Important factors making up the life situation for the interpretation placed upon the flood in Christian literature to the end of the second century include motifs suggested by the later O.T. writers; the LXX version; the allusions to the flood in the N.T.; and the allegorical interpretation of Scripture as a justification for the Christian message of salvation. The time had not yet arrived when churchmen composed detailed commentaries on O.T. books. From passing allusions and from scattered examples of detailed treatment of isolated passages, a picture can be formed which reveals that the second century was interested in the flood for its moral, polemical, and typological values. For the majority of writers the O.T. was a valid and literal record of the past. The interpretation given assumed and demanded that it be valid history. More interest was displayed, however, in the lessons to be drawn from this past than in the literal past itself.

We first examine the moral interest. The role played by Noah and the flood in the N.T. exercised a great influence over the treatment given these episodes by later writers. Noah is the exemplary righteous man, though not the first such man as Philo had contended (*Cong.* 90), for this honor is reserved for Abel (Heb. 11:4). The Ep. to the Hebrews sets forth Noah as an example of obedient faith who when warned of God concerning unseen things built an ark, saved his household, condemned the world, and became the heir of the righteousness that comes by faith (Heb. 11:7).[1] There can be little doubt that this picture of Noah has been influenced by Ez. 14:14, 20. Its general treatment of Noah's righteousness parallels the ideas of *Sir.* 44:17 and *Wisd.* 10:4.

In general, for writers of the second century "righteous Noah" continued to serve a moral purpose.[2] In the midst of an admonition

---

[1] Cf. Josephus, *Ant.* i. 3. 1-2, where it is less clearly implied that Noah shamed the world by throwing their skepticism into relief against his faith.

[2] The only exception is to be found in Iren., *Demonst.* 19. The epithet "just Noah" or "righteous Noah" is to be found in Philo, *Post.* 48, 173, 174; *Mig.* 125; *Conf.* 105; *Gig.* 3, 5; *Mut.* 189; II *Enoch* 34:3; Justin M., *Dial.* 138; *Const. Apost.* viii. 12. 24 (Funk, p. 502); Augustine, *c. duas ep. Pelagianorum* 3. 8 (*CSEL.* 60.

which is concerned to show the evils of faction and jealousy, of which
Cain, Dathan, and Abiram are examples, and at the same time concerned to exalt submission to the will of God, Noah along with
Enoch and Abraham becomes an example of obedience. Noah foretold a new beginning of the world and became the means through
whom the Master saved the living creatures. "The humility and
obedience of so many famous persons has served to improve not
only ourselves but also the generations before us" (I *Clem.* 9. 4; 19.
1).[1]) Clement has been strongly influenced by *Sir.* 44 ff. and Heb. 11.
A writer in the middle of the century exhorted from Ezekiel's doctrine
of individual responsibility in which Noah is an example (Ez. 14:14),
that unless one's baptism be kept pure he cannot expect to enter the
palace of God. No advocate shall be his if he has not pious and
righteous works (II *Clem.* 6. 8-9).[2])

    That Noah preached to his generation is not specifically stated in
the O.T.; however, this role which is also known for him in Jewish
writings,[3]) is set forth in II Pet. 2:5 with the phrase "herald of
righteousness." The preaching motif served the second century
for homiletical purposes. Clement of Rome urges repentance on the
basis that each generation had been given a place of repentance. Noah
preached repentance and those who obeyed him were saved (I *Clem.*
7. 6).[4]) He foretold "the beginning of a new world" (I *Clem.* 9. 4).
Clement does not enlarge further on the idea, but in using the term
παλιγγενεσία ("rebirth") he is using a technical Christian term which

---

494); *De consensu evang.* 1 (25) 39 (*CSEL.* 43. 38); cf. John Cassian, *Collatio VIII.*
21-23 (*CSEL.* 13. 2. 236-240). The epithets "the just" or "the righteous" man
are to be found in *Wisd.* 10:4; II *Enoch* 35:1 (Text B); Ps.-Clem., *Recog.* i. 29
(*PG.* 1. 1223); iv. 12 (*PG.* 1. 1320); viii. 50 (*PG.* 1. 1394); Ps.-Clem.,
Hom. viii. 17 (*GCS.* 42. 128); Chrysostom, *In Ep. I Cor.* hom. 34. 4 (*PG.* 61.
291); Sulpicius Severus, *Chron.* i. 3 (*CSEL.* 1. 5); Augustine, *De Catech.* 19. 32
(*PL.* 40. 334).

   [1]) Noah in a list of righteous worthies is also found in Origen, *Hom. in Ez.*
iv. 4, 5 (*GCS.* 33. 364-367); and in Cyril of Jer., *Catechesis* 16. 27 (*PG.* 33. 957A).

   [2]) This is the earliest evidence for what seems to be an established motif in
the preaching of the church; see J. Fink, *Noe der Gerechte in der Frühchristlichen
Kunst* (Münster/Köln: Böhlau-Verlag, 1955), pp. 75-76. Ezekiel is quoted in
Justin M., *Dial.* 44, 45; cf. 140. 3; Origen, *Hom. in Ez.* 4. 8 (*GCS.* 33. 368-369);
Cyprian, *Ep.* 75. 3 (*CSEL.* 3. 2. 811); Salvian the Presbyter, *De gubern. Dei* iii.
58 (*CSEL.* 8. 61); Aphraates, *Hom.* 23 (*TU.* III. 3. 374); Chrysostom, *In Ep. I
Thess.* c. 1, hom. 1. 4 (*PG.* 62. 598); *In Matt.* hom. v. 4 (*PG.* 57. 59); Augustine,
De peccatorum meritis et remissione 2. 10. 12 (*CSEL.* 60. 83-84); *Cant. R.* ii. 15. 2.

   [3]) Josephus, *Ant.* i. 3. 1; *Gen. R.* 30. 7; *Eccl. R.* 9. 15. § 1; *T. B. Sanh.* 108a-b;
Or. Sib. i. 177-233.

   [4]) Cf. Clement of A., *Strom.* i. 21. 135 (*GCS.* 15. 84).

has a connection with baptism (Mt. 19:28; Tit. 3:5; cf. Jno. 3:5). Despite its having been used by Philo (*Mos.* ii. 65) for the world after the deluge, it is entirely likely that Clement implies, without being specific, that Noah prefigures the Christian age.

Theophilus of Antioch informs us that:

Noah, when he announced to the men then alive that there was a flood coming, prophesied to them saying Come thither, God calls you to repentance (*Ad Autol.* iii. 19).[1]

In the third and later centuries pious imagination added details to the preaching motif for its own purposes. Methodius speaks of Noah's promising happiness and rest from evils to those who gave heed.[2] Hippolytus tells how Noah was commanded to make a wooden rattle on which he struck to attract the attention of the sons of Cain that he might tell them of the approach of the flood.[3] This preaching was repeatedly done.[4] Noah told Paul when the latter came to paradise that his message was "Repent for a flood of waters comes upon you." [5] The preaching went on for a hundred years,[6] but in each case Noah met with skepticism and contempt on the part of the people.[7]

To what extent the Christian interpretations of Noah's preaching are dependent on the phrase, "he condemned (κατακρίνειν) the world" (Heb. 11:7), it is not now possible to determine. The passage need imply no more than that the life of the pious is a standing rebuke to the skeptical and impious.[8]

Whether the preaching to the "spirits in prison, who formerly did not obey when God's patience waited in the days of Noah" (I Pet. 3:19-20) should be understood to refer to the spirit of Christ in the person of Noah preaching to the men of his generation or to preaching that took place during a journey of Christ to Hades between his death and resurrection is still a debated question.[9] The latter view had a

[1]) Cf. Ps.-Tertullian, *Carmen adv. Marc.* iii. 2 (*PL.* 2. 1071 A).

[2]) Methodius, *Conv. decem virg.* 10. 3 (*GCS.* 27. 125).

[3]) Hippolytus, *Arabic Frag. to Pent.*, Gen. 6:18 (*GCS.* I. 2. 88).

[4]) *Bk. of Adam and Eve* iii. 2, 4.

[5]) *Ap. of Paul* 50.

[6]) Augustine, *De catech.* 19. 32 (*PL.* 40. 334).

[7]) Chrysostom, *In Ep. I Thess.* c. 4, hom. 8. 2 (*PG.* 62. 442); see also Koran, Sura 11:27-49.

[8]) Cf. *Wisd.* 4:16; Mt. 12:41.

[9]) See the study by Bo Reicke, *The Disobedient Spirits and Christian Baptism* (København: E. Munksgaard, 1946), 275 pp.

certain vogue in some circles of the early church and is still popular.[1])
The grave theological difficulties which this doctrine presents, when
considered in the light of the teaching of Paul that men are to be
judged for deeds done in the body, are not considered in the literature
included in this survey.

The sins of the flood generation are detailed by Justin to be mur-
ders, wars, adulteries, intemperance, and every sort of vice (*Apol.* ii.
5).[2])

Equally as homiletical as the material just surveyed is the passing
remark made by Clement that "the animals entered with concord into
the ark" (I *Clem.* 9:4). [3]) Though typology had not developed
sufficiently in Clement's day to make the ark specifically a type of the
church, elements that later became specific are latent here. Clement is
really making the point that there should be harmony in the church.

Still a further homily is to be seen in Irenaeus' argument that there
was to be a resurrection of the flesh, insisting that the blood of the
righteous was to be required after, from the statement made to Noah,
"For your blood of your souls will I require, even from the hand of
beasts"; and again, "Whosoever will shed man's blood, it shall be shed
for his blood" (Iren., *Adv. haer.* v. 14. 1 (*ANF.* I. 541)). [4])

---

[1]) For the teaching of Marcion, see Iren., *Adv. haer.* i. 27. 3; cf. also *Gospel of
Peter* 10:42.

[2]) Aphraates, *Hom.* 18. 2 (*TU.* III. 3. 291), speaks of a time of special godlessness. The life of ease and denial that the world is governed by the providence
of God is mentioned, but it was the eating of blood that then resulted in cannibalism that sealed their doom, Ps.-Clem., *Recog.* iv. 10-11 (*PG.* I. 1319-1320);
Ps.-Clem., *Hom.* viii. 15 (*GCS.* 42. 128). They laughed at Noah as he built the
ark; see Ephraem Syrus, *Adv. Scrut. Rhythms* 56. 2; Chrysostom, *De statuis hom.*
20. 8 (*PG.* 49. 210); cf. *Bk. of Adam and Eve* iii. 2. Even their greatness of number
could not save them, Chrysostom, *In Ep. II Cor.* hom. 2. 4 (*PG.* 61. 398). The
statement that "the heart of man is evil from his youth" lent itself well as a proof
text that men are born children of wrath; see Jerome as quoted by Rufinus,
Apol. i. 38 (*PL.* 21. 576).

[3]) In contrast, Hippolytus, *Arabic Frag. to Pent.* 2 (*GCS.* 1. 2. 88), assumes
that it was only the stakes in the ark which kept the wild animals from the tame
ones.

[4]) Irenaeus quotes from the LXX; see H. B. Swete, *Intro. to O.T. in Gk.*
(Cambridge: U. Press, 1902), p. 415. Tertullian insisted that Moses was specifically
foreseeing the resurrection of the body, "since requisition will have to be made
therein of the blood of man" (*De res. carnis* 39; cf. 28 (*CSEL.* 47. 82, 65)). "How
will He require the blood of man at the hand of every beast unless because the
bodies of dead men will rise again?"; see John of Damascus, *De fide orth.* iv. 27
(*PG.* 94. 1221 A). Augustine, *Contra litt. Petil.* ii. 92. 209 (*CSEL.* 52. 135), cites
the case of one, Ursacius, slain in battle and devoured by birds and dogs, but he is
sure that God's promise contains consolation for him.

In polemics the flood served as a useful tool both in the struggle with Greeks and with Jews. The major cause of the flood in Genesis is the episode of the sons of God with the daughters of men. While the N.T. furnishes certain echoes of a fall of angels (II Pet. 2:4; Jude 6), the fact that it does not specifically deal with the sons of God left the four writers of the second century who allude to the episode free to follow the pattern set in the Pseudepigrapha which identifies the sons of God with angels.[1]) Codex Alexandrinus of the LXX reads ἄγγελοι in Gen. 6:2. Assuming a widespread knowledge of such a LXX reading, one has a ready explanation for the appearance of the idea in Philo (*Gig.* 6), Josephus (*Ant.* i. 3. 1), and in the church fathers.[2])

The episode, which formed a part of his anti-Greek polemic, served Justin in two ways. First, it gave an explanation for the origin of demons whom Justin believed to be the mixed offspring of the marriages (*Apol.* ii. 5).[3]) Second, it explained the widespread notion that sacrifice is demanded by God. The angels after their fall needed sacrifices and libations.[4]) The poets, being deceived, supposed it was God. According to Justin, the Father of all cannot be served in such ways (*Apol.* ii. 6). Athenagoras insists that the poets are mistaken even if what they say resembles the episodes of the Bible. In the course of the argument he insists that angels are free agents. Some fell into impure love of virgins and begot giants. The souls of the

---

[1]) I *Enoch* 6:1; *Jub.* 10:1-7; *T. Reub.* 5:6-7; cf. *T. Naph.* 3:5.

[2]) Justin M., *Apol.* ii. 5; Irenaeus, *Demonst.* 18; cf. *Adv. haer.* iv. 16. 2; iv. 36. 4; Athenagoras, *Supplic. pro Christ.* 24; Clement of A., *Paed.* iii. 2. 14 (*GCS.* 12. 244); *Strom.* iii. 7. 59 (*GCS.* 15. 223); note phrases, "angels who renounced the beauty of God for a beauty that fades," and "became incontinent, and were seized by desire so that they fell from heaven to earth." Tertullian used the episode as a support for his argument that virgins should wear veils, *Adv. Marc.* v. 8, 18 (*CSEL.* 47. 597, 642); cf. *Apol.* 22 (*CSEL.* 69. 61); *De virg. vel.* 1 (*CSEL.* 76. 89-90); *De cultu fem.* i. 2; ii. 10 (*CSEL.* 70. 60-62; 88-89); *De idol.* 9 (*CSEL.* 20. 38); *De orat.* 22 (*CSEL.* 20. 194). The angel interpretation is echoed by Cyprian, *De hab. virg.* 14 (*CSEL.* 3. 1. 197); Nemesius, *On the Nature of Man* 57 (*LCC.* 4. 420); Methodius, *De resurrectione* i. 37; iii. 19 (*GCS.* 27. 278; 417); Lactantius, *Div. inst.* ii. 14 (*CSEL.*19.162-163); Ambrose, *De virginibus* i. 8. 53 (*PL.* 16. 214 B); Sulpicius Severus, *Chron.* i. 2 (*CSEL.* 1. 4-5); Ps.-Clem. *Hom.* viii. 14 (*GCS.* 42. 127); and Petilian the Donatist; see Augustine, *c. litt. Petil.* ii. 18. 40 (*CSEL.* 52. 41-42).

[3]) The offspring are also called demons by *Jub.* 10:1-7; cf. Athenagoras, *Supplic. pro Christ.* 25; Tertullian, *Apol.* 22. 3-4 (*CSEL.* 69. 61); Lactantius, *Div. inst.* ii. 14 (*CSEL.* 19. 163).

[4]) Both of these ideas are likely taken by Justin from I *Enoch* 15: 11 and *Jub.* 10:1-7; 22:17.

giants are the demons that wander about the earth; while the angels involved haunt air and earth and are no longer able to rise to heavenly things. The demons lure men to offer sacrifices (*Supplic. pro Christ.* 24-26).[1])

Irenaeus repeats the story told in I *Enoch* 7:1 ff., making the fallen angels the teachers of wickedness to women. From the angels are learned the virtues of roots and herbs, dyeing in colors and cosmetics, discovery of rare substances, love-potions, aversions, amours, concupiscence, constraints of love, spells of bewitchment, and all sorcery and idolatry hateful to God (*Demonst.* 18).

The fundamental presupposition of the Gnostic, Heracleon, is identical with the previous three writers we have noticed; however the episode serves him for a different purpose. In the course of his allegory on the Gospel of John he interprets the phrase "He and his whole house believed" (Jno. 4:53) to imply that the angels of Gen. 6:2 would be saved.[2]) No cognizance is taken in the second century of the theological conflict between its accepted interpretation and the assertion of the N.T. that angels do not marry (cf. Mt. 22:30; Mk. 12:25; Lk. 20:35).

A further example of the tendentious nature of early Christian polemic on the flood may be seen in the treatment of Deucalion, the Greek flood hero. Here there was no O.T. or N.T. background to serve as a guide. Some apologists like Justin who had a high regard for Greek philosophy did not hesitate to follow the pattern set earlier by Philo (*Praem.* 23) and identify Noah with the Greek hero. The Jews knew him by one name and the Greeks by another, declared Justin (*Apol.* ii. 7. 2). Justin's attitude is in full harmony with his contention that pagans of the past who spoke truly enjoyed a measure of guidance by the *Logos* (*Apol.* i. 46; ii. 10, 13).

Athenagoras does not specifically mention Deucalion, but he, sharing with Justin esteem of pagan philosophy, attempts to gain a

---

[1]) The giants are the subjects of homiletical remarks on the part of several later writers. They carried on war with God; see Eusebius, *Praep. Evang.* vii. 8. 16 (*GCS*. 43. 1. 372). One of their major crimes, the eating of flesh, God had attempted to forestall by feeding them on manna; see Ps.-Clem., *Hom.* viii. 15 (*GCS*. 42. 127). They harass their neighbors and practice pillaging among men; see John Cassian, *Collatio VIII*. 21 (*CSEL*. 13. 2. 240). Augustine attempts to solve the problem by dissolving the connection between הנפלים and the marriages. There were giants before the marriages just as there have been giants since then right on down to present times; see *Civ. Dei* 15. 23 (*CSEL*. 40. 2. 111).

[2]) Cited by Origen, *Comm. in Iohann.* xiii. 60; trans. in R. M. Grant, *Second Cent. Christianity* (London: SPCK., 1946), p. 49.

hearing among the heathen by appealing to pagan poets. In the course of an argument explaining why divinity has been ascribed to men, he comments that the Sibyl says:

> It was the generation then the tenth,
> of men endow'd with speech, since forth the flood
> Had burst upon the men of former times,
> And Kronos, Japetus, and Titan reigned.
> (*Supplic. pro Christ.* 30; cf *Or. Sib.* iii. 108-125).

Athenagoras' general position would almost certainly demand that he identify the Jewish and Greek floods.

It would seem, however, that Tatian and Theophilus, though they knew of the trend, rejected the temptation. This attitude may well be a reaction to such charges as those of Celsus who said that Jewish writers falsify and recklessly alter the story of Deucalion.[1] Tatian challenged the Greek claims to leadership in the arts and letters and asserted that Moses is older than Homer. He traced out names of important Greek figures in the effort to prove his case. Two floods are mentioned. The first came in the time of Ogyges who was set forth as a contemporary of Moses. The flood of Deucalion came five names after Ianchus who was two names removed from Ogyges. This flood also preceded the fall of Troy by six names. Deucalion must have lived considerably after Moses.[2] Though Tatian does not specifically mention Noah's flood, his chronology would make it impossible for him to identify Deucalion with Noah (*Address to the Greeks* 39. 2).

The attitude of Theophilus of Antioch toward the identification of Noah and Deucalion also fits into his general denial of the claims of Greek religion and philosophy. He insists that the Greeks have not invented music, for the true inventors lived long before the flood. Theophilus claims to have dealt with Noah, whom he says some call

---

[1] Origen, *C. Celsum* i. 19; iv. 11, 42 (*GCS*. 2. 70, 281, 315). It is particularly distasteful to Origen that Celsus would call the raven a "crow" (κορώνη).

[2] Origen, *C. Celsum* iv. 11 (*GCS*. 2. 281), also attempts to prove that Moses antedates Deucalion. Hippolytus, *Elenchos* x. 30 (*GCS*. 26. 286), while admitting that there had been local inundations in Greece in the time of both Ogyges and Deucalion, asserts that neither the Egyptian, Chaldean, nor Greek historians knew of Noah's flood. This is essentially the course taken by Augustine, *Civ. Dei* 18. 8, 10 (*CSEL*. 40. 2. 277, 279). Lactantius, *Div. inst.* ii. 10 (*CSEL*. 19. 148), insisted that the Greeks have corrupted the Hebrew traditions and attempted to prove the fallacy of the Deucalion story on the basis that Prometheus was the first man. If Deucalion was his son, how could the population have increased sufficiently for the earth to need to be cleansed of wickedness?

Deucalion, with the beginning of civilization after the flood at Babylon with Nebroth (Nimrod) as king, and with the genealogies of Noah's sons in a work known as *The History* (*Ad Autol.* ii. 30-31). This work has not survived. In the course of his argument with Autolycus, he decries the Greek historians for their failure to mention events that happened before the flood (*Ad Autol.* ii. 33). He claims that the fulfilled prophecies show that the writers of the O.T. spoke by the divine spirit and that this fact should create a presumption that the biblical account of the antediluvian period is accurate. He ridicules Plato's account of a local flood in which some fled to the hills and saved themselves.[1]) He declares that other accounts speak of Deucalion and Pyrrha being preserved and repeopling the earth by flinging stones behind them.[2]) Still others say, he tells us, that Clymenus existed in a second flood. Theophilus concludes that all these stories are senseless and that Moses alone gives a true account of the universal deluge. It is to be noticed, however, that Theophilus has not escaped the Deucalion identification entirely, for a few lines further down he gives a false etymology based on Δεῦτε . . . καλεῖν:

Noah. . . prophesied to them saying, Come thither, God calls you to repentance. On this account he was fitly called Deucalion (*Ad Autol.* iii. 19).[3])

No less tendentious than the orthodox of the second century, but more far-fetched, was the polemical exegesis of the heretics. The Gnostics, in contrast to Marcion with his demand for literal interpretation, were generous users of allegory. Considerable support for their system was found in the flood narrative.

The Valentinians had a series of thirty aeons called the Triacontad by which they insisted that divinity had descended in order to have contact with the world. The thirty cubits of the height of the ark

---

[1]) Plato's account is found in *The Laws* 677A. Eusebius, *Praep. Evang.* 12. 15 (*GCS.* 43. 2. 103), paralleled Moses' account of history and the flood with that of Plato without making specific mention of Deucalion. Hippolytus, *Elenchos* x. 30 (*GCS.* 26. 286), and Augustine, *Civ. Dei* 18. 8, 10 (*CSEL.* 40. 2. 277, 280), reject the identification of the two flood stories by making the point that the Greek floods were merely local.

[2]) This episode is related by Pindar, *Olympian Odes* 9. 40-46. Deucalion is a son of Prometheus who built a chest upon the advice of his father when Zeus decided to bring a flood on the greater part of Greece. All men died except a few who escaped to the mountain tops. See J. Skinner, *A Critical and Exegetical Commentary on Genesis* (N. Y.: Scribner's, 1910), p. 179; Apollodorus, i. 7. 2 ff.; Ovid, *Met.* 1. 244-415; Plutarch, *De sollert. an.* 13.

[3]) Cf. Ps.-Clem., *Recog.* viii. 50 (*PG.* 1. 1394).

represented the entire Triacontad (Iren., *Adv. haer.* i. 18. 4). The first eight aeons of the Triacontad are called the Ogdoad. Among other eights of the O.T., they found that the eight persons saved in the ark from the deluge clearly indicated the Ogdoad which brought salvation (Iren., *Adv. haer.* i. 18. 3).

In the system of the Ophites, the same general pattern is to be seen. Peculiar to their system, however, is the idea that the name for the first descendant from the mother, the Holy Spirit, was called Ialdaboath. Ialdaboath, being incensed that men did not worship him as God, sent the flood. Sophia, however, opposed him, saved Noah and his family by means of the besprinkling of light that proceeded from her, and then refilled the earth (Iren., *Adv. haer.* i. 30. 10).[1]

The Sethians, like other Gnostics, assumed that the world was created by inferior angels rather than by the supreme God. In the myth, two angels had intercourse with Eve and produced Cain and Abel. Cain was slain as a result of strife between angels. Then the mother (the power of all powers), in order to destroy the power of these angels, caused Seth to be born of Adam. Seth had a spark of power that would enable him to resist angelic power, as well as to enable him to become the ancestor of a pure race; however, the intermarriage of the races brought corruption. The mother sent the flood to destroy the corrupt brood. Other angels frustrated her plan by seeing that some of the race she wished to destroy (Ham and seven souls) got into the ark. In this manner the seed of malice did not perish, but survived to fill the earth. The resulting confusion made the later descent of Christ necessary. Some Sethians thought that Christ was identical with Seth.[2]

No less clear in its tendentious nature is the impugning of Noah's righteousness furnished by the heretic Marcion who is primarily concerned with combatting the orthodox. In his denial that the God of the O.T. was the supreme God, Marcion inverted values of the O.T. to make those who served God into sinners. When Jesus descended into Hades he had a ready reception from Cain, the Sodomites,

---

[1] Cf. George Salmon, "Ophites," *A Dictionary of Christian Biography*, IV, 87.
[2] Ps.-Tertullian, *Against all Heresies* 8, trans. in R. M. Grant, *Second Cent. Christianity* (London: SPCK., 1946), pp. 130-131. Other later allegorists found in the Sons of God episode the doctrine taught that the nutritive powers of the soul descend from heaven to earth; see Alexander of Lycopolis, *De placitis Manichaeorum* 25 (*PG.* 18. 446); or that souls yet unborn desired the corporeal life of men; see Origen, *C. Celsum* 5. 55 (*GCS.* 3. 58); cf. the comments of Jerome, *Ep.* 51. 4 (*CSEL.* 54. 402).

and Egyptians; while Abel, Enoch, Noah, and other righteous men did not partake of salvation, supposing that their God was merely tempting them (Iren., *Adv. haer.* i. 27. 3 (*ANF*. 1. 352)). Marcion is a unique figure in his denial of Noah's salvation.

Justin found "righteous Noah" particularly useful in his anti-Jewish polemic. Unlike the rabbis who insisted that the patriarchs observed the Law before it was given at Sinai, the Christian apologists used Noah to demonstrate that Law observance was unnecessary. Justin insisted that circumcision, Sabbath keeping, and food laws do not make one righteous. Adam was created uncircumcised; other early patriarchs were uncircumcised; and Noah, uncircumcised, along with his children, went into the ark (*Dial*. 19. 4).[1]) Justin's general position is that the Law was given to the Jews as an extra burden to keep them in line. He insists that their proneness to sin made it necessary.

Equally polemical is Justin's argument against the food laws. Noah, a just man, was permitted to eat of every kind of flesh except that which had the blood that dies of itself.[2]) He emphasized the phrase "as the green herb" (Gen. 9:3). Trypho in the *Dialogue* used "as the green herb" as a proof text that as some herbs are not eaten, so some animals are not eaten. It is widely thought that Trypho is a "straw man." That the rabbis ever applied the laws of clean and unclean to

---

[1]) Cf. Iren., *Adv. haer.* iv. 16. 2; Tertullian, *Adv. Judaeos* 2 (*CSEL*. 70. 257-258); Cyprian, *Testimonies* 1. 8 (*CSEL*. 3. 1. 45).

[2]) Influenced by the Apostolic Letter, Acts 15, several of the church fathers consider the prohibition against eating blood binding; see John of Damascus, *De Fide orth*. iv. 27 (*PG*. 94. 1221A); Sulpicius Severus, *Chron*. 1. 4 (*CSEL*. 1. 5); Aphraates dates the prohibition even back to Adam; see *Hom*. 15. 4 (*TU*. 3. 3. 261). Tertullian, *De jejunio* 4 (*CSEL*. 20. 278) considers that one would be eating the soul if he ate blood. Any bishop or deacon or other sacerdotal person who ate blood should be deprived of his position, while one of the laity would be suspended from the church; see *Const. Apost*. viii. 47. 63 (Funk, p. 582).

Ps.-Clem., *Recog*. i. 30 (*PG*. 1. 1224), erroneously states that the prohibition was given in the twelfth generation after man had begun to multiply. In Augustine's day the church was divided over whether Acts 15 alluded to the prohibition of eating blood given to Noah, or whether it prohibited murder. Augustine, himself, feels that the apostles were merely legislating for the period when both Jewish and Gentile elements were in the church. Now that it is predominantly Gentile, no one feels bound to abstain from birds or hares whose necks have been broken without shedding blood. One who is afraid to eat is laughed at by the rest. Augustine's proof text is, "Not that which enters the mouth defiles, but that which comes out"; see *C. Faustum* 32. 13 (*CSEL*. 25. 772-773). A highly allegorical treatment of Gen. 9:3 is to be found in Gregory of Nyssa, *De hominis opificio* 15 (*PG*. 44. 177 A).

plants cannot be demonstrated from Jewish sources.[1]) In the argument, Justin returned that the distinction between herbs is not that one is clean and another is unclean, but rather that some are bitter or poisonous or prickly. God then commanded the Jew to abstain from unclean animals because after having eaten manna in the wilderness, they showed their lack of faith by making the golden calf (*Dial.* 20).[2])

Trypho, when crowded into a corner, admitted that the patriarchs, including Noah, will be saved without keeping the demands of the Law: Sabbath, circumcision, observing months, and the various lustrations (*Dial.* 46).

Justin further argued that the Jew had deceived himself in thinking that through being a descendant of Abraham he should have blessings, for Ezekiel had said, "If Noah, Jacob (*sic.*), and Daniel would beg either sons or daughters, the request would not be granted them" (*Dial.* 44; cf. 140. 3). The Christians are not to be despised, but really are the nation promised to Abraham, of whom Noah was the father, as well as of all men (*Dial.* 119. 4).

In reply to Trypho's question whether keepers of the Law would be saved if they live in the same manner as Jacob, Enoch, and Noah, Justin replied that some things in the Law are naturally good. These, of course, those under the Law must keep; and if they do, they will be saved by Christ in the resurrection along with the righteous men before them: Noah, Enoch, and Jacob (*Dial.* 45). In the narrow space of two sections Justin uses Noah, Jacob, and Daniel and also Noah, Enoch, and Jacob as examples of three particularly righteous men who are saved by their faith—saved by righteousness apart from the law.

---

[1]) A. H. Goldfahn, "Justin Martyr und die Agada," *Monatschrift für Geschichte und Wissenschaft des Judentums*, 22 (1873), 57-58.

[2]) An appeal to Gen. 9 becomes a standard reply in anti-Jewish polemic to be found in Clement of A., *Paed.* ii. 1. 16 (*GCS.* 12. 165); *Const. Apost.* vii. 20 (Funk, p. 404); Jerome, *Adv. Jovin.* i. 5 (*PL.* 23. 226). Augustine flatly states that it is not the uncleanness of meat that he fears, but the uncleanness of lusting, *Conf.* 10. 31. 46 (*CSEL.* 33. 261); also cited in Possidius, *Life of Augustine* 22 (*F. of Ch.* 15. 99).

It is interesting that the *Midrash to Psalms* 146. 7 admits that all animals are clean for the *bene-Noah*. The limitation was later placed to see who would accept God's will and who would not; cited in Goldfahn, *op. cit.*, p. 58.

The statement of Genesis further entered into the polemics of Christians in questions regarding asceticism. Clement of Alexandria reduces the argument of his opponent to absurdity by pointing out that if one should refrain from sexual relations in spite of the command to multiply, then he should abstain from food altogether in spite of all things being given for food, *Strom.* iii. 37 (*GCS.* 15. 212).

The marked christological tendencies observable in the second century exegesis serve both to affirm the unity of the O.T. and N.T. revelation and as a reply to the Jew. Justin insisted that it is really Christ rather than the ineffable God that is to be understood as appearing to the patriarchs. Both his philosophical doctrine of God and his Christology are reflected in his statement that it was Christ who closed the ark of Noah from without (*Dial.* 127). This same line of thought is followed by Irenaeus (*Adv. haer.* iv. 36. 4) who has the Son of God bring the deluge and by Melito who in discussing faith lists some episodes in the O.T. in which the *Logos* played a part. The *Logos* led Abraham, was bound with Isaac, sold with Joseph, and "he was Noah's pilot." [1]

For Justin, the fact that the whole earth was covered fifteen cubits implies that the story is intended for all who are obedient to God and not merely for the Jew (*Dial.* 138). Both Justin and Irenaeus found Christ to be the fulfillment of the promise made that God would enlarge Japheth and place him in the tents of Shem, for Christ preached peace to those near and those afar off (*Adv. haer.* iii. 5. 3).[2]

Christian treatment of the flood differs most markedly from the other literary groups covered in this study in its use of typology. Typology as it applied to the flood should not be considered in isolation from its application to the rest of the O.T.[3] Back of this kind of exegesis is a theory of history as prophecy and fulfillment,[4] in which the secret counsel of God, unknown in times past has now

---

[1] Melito, *Frag.* 13; trans. in R. M. Grant, *Second Century Christ.* (London: *SPCK.*, 1946), p. 77. Further examples of this tendency are to be seen in those writers who assert that it was Christ who repented that he made man; see Tertullian *Adv. Prax.* 16 (*CSEL.* 47. 257); Christ commanded Noah and family to enter the ark, opened the cataracts of heaven, and broke up the great deep to bring on the flood; see Athanasius, *Oratio III contra Arianos* 45 (*PG.* 26. 417 C-420). Christ reconciled the animals in the ark; see Ephraem Syrus, *Hymns on the Nativity*, Hymn V (*NPNF.* ser. ii. 13. 238). It would be a mistake, however, to suppose that these writers always make this shift from God to the Son as the active agent in the flood episode; see Chrysostom, *In Ep. ad Col.* c. ii, hom. v. 4 (*PG.* 62. 336); Ephraem Syrus, *Nisibene Hymns* i. 10 (*NPNF.*, ser. ii. 13. 168); Peter Chrysologus, *Sermo* 147 (*PL.* 52. 594 D).

[2] Cf. *Demonst.* 21 and Justin, *Dial.* 139. That the promise involved the displacing of the Jews in Palestine by the Gentiles is also known to the Syrian Fathers; see A. Levene, *op. cit.*, p. 85.

[3] Typology is considered by G. W. H. Lampe and K. J. Woollcombe, *Essays on Typology* (London: SCM. Press, 1957), 80 pp.

[4] R. L. P. Milburn, *Early Christian Interpretations of History* (N. Y.: Harper and Bros., 1954), p. 23; cf. E. E. Ellis, *Paul's use of the O.T.* (Grand Rapids: Eerdmans, 1957), pp. 126-135.

been made known in Christ. He who formed the world determined that all things "would center in the Son of God; God predestinating the natural man to be saved by the spiritual man" (Iren., *Adv. haer.* iii. 22. 3).[1]) This conviction is quite important in understanding how early Christians justified the christological interpretation of the O.T.

Already in the O.T. the idea is set forth that God's great acts of the past enable Israel to understand the present. Such pictures are to be seen in the idea of the return to the wilderness of Hos. 2:14 or in the combination of creation, exodus, and return from exile of Is. 51:9-11. It was the N.T., however, that was the most influential in legitimizing typology for the second century church. Paul asserted that a veil lay on the minds of the O.T. reader which was removed only if one turned to Christ (II Cor. 3:14). It was only natural that the churchman with his conviction of the unity of God's revelation should find meanings not previously seen. Paul further asserted that Adam was a type of that to come (τύπος τοῦ μέλλοντος; Rom. 5:14). The Red Sea and the wilderness experience contained types (τύποι; I Cor. 10:6) "for us." Without specifically using the word, the typological interpretation is used for the passover (I Cor. 5:7) and for the high priest on the day of atonement (Heb. 9). To trace out further these ideas would carry us farther afield than suits our purpose at this time.

Beyond the general acceptance of typology, the specific application to the flood is mediated by the assertion in I Pet. 3:21 that baptism is the like figure (ἀντίτυπος) to the flood. Little less important is the comparison between the days of Noah and those of the Son of Man where the indifference of guilty sinners at the former time is the type of those of the latter (Mt. 24:37; Lk. 17:26). A comparison is also made between the flood of water and the end of the world (II Pet. 3:6). From these beginnings, typology becomes, along with the argument from prophecy, a main line of attack on Judaism. It also serves, however, as a confirmation of the unity of the O.T. and N.T., and as a device to remove difficulties in the O.T. An unnamed elder from Asia who is quoted in Irenaeus insisted that manifest error in the life of a patriarch is not to be considered blameworthy unless the Scriptures censure him. One should, instead, seek the type hidden in the episode. To fail to take this attitude toward the patriarchs, he insisted, was to be like Ham who laughed at his father's shame and fell into wickedness. Since the Lord's coming the patriarchs' sins

---

[1]) See G. W. H. Lampe and K. J. Woollcombe, *op. cit.*, p. 29.

have been remitted. They rejoiced to see the Lord's day (Jno. 8:56; Iren., *Adv. haer.* iv. 31. 1).

Of second century writers, it is in Justin that this typological treatment of the flood is most obvious. Justin introduces his discussion of what Daniélou calls "sacramental typology" [1]) by a strange twist on Is. 54:8, 9: "In the deluge of Noah I saved thee." The mystery of mankind who are to be saved is to be found in the deluge, says Justin. Righteous Noah and the total of eight persons (Noah and his wife, their three sons and their wives) were a type of the eighth day of the week on which Christ arose from the dead. Christ has become the chief (ἀρχή) of a new race which has been regenerated by him. For them he has prepared a place of rest (ἀνάπαυσις) at Jerusalem. The water and the wood which saved Noah, along with his faith, prefigure baptism, the cross, and the faith of Christians. Since the whole earth was covered fifteen cubits, it is obvious, argues Justin, that the story is for all who are obedient and not merely for the Jew (*Dial.* 138).[2])

Less directly connected with a N.T. passage, but no less christological, is Justin's exposition of what he calls the mystery contained in the blessings and curses of Noah. The prophetic spirit did not curse the son who had been blessed by God,[3]) despite his deriding his father's nakedness, so the curse began with the son's son and was to pass through his whole race.[4]) But in reality, Noah was foretelling that the Shemites would dispossess the Canaanites and would in turn be dispossessed themselves by the Japhethites; hence, says Justin, the Jew has lost the land of Palestine.[5]) Just as in the curse Canaan was delivered into servitude, Christ came calling men to friendship, and

---

[1]) J. Daniélou, *Sacramentum Futuri* (Paris: Beauchesne et ses Fils, 1950), pp. 74-75.

[2]) The only other treatment of the verse from Isaiah revealed in the course of this study of Christian literature is Aphraates, *Demon.* 21. 6 (*NPNF.* ser. ii. 13. 395), who interprets the passage literally.

[3]) Justin borrows this idea from the Haggadah; see *Gen. R.* 36. 7. It is also known to Ephraem Syrus, *Comm. in Gen.* 7:3 (*CSCO.* 72. 51-52); See D. Gerson, *Die Commentarien des Ephraem Syrus im Verhältniss zur jüdischen Exegese* (Breslau: Schlechter'schen Buchhandlung, 1868), p. 27.

[4]) It is the general view that the curse was not limited to the individuals involved but rather concerned their descendants, though there is not the slightest indication in Scripture that this is true. See *Wisd.* 12:11; Ps.-Clem., *Recog.* i. 30 (*PG.* i. 1224); Vincent of Lerins, *Commonitorium* 7 (*PL.* 50. 647).

[5]) Justin quotes Gen. 9:24-27 from the LXX; see H. B. Swete, *Intro. to the O.T. in Greek* (Cambridge: University Press, 1902), p. 418. He understands Japheth to be the subject of the ambiguous phrase of Gen. 9:27 as does *T. Ps.-Jon.* [T]ub. 7:12 and *T. Onkelos* take the subject to be God.

those who acknowledge him shall dwell together in that land in eternal and incorruptible inheritance (*Dial.* 139). Justin enlarges on the idea by declaring Jacob a type. His two wives and sons indicated beforehand that Christ would receive all men. Of Japheth's race, the descendants of Canaan equally with the free descendants would be fellow heirs. Trypho, says Justin, does not understand this action because he drinks at the broken fountain of tradition (*Dial.* 140). Justin had earlier argued that whereas Noah gives two sons the third son as a servant, Christ comes to restore both the free sons and the servants among them, conferring the same honor on all of them who keep his commandments (*Dial.* 134).

The flood as a type of the times of the end, we have already seen arising in Is. 24:1, 4-5. This motif furnishes two separate pictures for eschatology. The first is that of the end as a time of wickedness which is developed in the gospels (Mt. 24:37; Lk. 17:26). The second is that of the destruction which develops into the idea of the flood of fire (II Pet. 3:6).

The first of these ideas is expounded by Irenaeus. The beast of Revelation is the recapitulation of all the wickedness which took place prior to the deluge[1]) due to the apostasy of the angels as well as to the error of devising idols since the flood. The beast's number is 666 which is quite appropriate since Noah was six hundred years old when the deluge came. His age, when taken with the sixty cubits of Nebuchadnezzar's image plus the six cubits of its breadth, gives the total of 666. In him, then, is summed up the apostasy of six thousand years of unrighteousness (Iren., *Adv. haer.* v. 29. 2).

Irenaeus also develops the second idea as he compares the destructions of the flood and of Sodom with that to come. Here are reflected the ideas we have earlier seen in the O.T. of a punishment on sin and of a remnant saved by grace (Iren., *Adv. haer.* iv. 36. 3-4). The concept is further taken up by Pseudo-Melito who, in setting forth an idea quite similar to that seen in Josephus (*Ant.* i. 2. 3), speaks of three deluges the world is to suffer. Those of wind and water are already passed, while that of fire is still to come (Ps.-Melito, *Apology*).[2]) This type is likely in the back of the mind of Gaius of Rome when he

---

[1]) For Irenaeus' doctrine of recapitulation, see J. Lawson, *The Biblical Theology of St. Irenaeus* (London: Epworth Press, 1948), pp. 140-198.

[2]) Text in W. Cureton, *Spicilegium Syriacum*, p. 50, l. 33 ff.; cf. George Salmon, "Melito," *A Dictionary of Christian Biography*, William Smith and Henry Wace, editors, III, 895.

argued that just as the heavenly bodies were not taken away in the flood, so it would be at the end of the world.[1]) In view of the fact that the flood is so important to Justin, we are not surprised when he also takes up this type. The fire of judgment will dissolve all things just as the waters of the flood formerly left no one but Noah and his family (*Apol.* ii. 7. 2). This catastrophe is delayed in the present age on account of the race of Christians as Noah's flood was delayed during Noah's preaching. Thus the themes of delay and of the long-suffering of God are continued in Christian typology.

Three writers without giving up tendentious elements begin to move in the direction of a systematic treatment of portions of the flood episode. The first of these is a heretic, Apelles, about A.D. 130. Apelles, a disciple of Marcion, maintains his master's contempt toward the O.T. He sets out to prove that the writings of Moses contain no divine wisdom and were not a work of the Holy Spirit. Eusebius accuses him of committing "countless impieties against the law of Moses, blaspheming the divine word in a multitude of books" (*H.E.* v. 13. 9). Apelles, true to his system, magnifies the difficulties in the biblical account of the flood:

> In no way could it have been accomplished that in so short a time so many kinds of animals and their foods, which were to last for a whole year, should be taken aboard. For when two by two the impure animals, i.e., two males and two females of each—that is what the repeated word means—and seven by seven the pure animals, that is seven pairs, are described as led into the ark, how, he says could that space which is described be made big enough to take even four elephants alone? And afterwards he contradicts single points, and on everything adds these words: it is clear that the story is false; but if it be so, it is clear that this Scripture is not from God (Origen, *Hom. in Gen.* ii. 2). [2])

Despite the views of Apelles, his comments are important both for their lack of allegory and for their raising questions which really are fundamental. How were the animals fed and how could the ark hold

---

[1]) *Dial. with Proclus*; trans. in R. M. Grant, *Second Cent. Christ.* (London: SPCK., 1946), pp. 105-106.

[2]) Translation in R. M. Grant, *op. cit.*, p. 84. Similar skepticism over the ability of the ark to hold the animals was expressed by Celsus; see Origen, *C. Celsum* iv. 41 (*GCS.* 2. 314-315). Origen replied by pointing out that the unbelievers had considered only one floor of the ark, and by suggesting that since Moses was trained in Egypt, the cubit he had in mind could stand for six or even 300 ordinary ones (*Hom. in Gen.* ii. 2 (*GCS.* 29. 29-30)); but elsewhere he gives the traditional measurements without indicating that they were unusual. Cf. Augustine, *Civ. Dei* 15. 27 (*CSEL.* 40. 2. 120).

them all? Also the question of how many animals there really were is a vital question and has perplexed Bible students in all ages.

The earliest of the orthodox to show any real concern about expounding the flood as a historical event, though not even he is free from allegorical or hortatory purposes, is Theophilus of Antioch. Theophilus insists that Moses gives the true account of a universal deluge.

Neither does he make out that there was a second flood; on the contrary, he said that never again would there be a flood of water on the world; as neither has there been, nor shall ever be. And he says that eight human beings were preserved in the ark, in that which had been prepared by God's direction, not by Deucalion, but by Noah; which Hebrew word means in English "rest" [ἀνάπαυσις],[1]) as we have elsewhere shown that Noah, when he announced to men then alive that there was a flood coming, prophesied to them, saying, Come thither, God calls you to repentance. On this account he was fitly called Deucalion. And this Noah had three sons (as we mentioned in the second book), whose names were Shem, and Ham, and Japheth; and these had three wives, one wife each; each man his wife. This man some have surnamed Eunuchus. All the eight persons, therefore, who were found in the ark were preserved. And Moses showed that the flood lasted forty days and forty nights, torrents pouring from heaven, and from the fountains of the deep breaking up, so that the water overtopped every high hill 15 cubits. And thus the race of all men that then were was destroyed, and those only who were protected in the ark were saved; and these, we have already said, were eight. And of the ark, the remains are to this day to be seen in the Arabian mountains. This, then, is the sum of the history of the deluge (Theophilus, *Ad Autol.* ii. 19 (*ANF.* II. 116-117)).

It is to be noticed that Theophilus stresses the universality of the flood,[2]) and the fact that it will not be repeated. He seems to have some knowledge of the rabbinic legend that Noah was a eunuch (*T.B. Sanh.* 70a), as can be seen from his suggestion that Noah is surnamed Eunuchus. Theophilus takes up the legend, earlier reflected

---

[1]) The idea that Noah means "rest" is a very important idea in Christian treatments of the flood. Ephraem Syrus remarks, "Noah was refreshed in rest that his dwelling place should give rest according to his name" (*Nisibene Hymns* i. 10). Again he says, "In the stead of the Lord afar off, the type at hand afforded quiet" (*Hymns on the Nativity* I (*NPNF.* ser. ii. 13. 225)). Aphraates remarks: "Then the blessing was guarded in the man of 'rest,' in Noah" (*Hom.* 23 (*TU.* III. 3. 381)); cf. S. Funk, *Die haggadischen Elemente in den homilien des Aphraates* (Wien: Selbstverlag des Verfassers, 1891), p. 25.

[2]) Other sources with phrases stressing the universal nature of the flood are III *Macc.* 2:3-4; II *Enoch* 34:3; IV *Macc.* 15:31-32; Augustine, *Civ. Dei* 18. 8, 10, 22 (*CSEL.* 40. 2. 277, 280, 296).

in Josephus (*Ant.* i. 3. 6) and quite common in later literature, that the remains of the ark had survived until his time.[1]) It would, however, be hard to harmonize their being in Armenia, as Josephus thought (*Ant.* i. 3. 6), with the Arabian mountains of Theophilus.

The nearest complete survey of the flood comparatively free from excessive hortatory or allegorical tendencies, though not from christological ones, to be found in the second century is that given in Irenaeus' *Demonstration of the Apostolic Preaching.*[2]) Following a survey of the early chapters of Genesis made for the purpose of explaining the grounds of his faith to his friend Marcianus, Irenaeus comes to the union of the daughters of men with angels. These angels taught women the virtues of roots, herbs, dyeing in colors, cosmetics, and lovepotions; concupiscence, sorcery, idolatry, and other evils flourished[3]). Thus righteousness grew more feeble, while wickedness spread (par. 18). In the tenth generation from Adam,[4]) Noah alone was righteous. He and his sons and the wives of the four were alone preserved in the ark. From Shem, Ham, and Japheth came the beginning of the race of mankind after the flood (par. 19). Ham the youngest son (as the LXX, Gen. 9:24),[5]) being guilty of impiety, received a curse which involved the whole race.[6]) Shem and Japheth for their piety received a

---

[1]) Hippolytus, *Elenchos* x. 30 (*GCS.* 26. 286); *Arabic Frag. to Pent.* 4 (*GCS.* 1. 2. 91), believes certain relics are on the ridges of the mountains which no one has been able to reach because of a demon who throws down the one who tries to ascend it. There are also violent winds and storms.

The efforts to find relics of the ark in recent years would fill a book in itself. Some of these are summarized by A. Parrot, *The Flood and Noah's Ark* (London: SCM. Press, 1955), pp. 63-67. The most recent effort is to be seen in "Noah's Ark?" *Life*, 49 (Sept. 5, 1960), 112-114.

[2]) J. Armitage Robinson, trans., *St. Irenaeus. The Demonstration of the Apostolic Preaching* (London: SPCK., 1920), pp. 85-90.

[3]) Cf. I *Enoch* 7:1 ff.

[4]) Allusions to the ten generations are made by Philo, *QG.* i. 87; Athenagoras, *Supplic. pro Christ.* 30; Irenaeus, *Demonst.* 19; *Gen. R.* 34. 5; *M. Aboth* 5. 2; *Eccl. R.* 7.19. §2; *Num. R.* 14. 12. Basil for some reason counts only seven generations from Cain to the deluge, *Ep.* 260. 5 (*PG.* 32. 974A); the four generations from Adam to Noah in Victorinus, *De fabrica mundi* 3 (*CSEL.* 49. 4), are arrived at on dogmatic grounds.

[5]) Ham as the youngest son is known to Josephus, *Ant.* i. 4. 1; cf. i. 6. 3; *Jub.* 7:10; Justin M., *Dial.* 139; Ramban, *EBI.* II, 71. He is considered the middle son by Origen, *Selecta in Gen.* 61 (*PG.* 12. 108); Cyprian, *Ep.* 63. 3 (*CSEL.* 3. 2. 702); cf. Augustine, *Civ. Dei* 16. 1 (*CSEL.* 40. 2. 123); and Ephraem Syrus, *Comm. in Gen.* 7:3 (*CSCO.* 72. 51).

[6]) Cf. Lactantius, *Div. inst.* ii. 13 (*CSEL.* 19. 161). This may be the view of Ambrose, *Ep.* 58. 12 (*PL.* 16. 1231), who says, "The one who mocked him remained exposed to the shame of everlasting disgrace." Cf. the views of some of the rabbis who say that Noah really meant to curse Ham; *Num. R.* 10.

blessing. Irenaeus read Gen. 9:24 "Cursed be Ham the child, a servant shall he be unto his brethren." He read v. 29: "Blessed be the Lord, the God of Shem; and Ham shall be his servant" (MT. reads "Canaan," but one ms. of the LXX has *Cham*). The blessing meant, according to Irenaeus, that God would be the particular object of worship of Shem; and it is carried out in Abraham who is the tenth generation of the race of Shem.[1]) Irenaeus also read the blessing on Japheth with "Ham" rather than "Canaan" as the servant. This blessing is fulfilled in the call of the Gentiles into the church, declares Irenaeus. To dwell in the tents of Shem means to receive the inheritance of the fathers (*Demonst.* 21; cf. Justin M., *Dial.* 139).

Following the flood, God made a covenant with all the world to destroy the earth no more. This Irenaeus proves by quoting Gen. 9:14 f.[2])

Man had previously been vegetarian, but now since he was blessed for multiplication and increase,[3]) he could eat flesh.[4]) Gen. 9:1 ff. is quoted in proof. Murder was prohibited, for man is in God's image, and the image of God is the Son who has now been manifest that he might make this fact known (cf. Iren., *Adv. haer.* v. 14. 1).[5]) It was by

---

2. Some make an effort to say that the curse on the son was a punishment of the father; see Augustine, *Civ. Dei* 16. 1, 2 (*CSEL.* 40. 2. 123-125); Gregory the Great, *Ep.* 45 (*PL.* 77. 1157 C).

[1]) Cf. *Adv. haer.* iii. 5. 3. The same interpretation is to be seen in the Syrian Fathers; see A. Levene, *op. cit.*, p. 85.

[2]) Cf. *PRE.* 23; *Gen. R.* 34. 6; *Lam. R.* 5. 21. § 1; *T. B. Sanh.* 99a where Is. 54:9 is cited as a proof text; cf. also *Jub.* 6:1-5 and Ps.-Philo, *Bib. Ant.* iii. 9 for other allusions to the covenant. Man's sins in each generation would bring a flood were it not for God's promise; see Ps.-Clem., *Recog.* viii. 50 (*PG.* 1. 1934-1935). God had "made known His grace that He would not again overwhelm all flesh by the waters of the flood," commented the Syrian Fathers; see A. Levene, *op. cit.*, p. 84.

Further allusions made to the covenant in passing are found in Iren., *Adv. haer.* iii.11. 8; Cyril of Jer., *Catech.* iii. 5 (*PG.* 33. 433 A); Ephraem Syrus, *Nisibene Hymns* i. 1. 2 (*NPNF.* ser. ii. 13. 167); and *Acts of Andrew and Matthias* 20 (*ANF.* 8. 521).

[3]) It is obvious that the Scripture statement must needs enter the controversies on asceticism in the later church. Jovinianus, as cited by Jerome, *Adv. Jovin.* i. 5 (*PL.* 23. 226), insisted that a blessing had been placed on procreation. The same type of argument is made by Augustine's opponent; see *De nuptis* ii. 9. 21 (*CSEL.* 42. 273). In a different controversy, Jerome insisted that Origen, by his doctrine that human spirits were previously angels, made the blessing a curse since procreation made angels leave celestial realms; see *Ep.* 51. 4 (*CSEL.* 54. 402).

[4]) For the controversy over whether the antediluvians were vegetarians, see the chapter on rabbinic interpretations.

[5]) In no place in the O.T. or N.T. is an appeal directly made to the command

this covenant that men multiplied, springing up from the three (*Demonst.* 22).[1])

This survey has revealed that there was very little concern in the second century to give either systematic or scientific exegesis of the flood narrative. The general tendency is to see in it that which the writer has accepted on other bases. This is true both of the orthodox and the heretic. All the presuppositions are not traceable, but the allusions to the flood made in the N.T. are quite determinative for most writers. The christological meaning of the O.T. is always presupposed. Some motifs which occur more than once may have been fairly standardized. Among these are the role assigned to "righteous Noah"; the preaching of Noah; Noah as a type of Christ; the flood as a type of baptism; the flood as a type of the times of the end; and finally, Noah's blessing as a promise of the preaching of the Gospel to the Gentiles.

---

given to Noah as a basis for the prohibition of murder; see Ex. 20:13; Rev. 21:8. Nevertheless, the idea is not altogether unknown to the church fathers; see Tertullian, *De res. carnis* 28 (*CSEL.* 47. 65); *De jejunio* 4 (*CSEL.* 20. 278); Sulpicius Severus, *Chron.* 1. 4 (*CSEL.* 1. 5); Aphraates, *Hom.* 3. 3 (*TU.* 3. 3. 44); *Const. Apost.* ii. 42. 6 (Funk, p. 135); Chrysostom, *In Matt. Hom.* 74. 2 (*PG.* 58. 682); Hilary, *De Trin.* iv. 19 (*PL.* 10. 111-112).

[1]) It is to be noticed that Irenaeus makes no allusion to Noah's post flood sacrifice. Passing allusions to this act and its acceptance, without further interpretation, are to be found in: *Const. Apost.* vii. 37. 2 (Funk, p. 436); Gregory of Nazianzus, *Ep.* 153 (*PG.* 37. 260 B); John of Damascus, *De fide orth.* iv. 16 (*PG.* 94. 1169 B); Augustine, *Civ. Dei* 15. 16 (*CSEL.* 40. 2. 95); Aphraates, *Hom.* 18. 2 (*TU.* iii. 3. 291).

CHAPTER SIX

THE RABBINIC NOAH

The Mishna, Tosefta, and other early sources contain only scanty, passing references to the flood. Were we dependent on them alone, this section of our study would be impossible. The lion's share of material dealing with the flood in rabbinic sources in the period we are concerned with is to be found in the Babylonian Talmud, *Sanhedrin*, and in the Midrash, *Genesis Rabbah. Genesis Rabbah* is an expository commentary of a homiletic nature, following the text of Genesis verse by verse. While the final compilation may not have taken place until the fifth century A.D., some early material is contained in it. [1] In this study this Midrash is cited according to the divisions of the Soncino edition..

Rather than a single homogeneous picture of the flood, the rabbinic sources give us an account of continuous differing opinion. It is necessary to record these divergent views without attempting to harmonize them. There are many repetitions of the same sayings in different contexts. The saying is at times ascribed to different authorities and is often repeated in later generations. Since the date at which a view was held may be of some importance, we have attempted to follow Moore's system of indicating the provenience and date of various materials. [2] In many cases since names are similar and since views are often not identified with individuals, dates cannot be determined.

The rabbis believed that certain passages of Scripture outside the book of Genesis spoke of Noah and the flood. Ps. 1 spoke of Noah and his righteousness, of the wickedness of the generation of the flood, and of the three sons: Shem, Ham, and Japheth. [3] The three friends of Job, according to R. Johanan (PA. 2) and Rabbi (T. 5), in the descriptions recorded in Job 21, 24, and 36, expounded

---

[1] G. F. Moore, *Judaism* (Cambridge: Harvard U. Press, 1946), I, 163-166.

[2] *Ibid.*, II, 481-486; T = Tanna; BA = Babylonian Amora; PA = Palestinian Amora. The figures indicate the generation or the date.

[3] *Gen. R.* 26. 1. *Midrash Tehillim* 1. 12 (*EBI.* II, 4-5). Certain church fathers applied this Psalm to Christ; see R. Loewe, "The Jewish Midrashim and Patristic Exegesis of the Bible," *Studia Patristica*, K. Aland and F. L. Cross, eds. (Berlin: Akademie Verlag, 1957), p. 500.

the sins of the generation of the flood. [1]) Likewise, certain passages from Ecclesiastes 1:11-15; 9:14-15 and from Proverbs 10:25; 11:30, 31 were found applicable. [2])

The hermeneutic principles expounded by Hillel, Akiba, and Ishmael were frequently used in expounding the flood material. Most frequently applied was the *gezera shavah* which is an analogy based on a word. When a word occurs in two separate contexts, that which is said in one may be applied to the other. [3]) Etymologies may explain a word. The rabbis assume that there is no chronological order in Torah. [4]) There is no redundancy without some hidden meaning being indicated. [5]) The idea of punishment, measure for measure, is prominent as can be seen when hot water comes to punish men for heated lust or when God is unmerciful because men have been unmerciful.

The rabbis at times use allegory. Certain details in the construction and dedication of the tabernacle were interpreted to symbolize details of past history. The golden pan of ten shekels in the dedicatory offerings, Num. 7:56, symbolized the ten generations from Adam to Noah, both of whom were righteous and kept the commandments. The one silver basin (מזרק אחד כסף, Num. 7), said R. Shemayah (T.), equals by gematria 520, which refers to the 500 years of Noah's life, Gen. 5:32. The extra twenty years reflect that the warning of the flood had been given twenty years before Noah begat his children. The silver in the vessel alludes to the commandments Noah gave. [6])

For the rabbis, the tetragrammaton when it occurs, designates the attribute of mercy of God. The alternation of the divine name in the flood narrative gave grounds for some homiletical remarks. In Gen. 6:7 "The Lord" says He will blot out man. These wicked men had turned the attribute of mercy into judgment, but it is "Elohim," the attribute of judgment, which remembers Noah when he is in the ark, Gen. 8:1. Judgment had been turned into mercy by Noah's feeding the animals. [7])

---

[1]) *Gen. R.* 26. 7; *Num. R.* 21. 23; 9. 24; *Lev. R.* 7. 6; *T. B. Sanh.* 108a.
[2]) *Eccl. R.* 9. 14-15. § 1; 1. 11. § 1; 1. 13. § 1; *Gen. R.* 30. 1, 6.
[3]) M. Mielziner, *Intro. to the Talmud* (Cincinnati: Bloch Pub. Co., 1894), pp. 142-152.
[4]) *Num. R.* 9. 18.
[5]) M. Mielziner, *op. cit.*, pp. 123-128.
[6]) *Num. R.* 14. 12.
[7]) *Gen. R.* 33. 3; cf. the discussion of this topic in the section on Philo, *supra*, pp. 50-51.

Ten generations [1]) covering a period of 1656 years [2]) passed between the creation and the time of Noah. These were all evil and
continuously provoked the Lord sorely, but because He is long-
suffering, the flood was delayed.[3]) The coming of the flood was
predicted as early as the time of Lamech, Gen. 4:23 ff., by his wives. [4])
The righteousness of ones like Methuselah delayed its arrival. [5])

Noah, son of Lamech, was among those few characters who were
born circumcised. [6])

The rabbis were well aware of the problem of the name of Noah
and offered numerous interpretations. R. Johanan (PA. 2) commented
that the name does not correspond to the explanation nor the explanation to the name and suggested that the text needs יניחנו
("He will give us rest") or that Noah should be called נחמן. Another
suggests that Noah brought ease, in that from this time on the cow
and the furrow, unlike they had done since the time of Adam, obeyed
the plowman. [7]) Resh Laḳish (PA. 2) proposed that from the time
of Adam a flooding of graves twice a day had taken place, but now these
had rest.[8]) R. Eleazar (PA. 2) connects the name with the ריח הניחה
of Noah's postdiluvial offering. [9]) R. Jose b. R. Ḥanina (PA. 2)
connects the name with the resting of the ark, Gen. 8:4.[10]) R. Johanan
(PA. 2), supported by R. Joshua, though disputed by R. Jonathan
(PA. 1) and R. Eliezer (PA. 3), further suggests that there is a connection with the failure of the planets to function during the flood.
The exact connection is not enlarged upon.[11]) Even from Noah's
name, there was an indication that good was to come into the world.[12])

---

[1]) *Gen. R.* 34. 5; *M. Aboth* 5. 2; cf. *Eccl. R.* 7. 19. § 2; *Num. R.* 14. 12.

[2]) *Seder Olam*, ch. 1 (*EBI.* I, 177, § 49).

[3]) ארך אפים: *M. Aboth* 5. 2; cf. *Num. R.* 5. 3; 14. 6; *Gen. R.* 26. 5.

[4]) *Gen. R.* 23. 4.

[5]) *ARN.* 32.

[6]) *ARN.* 2; cf. *Gen. R.* 26. 3; *Deut. R.* 11. 10. Others born circumcised are
Shem, Seth, Moses, Jacob, Joseph, Balaam, Samuel, David, Jeremiah, and
Zerubbabel. Contrast the argument of Justin, *supra*, p. 110.

[7]) *Gen. R.* 25. 2; an analogy on the root נוח here and Ex. 23:12.

[8]) *Gen. R.* 25. 2; an analogy on the root נוח here and Is. 57:2.

[9]) *Gen. R.* 25. 2; 33. 3; this etymology was known to Ephraem Syrus; see L.
Ginzberg, *Die Haggada bei den Kirchenvätern* (Berlin: S. Calvary and Co., 1900),
pp. 73-74.

[10]) *Gen. R.* 25. 2; 33. 3.

[11]) *Gen. R.* 25. 2; 33. 3; 34. 11; this was perhaps known to Jerome, *Heb. Quaest.
in Gen.* 314 (*PL.* 23. 996); also cited in L. Ginzberg, *Die Haggada bei den Kirchenvätern* (Berlin: S. Calvary and Co., 1900), p. 74.

[12]) *Tos. Sotah* 10 (*EBI.* I, 179, § 54). Rashi makes an effort to connect the name

Noah begat his first child at a much more advanced age than his predecessors. R. Shemayah (T.) said he had neglected the command to be fruitful and multiply because he had observed the wickedness of the generation about him and did not wish to produce children. [1] According to this view, he did not marry nor were children born until 20 years after the initial warning of the coming flood had been given. [2] A divergent view is given by R. Judan (PA. 4) who contended that God had rendered Noah sterile during his early years lest he should have to build many arks if his children were righteous, or suffer great grief should they prove wicked. [3]

The rabbis are not greatly concerned with Noah's wife. In *Sefer ha-Yashar* her name is Naamah, daughter of Enoch, [4] but R. Abba b. Kahana (PA. 3) says that Naamah, sister of Tubal-Cain, Gen. 4:22, was Noah's wife. He derives her name from her pleasing (נעימים) deeds, [5] but the rabbis refused this identification. The same favorable view of her character is seen in the *Midrash Hagadol* where the phrase from Prov. 31, "woman of valor," is applied to her. [6] This is ob-

---

with the invention of wine by Noah and its comfort to the worker, *EBI.* I, 178-179.

[1] *Num. R.* 14. 12; cf. Ps.-Philo, *Bib. Ant.* i. 22, where Noah is said to be 300 yrs. old.

[2] *Num. R.* 14. 12; *Tanhuma Yashan B'reshith* 39 (*EBI.* I, 181, § 63); cf. *Sefer Hayashar Noah* (*EBI.* II, 17, § 54); *Bk. of Adam and Eve* iii. 1; Ephraem Syrus, *Comm. in Gen.* 6:1 (*CSCO.* 72. 43); see L. Ginzberg, *op. cit.*, pp. 74-75; it is this tradition that Aphraates is following when he insists that it was not a question of sterility. Noah did not marry until the command to build the ark came, *Hom.* 13. 4 (*TU.* III. 3. 200); cf. S. Funk, *Die haggadischen Elemente in den Homilien des Aphraates* (Wien: Selbstverlag des Verfassers, 1891), p. 26.
That the first warning came in the 480th year is a widespread view (*Seder Olam* 28; RaSaG and Rashi; see *EBI.* I, 185-186) which was known to the early Syrian Fathers who comment: "God determined to do these things in the 480th year of Noah. But the Scripture mentions this afterwards, so that the scheme and order of the generations should not have been broken up had this been mentioned in its place"; see A. Levene, *op. cit.*, p. 81. Julius Africanus assumes that the 120 years refers to those who were 20 years old when the warning came (*Chron.* 4 (*PG.* 10. 68)). Augustine proposes that Scripture uses the round number 500 when in reality it was the 480th year (*Civ. Dei* 14. 24 (*CSEL.* 40. 2. 115)). Aphraates, on the contrary, assumes that God shortened the promised time twenty years when the flood generation had demonstrated their contempt for God (*Hom.* ii. 8 (*TU.* III. 3. 26)).

[3] *Gen. R.* 26. 2; cf. Rashi (*EBI.* I, 180).

[4] *EBI.* II, 18.

[5] *Gen. R.* 23. 3.

[6] *EBI.* II, 19, § 5. The phrase from IV *Ezra* 3. 11, "all the righteous, his

viously the view of the Midrash where the reason for Abraham's figure of ten in pleading for Sodom is due to the fact that eight could not deliver the prediluvian peoples. [1])

R. Levi (PA. 3), though some authorities say it was R. Jonathan (T.), thought that the phrase "and it came to pass" in the story indicates the approach of trouble. [2])

Gen. 6:1, החל is expounded by R. Simon (T. 4) "when man rebelled," even as he rendered other occurrences of this same root in Gen. 4:26; 10:8; 11:6. [3])

The בני־האלהים were understood by some rabbis to be "sons of judges." [4]) This view is perhaps first encountered in the argument of Trypho who rejects the idea of a fall of angels. [5]) R. Simeon b. Yoḥai (T. 4), cursing all who called them "sons of God," explains that real demoralization begins with leaders. R. Ḥanina (PA. 3rd cent.) and Resh Laḳish (PA. 2) explain that they are called "sons of God" because they lived long without trouble. [6])

R. Huna (PA. 3, 4) in R. Jose's (BA. 3) name said they lived long so that men could understand astronomical calculation. [7]) The rabbis said that it was in order that they might receive the punishment of two generations, theirs and that of the preceding one. [8]) An entirely divergent view makes the בני־האלהים sons of Cain who were strikingly tall and beautiful. [9])

---

descendants," may also reflect a favorable view; cf. also Ps.-Clem., *Recog.* iv. 12 (*PG.* 1. 1320) which describes Noah as "righteous with his house."

[1]) *Midrash Hagadol*, Noah (*EBI.* II, 20, § 7); but in Ramban the family is only saved for Noah's merit (*EBI.* II, 33).

[2]) *T. B. Megilla* 10b.

[3]) *Gen. R.* 26. 4; 23. 6.

[4]) This view is probably suggested by certain passages where judges are called "gods" or placed in close juxtaposition with God, such as: "You shall bring him before God unto the judges," Ex. 4:16; 7:1; 21:6; 22:8, 9; I S. 2:25; Ps. 82:1. This general interpretation can be traced through the commentators of the Middle Ages, such as Rashi; see *EBI.* I, 182-183.

[5]) Justin M., *Dial.* 79. In contrast, the angel interpretation is not entirely absent from rabbinic literature. *Midrash Aggadah, B'reshith*, says that the angels Uzza and Uziel came to earth to demonstrate that they would not sin as man had sinned. After their fall, they desired to return to heaven, but God refused them (*EBI.* I, 183, § 10; cf. *PRE.* 22). The same idea, minus the names, is recited by Christian writers: Lactantius, *Div. inst.* ii. 14 (*CSEL.* 19. 162-163); and Ps.-Clem., *Hom.* viii. 12-13 (*GCS.* 42. 126).

[6]) *Gen. R.* 26. 5; cf. *Midrash Siphre to Numbers* 11: 3 (86).

[7]) Cf. Josephus, *Ant.* i. 3. 9, where antediluvians are said to be interested in astronomy.

[8]) *Gen. R.* 26. 5.

[9]) Intro. to *Aggadath B'reshith* (*EBI.* I, 183, § 7). This line of thought is followed

נפלים is an alternate name for עֲנָקִים, זַמְזֻמִּים, גְּבֹרִים, רְפָאִים, אֵמִים, and עַוִּים. These terms are usually taken in the English versions to refer to aboriginal inhabitants of Palestine, but the Midrash explains them in terms of the destruction they wrought. They are גְּבֹרִים because of their size; זַמְזֻמִּים because of their mastery of war; עֲנָקִים because they were loaded with chains; אֵמִים because they brought dread to all who saw them; רְפָאִים because all melted like wax who saw them; and עַוִּים because they cast the world into ruin. נפלים implies that they hurled the world down, fell down themselves from the world, and filled the world with abortions through their immorality. All of these pun upon נפל "to fall" or "to fall upon." [1]

The men of renown (אנשי–השם) were really ignoble, said R. Aḥa (PA. 4), but were designated אנשי–השם because they desolated (השימו) the world. R. Samuel b. Naḥman (PA. 3) said it referred to those men mentioned in the preceding chapter of Genesis. [2]

The time prior to the flood was a time of prosperity and ease. One had to sow grain only each forty years. He was unafraid of animals and had spring weather all year long. [3] Women bore children after a pregnancy of three days, according to R. Levi (T. 4), though the rabbis said it was only one day, and children could walk and talk immediately. [4] The phrases of ease and prosperity used by Job's friends for the wicked man, Job 21:9-14, 23; 36:11; etc., describe them. [5] But the great boons of God were only met with by a practical

---

by the later commentator ShaDaL: "The iniquitous male descendants of Cain (called *b'nei 'elohim* because they were giants) saw righteous women of the stock of Seth; or the uncouth barbarians saw the refined daughters of civilized man" (*EBI.* I, 183). For a more recent exposition of this view, see J. W. Dawson, "Sons of God and Daughters of Men," *The Expositor*, ser. V, 4 (1896), 201-211.

The first identification of the בני–האלהים with Sethites in Jewish sources is made by Ibn Ezra; see L. Ginzberg, *Die Haggada bei den Kirchenvätern* (Berlin: S. Calvary and Co., 1900), p. 76, though it is entirely possible that *Pirke de R. Eliezer* 22 knew of it when it speaks of the angels seeing the daughters of Cain walking about naked with painted eyes and of their marrying them. This Midrash quotes a saying from R. Simeon that Seth was the ancestor of all the righteous and that Cain was the ancestor of all the wicked. In recent discussion, J. H. Hertz explains that "Sons of God" means those who serve and obey Him (Ex. 4: 22; Deut. 14:1; 32:5; Is. 1:2; Hos. 2:1). The episode in Genesis is the first warning against intermarriage with idolaters (*The Pentateuch and Haftorahs* (N.Y.: Metzudah Pub. Co., 1941), I, 19).

[1] *Gen. R.* 26. 7; cf. Rashi (*EBI.* I, 186).

[2] *Gen. R.* 26. 7.

[3] *Gen. R.* 34. 11. The Christian Ps.-Clem., *Hom.* viii. 15 (*GCS.* 42. 128) further develops their life of ease by having them eat manna.

[4] *Lev. R.* 5. 1; *PRE.* 22.

[5] *T. B. Sanh.* 108a; *Mekilta, Shirata* 2. 15 f.

skepticism on the part of the people who insisted that they had all they needed. Their wells and rivers supplied the water they used, so that they were not even dependent on God for rain.[1]) They said, "What is the Almighty that we should serve Him?" [2]) and "Depart from us." [3]) This skepticism extended to their insistence that they would be able to escape from a flood of fire by a substance, אליתא or from one of water by iron plates with which to cover the earth if it came up from below, or to escape water from heaven by עקב. Skepticism made them unreceptive to Noah's preaching. [4]) As their prosperity increased they did not offer a single sacrifice or honor God. [5]) R. Ḥanina (c. 225), interpreting the phrase "the wickedness of man was great," said that their wickedness waxed ever greater and greater. [6])

The bill of particulars of the sins of the generation included covetousness of the eye-ball, according to R. Jose (c. 150), son of the Damascene. [7]) Another authority notes that they turned their eyes from the lofty to the low. [8]) But special stress is put on licentiousness [9]) and whoredom, the latter of which R. Samlai (A. 2) insisted always brought punishment on men regardless of guilt.[10]) Under this category may be included a number of sexual perversions: spilling their seed on trees and stones;[11]) the *jus primae noctis*; intercourse with married women, males, and beasts;[12]) incest;[13]) and sexual enjoyment without intention to procreate.[14]) Women were seized from their husbands.[15]) R. ʿAzariah (c. 380) in R. Judah's (T. 4) name, tells of their taking two wives, one of whom they rendered sterile for purposes of pleasure. [16]) R. Huna (PA. 3, 4) in the name of R. Jose (BA. 3) insisted that composing nuptial songs

[1]) *T. B. Sanh.* 108a; *Num. R.* 9. 24.
[2]) *Gen. R.* 38. 6; *Lev. R.* 7. 6; *Eccl. R.* 5. 2, § 1.
[3]) *Num. R.* 21. 23; *Lev. R.* 4. 1; *Ex. R.* 15. 7.
[4]) *T. B. Sanh.* 108a-b.
[5]) *Num. R.* 21. 23.
[6]) *Gen. R.* 27. 3.
[7]) *T. B. Sanh.* 108a.
[8]) *Mekilta, Shirata* II. 23-24.
[9]) *Lev. R.* 12. 5.
[10]) *Lev. R.* 23. 9.
[11]) *Gen. R.* 26. 4.
[12]) *Gen. R.* 26. 5.
[13]) *PRE.* 22.
[14]) *Gen. R.* 30. 2.
[15]) *Sefer Hayashar*, Noah (*EBI.* II, 17).
[16]) *Gen. R.* 23. 2.

in honor of sodomy and bestiality was the final straw. [1]) Since the word "great" is used both in connection with the sin of Sodom and that of the generation of the flood, by analogy one can conclude that all which was done in one was done by the other. [2]) The corruption extended to "all flesh" so that there was no regard for species lines even among animals. R. Johanan (PA. 2) and R. ʿAzariah (c. 380) insist in R. Judah's name (T. 4) that the dog mated with the wolf, the wolf with the peacock, and man with animals. [3]) Even the earth was lewd in that when wheat was sown, it produced pseudo-wheat. [4]) R. ʿAzariah (c. 380) in the name of R. Judah son of R. Simeon (PA. 4) and R. Joshua b. Levi (PA. 1) in the name of Bar Kappara (T. 5) insisted that God is not longsuffering toward whoredom; hence the flood came. [5])

The generation failed to execute justice. R. Aha (PA. 4) said God wanted to give them Torah, suffering, the sacrificial service, and prayer, which they refused to receive. [6]) They forgot to be merciful to fellow man; hence God in measure for measure forgot to be merciful to them. [7])

With many, as with R. Johanan (PA. 2), however, it was robbery that finally sealed the doom of the generation. [8]) This they derived from the word חמס, which is defined as theft of that which is worth more than a פרוטה, the smallest coin. [9]) The Midrash proceeds to enlarge on how they successively stole less than the value of a פרוטה from the produce of the farmer so that they would not be liable to court proceedings, but at the same time they ruined the farmer. R. Levi (PA. 3) would insist that under the term חמס we should also understand idolatry, incest, and murder, as well as its literal meaning which is robbery.[10]) That they engaged in robbery seems derived also from the application of Job 24:2 to their conduct.[11])

---

[1]) *Gen. R.* 26. 5; *Lev. R.* 23. 9.
[2]) *T. B. Sanh.* 108a; cf. *Gen. R.* 27. 3; 49. 5; *J. Baba M.* 4. 2 (*EBI.* II, 6-7, § 22).
[3]) *T. B. Sanh.* 108a; *Gen. R.* 28. 8.
[4]) *Gen. R.* 28. 8.
[5]) *Lev. R.* 23. 9.
[6]) *Ex. R.* 30. 13.
[7]) *Gen. R.* 33. 5.
[8]) *T. B. Sanh.* 108b; *Gen. R.* 31. 1, 2, 3, 4; *Gen. R.* 38. 6; *Eccl. R.* I. 13. § 1; cf. Rashi (*EBI.* II, 8).
[9]) *Gen. R.* 31. 5.
[10]) *Gen. R.* 31. 6; cf. the deeds of the giants set forth by John Cassian, *Collatio VIII.* 21 (*CSEL.* 13. 2. 240).
[11]) *Eccl. R.* 3. 10. § 1.

The generation is accused of pursuing after Noah [1]) and of calling him a contemptible old man. [2]) Even after he entered the ark they would have done him harm had God not shut the door. [3]) So great did their sin become that the *Shekina* ascended from the third heaven, whither it had been driven by previous sins, to the fourth heaven. [4]) God withdrew the light he had made the first day of creation and stored it up for the righteous in the world to come. [5]) That the evils continued all night, as well as "all the day" which the text states, is attained by applying Eccl. 2:23 and Job 24:14, 16 to the people of that generation. [6]) Even their prayer was to no avail. [7]) The evil inclination increasingly masters a man from day to day, said R. Isaac (PA. 3). [8]) This evil inclination is identical with Satan, said Resh Laḳish (PA. 2). [9]) There was no hope of good in them from the rising to the setting of the sun.[10])

Being guilty of such sins, it was a question whether they would have a share in the world to come. In the Mishna, premised on Gen. 6:3, it is asserted that they will neither have a portion, nor will they stand at the judgment since they had already been judged in the flood itself.[11]) This takes "spirit" and "judge" (ידין) as though they were asserting two separate ideas.[12]) R. Nehemiah (T. 4) arrives at the idea of no judgment by applying phrases of Ps. 1:5 to them,[13]) but the sages replied to him that they would stand in the congregation of the wicked. R. Joḥanan (PA. 2) argued from "they vanish away" (Job 6:17), that they are absolutely destroyed and have no portion in the world to come.[14]) R. Akiba (T. 3) derived the idea from the

---

[1]) *Lev. R.* 27. 5; *Eccl. R.* 3. 15. § 1.

[2]) *Gen. R.* 30. 7.

[3]) *Gen. R.* 32. 8; *Sifre Debarim* 337 (*EBI.* II, 26, § 20); *Tanḥuma Yashan*, Noah 1. 10 (*T. S.* 7. 76). This Haggadah was known to Ephraem; see L. Ginzberg, *Die Haggada bei den Kirchenvätern* (Berlin: S. Calvary and Co., 1900), p. 81.

[4]) *Gen. R.* 19. 7; *Cant. R.* 5. 1. § 1; *Num. R.* 13. 2.

[5]) *Ruth R.*, Proem VII. v; *T. B. Haggigah* 12a; *Ex. R.* 35. 1; *Lev. R.* 11. 7; *Num. R.* 13. 5.

[6]) *Gen. R.* 27. 2-3.

[7]) *Ex. R.* 22. 3.

[8]) *T. B. Sukkah* 52a.

[9]) *T. B. Baba Bathra* 16a.

[10]) *Gen. R.* 27. 3.

[11]) *M. Sanh.* 10. 3; cf. *Lev. R.* 4. 1. A number of explanations of Gen. 6:3 are proposed in the Midrash which presuppose that ידון comes from דין; see *ARN.* 32; *PRE.* 34.

[12]) *T. B. Sanh.* 107b; cf. *J. Sanh.* ch. 10, hal. 3.

[13]) *T. B. Sanh.* 107b-108a.

[14]) *Gen. R.* 28. 8.

phrase "upon the face of the ground," Gen. 6:7, which he referred
to the next world. [1]) R. Aḥa (PA. 4) deduced their doom from the
phrase: "There is no more a remembrance of former times." [2])
In the Gemara, R. Judah b. Bathyra (T. 2) is said to have maintained
from the phrases of Gen. 6:3 that they would neither be resurrected
nor judged. [3]) This is the view anonymously set forth in the Mishna.
Others connected ידון with נדנה (sheath) to arrive at the idea that
they would not rise at the judgment, for the soul would not return
to its sheath. [4]) R. Ishmael (T. 3) and R. Ḥiyya b. Abba (PA. 3)
agree that there would be no filling of their bodies with God's spirit
when other men are filled with it. [5])

R. Judah b. Bathyra (T. 2), however, also took the phrase of Gen.
6:3 to infer that the flood would never be repeated—God would
never again (לעלם) judge (דין) men with this judgment. [6]) R. Simeon
b. Laḳish (PA. 2) emended ידון to ירון to deduce that God would
not allow his angels to sing at the destruction of that generation. [7])

The rabbis understood the 120 years, Gen. 6:3, in several ways.
It was a period given to the generation to repent, say some. [8]) During
this time Noah planted cedars, cut them down, and worked on the
ark. [9]) It corresponds to the time the body in the grave becomes a

---

[1]) T. B. Sanh. 108a; cf. Tos. Sanh. 13. 6.
[2]) Eccl. R. 1. 11. § 1.
[3]) T. B. Sanh. 108a; cf. Gen. R. 32. 1.
[4]) T. B. Sanh. 108a.
[5]) Gen. R. 26. 6.
[6]) Gen. R. 26. 6; cf. T. Ps.-Jon.; Jer. Targ.; and Ps.-Philo, Bib. Ant. iii. 2
for other examples of דין.
[7]) Lam. R., Proem 24. For further miscellaneous references to the generation
of the flood as a time of sin and its punishment, see: Mekilta, Baḥodesh 10. 20;
Gen. R. 22. 6; 28. 5; 51. 8; 52. 6; Ex. R. 5. 22; 17. 4; Num. R. 16. 25; Eccl. R.
2. 2. § 1; 2. 21. § 1; 2. 23. § 1; 3. 14. § 1; 4. 2. § 1; 5. 8 f.. § 4; Lam. R., Proem
24; Cant. R. 1. 4. § 3; cf. T. B. Taʿanith 27b; Megilla 31b; Kiddushin 13a; Sanh. 38b.
[8]) Mekilta, Shirata 5. 37-39; Gen. R. 30. 7; cf. Mekilta, R.S. 32; ARN. 32;
Sifre, Numbers 43, end; cited in L. Ginzberg, Legends of the Jews, V, 174; Sefer
Hayashar, Noah (EBI. II, 17, § 54). This view is continued by the medieval commentators: Sforno (EBI. II, 9); RaSaG; and Rashi (EBI. I, 186). Certain of the
church fathers repeat this Haggadah: Jerome, Quaest. Heb. in Gen. 6:3 (PL.
23. 997); Aphraates, Hom. ii. 8 (TU. III. 3. 26); see L. Ginzberg, Die Haggada bei
den Kirchenvätern (Berlin: S. Calvary and Co., 1900), pp. 77-78; M. Rahmer, Die
hebräischen Traditionen in den Werken des Hieronymus (Breslau: Schletter'schen
Buchhandlung, 1861), p. 23; S. Funk, Die haggadischen Elemente in den Homilien
des Aphraates (Wien: Selbstverlag des Verfassers, 1891), p. 27; Cyril of Jerusalem,
De Catech. ii. 8 (PG. 33. 391 B).
[9]) Gen. R. 30. 7.

spoonful of dust. [1]) It was to allow Methuselah to complete his life span. [2]) Some, by a gematria based on בשגם and משה, saw a special reference to Moses who lived 120 years. [3]) A quite divergent view, however, treats the figure as a reduction of the life span: "they have never been restored to their original number." [4])

The repentance of God, Gen. 6:6, created certain difficulties lest it should be taken to imply either lack of foresight on the part of God or attribute to Him that from which by definition He is exempt. [5])

---

[1]) *J. Nazir* 7. 2 (*EBI.*, I, 185, § 19).

[2]) *Midrash Hagadol*, Noah (*EBI.* II, 9, § 28; cf. II, 22, § 11).

[3]) *Gen. R.* 26. 6; *T. B. Ḥullin* 139b; cf. Philo, *Gig.* 55-56; Ps.-Philo, *Bib. Ant.* 9. 8; see S. Rappaport, *Agada und Exegese bei Flavius Josephus* (Wien: Alex. Kohut Memorial Foundation, 1930), p. 95.

[4]) *Eccl. R.* 1. 15. § 2. Later commentators who continued this view include Abrabanel, RaNHaW, and Hertz; see *EBI.* I, 186. Josephus may have held it (*Ant.* i. 3. 2); Philo knew of it, but rejected it (*QG.* i. 91). The *Bk. of Jubilees* 23:9-11 presents the idea that the human life span has greatly decreased since the flood, but no connection is made with the 120 years. The Christian writer Hippolytus (*Frag. in Ps.* 4 (*PG.* 10. 716)) is vague, but must make some such connection when he equates the 120th Psalm with this 120 years and says, "This is the perfection of the life of man." Lactantius, *Div. inst.* ii. 13 (*CSEL.* 19. 160), remarks: "That the length of life might not again be a cause of mediating evils, [God] gradually diminished the age of man by each successive generation, and placed a limit at 120 years, which it might not be permitted to exceed." All of these interpreters are involved in the difficulty that men after the flood frequently exceeded 120 years.

[5]) Christian exegesis also felt this difficulty; see R. Loewe, "The Jewish Midrashim and Patristic Exegesis of the Bible," *Studia Patristica* I, 495-496 (*TU.* 63). Aphraates, *Hom.* 13. 6 (*TU.* III. 3. 204), declares that only fools take these statements literally.

Certain heretics attempted to prove by the passage that the God of the O.T. is imperfect; see Ps.-Clem., *Hom.* iii. 39 (*GCS.* 42. 71). When Origen is pressed by Celsus, he denies that the passage says that God repents. He proceeds to follow a reading previously referred to by Philo, *Immut.* 70, 72: "God was angry that He made man... God considered in His heart... For I was angry that I made them." Cf. Origen, *C. Celsum* vi. 58 (*GCS.* 3. 129); Augustine, *Civ. Dei* 15. 24 (*CSEL.* 40. 2. 115). Exactly how this alleviates the problem in any way is not clear.

Other church fathers move in quite a different direction, as Philo also had done in one passage (*Immut.* 52), and say that Scripture adapts itself to man's understanding and in a figurative way speaks of God in human terms; see Salvian the Presbyter, *De gubern. Dei* i. 31-32 (*CSEL.* 8. 15-16). Augustine comes to this position after juggling the passage with the phrase: "God had thoughts and second thoughts." He wants us to know that God's anger is simply the divine judgment passing sentence on sin, *Civ. Dei* 15. 24-25 (*CSEL.* 40. 2. 115-116); *De trin.* i. 1, 2 (*PL.* 42. 820).

Tertullian short-circuits the whole problem presented to him by Praxeas by transferring these emotions to the Son. Tertullian is the heir of the type of exegesis found in the apologists who saw the Son in all O.T. passages where God is said to do, see, hear, or feel anything. Since the Son becomes a man, it was

One rabbi suggests that God is like a father who rejoices at the birth of a son though he knows the son will someday die. Each thing comes at its own time. God makes the world though He knows that it will later turn out evil. [1]

The repentance of the Lord, Gen. 6:6, implies, says R. Judah (T. 4), that God declared it was a mistake to have made man out of earthly elements, since it led him to sin. R. Aibu (PA. 4) insists that it was a mistake to put the evil urge in man. R. Nehemiah (T. 4) and R. Levi (PA. 3) take נחם in the sense of "comfort." God was comforted that man was only of earth, for now he could not also make the heavens revolt. [2] R. Dimi (BA. 4) understood God to be comforted that there were graves for such evil ones; while others say it means they do not deserve such honorable burials. [3]

That God was grieved at his heart, Gen. 6:6, implies that since He was His own architect, He had no one to complain against. [4] R. Joshua b. Levi (PA. 1) took the passage literally to mean "grieve." [5] Premised upon Gen. 6:17, "I, behold I," it is asserted that God alone brought the flood. [6]

The decree to destroy the whole earth with animals included was understood by R. Azariah (PA. 4) upon the authority of R. Judah (T. 3) to follow as a natural result of the corruption of animals who interbred across species lines. The earth was so corrupt that when wheat was sown, it produced pseudo-wheat. [7] Others considered that the animals and the world led to man's downfall, hence were punishable. [8] One tanna, on the authority of R. Joshua b. Karka (T. 2), taught that the animals were created only for man's benefit.

---

not out of order for him to experience human emotions or to lack foresight, *Adv. Prax.* 16 (*CSEL.* 47. 257).

[1]) *Gen. R.* 27. 4. Later commentators Ibn Ezra and RaMBaN readily admit the anthropomorphism (*EBI.* I, 190).

[2]) *Gen. R.* 27. 4; cf. Rashi (*EBI.* I, 190).

[3]) *T. B. Sanh.* 108a.

[4]) *Gen. R.* 27. 4.

[5]) *Gen. R.* 27. 4.

[6]) *Num. R.* 11. 7; cf. *T. Onkelos*, Gen. 7:16, where God acts through His *memra* and cf. Christian exegesis where the *Logos* is responsible.

[7]) *Gen. R.* 28. 8; *Sefer Hayashar*, Noah (*EBI.* II, 17, § 54); Rashi (*EBI.* II, 8; I, 192). Very little space is spent by the church fathers on this question. Augustine asserts that there is no question of punishing irrational animals as though they were guilty of sin; he in so doing moves in an opposite direction from those rabbis who insisted that animals were also corrupted. The mention of animals in the decree of destruction is merely to show the extent of the calamity, *Civ. Dei* 15. 25 (*CSEL.* 40. 2. 116).

[8]) *Gen. R.* 28. 6; 31. 7.

With man destroyed, they were no more of value; hence they were destroyed. [1])

Noah lived through three wicked generations: that of Enoch, that of the flood, and that of the separation. [2]) While "one man among a thousand," Eccl. 7:28, applied to Noah, [3]) and while a distinction is made by R. Eleazar b. 'Azariah (T. 2) between the limited tribute paid to him in his presence and that said of him in Gen. 6:9, [4]) on the whole there is a general tendency to limit the righteousness of Noah. R. Judah (T. 3) insisted that it was only in comparison with the wicked of his generation that he was righteous, but compared with Moses and Samuel, he would not have been called righteous. [5]) In the Talmud this view is ascribed to R. Johanan. [6]) The opposing view is presented by R. Nehemiah (T. 4) who insisted that if righteous in a bad generation, he would have done even better if he had been in the time of Moses. [7]) This concept is the view of Resh Lakish (PA. 2) in the Talmud. [8])

In keeping with the view of limited righteousness, R. Judah compared the phrase "walked with God" to an invitation to a child, "Walk with me," while to an adult one would say, "Walk before me." "Noah's moral fiber was weak," he said. R. Nehemiah (T. 4), with less stress on the moral weakness, illustrated it by a king's friend who is sinking in mud in dark alleys and is invited to walk with the king. [9]) R. Johanan further stressed Noah's weakness when he asserted that Noah lacked faith and had the water not reached his ankles, he would not have entered the ark.[10]) R. Isaac (PA. 3) spoke of the ark cleansing Noah.[11])

In this connection, an interesting debate recorded between Noah and Moses over the relative greatness of the two concedes that

---

[1]) *Gen. R.* 28. 6; *T. B. Sanh.* 108a; cf. Rashi (*EBI.* I, 192); Philo, *QG.* i. 94; ii. 9.
[2]) *Gen. R.* 26. 1.
[3]) *Gen. R.* 28. 4.
[4]) *Gen. R.* 32. 3; *Sifre, Bamidbar* 102 (*EBI.* II, 4, § 10); *T. B. Erubin* 18b.
[5]) *Gen. R.* 30. 9; cf. Philo, *Abr.* 36; Origen, *Num. Hom.* 9. 1 (*GCS.* 30. 56); Jerome, *Quaest. Heb. in Gen.* 316 (*PL.* 23. 997); L. Ginzberg, *Die Haggada bei den Kirchenvätern* (Berlin: S. Calvary and Co., 1900), p. 78; M. Rahmer, *Die hebräischen Traditionen in den Werken des Hieronymus* (Breslau: Schletter'schen Buchhandlung, 1861), pp. 23-24.
[6]) *T. B. Sanh.* 108a.
[7]) *Gen. R.* 30. 9.
[8]) *T. B. Sanh.* 108a.
[9]) *Gen. R.* 30. 10.
[10]) *Gen. R.* 32. 6.
[11]) *Gen. R.* 31. 9.

Moses is greater because he was able to save both himself and his generation, while Noah saved only himself and his family. [1]) With this agrees the view of R. Berekiah (PA. 4-5) who insisted that Moses was more beloved than Noah. [2])

R. Simon (PA. 2-3) stressed that it was Noah who "found grace" rather than God's finding it in him. [3]) R. Hanina b. Papa (PA. 3) insisted that Noah possessed less than an ounce of merit, but was saved because of a special act of grace which came because Moses was to be descended from him. [4]) This is arrived at by an analogy based on gematria of בשגם, Gen. 6:3, and of Moses. The rabbis arrived at the same conclusion from the 120 years compared with the duration of Moses' life. R. Simon (PA. 2-3) insisted that God shows mercy to forebears on account of their descendants. [5])

R. Abba b. Kahana (PA. 3), by departing from the accepted punctuation, read Gen. 6:7-8, "I repent that I made them and Noah," to arrive at the idea that though Noah did not deserve to be spared, he found grace and so escaped. [6]) This view is attributed to the school of R. Ishmael (T. 3) in the Talmud. [7])

Nevertheless, from the repetition of Noah's name, Gen. 6:9, R. Abba b. Kahana (PA. 3) deduced that he would have a part in the world to come. [8]) Others deduced from the repetition that he was a comfort (נייחה) to himself, to his fathers, to his children, and to the world. [9])

The generations of Noah were life, righteous actions, and good deeds.[10]) The redundant "was" (היה), Gen. 6:9, indicated, according to R. Johanan (PA. 2), that he remained unchanged from the beginning to the end. He was destined for a miracle.[11]) But elsewhere he insists that he was predestined to recognize his creator.[12]) R. Levi (PA. 3),

---

[1]) *Deut. R.* 11. 3.
[2]) *Gen. R.* 36. 3.
[3]) *Gen. R.* 29. 3.
[4]) *Gen. R.* 26. 6; 29. 1.
[5]) *Gen. R.* 29. 5. The Soncino edition attributes the statement to R. Abbahu (PA. 3).
[6]) *Gen. R.* 28. 8; 29. 1; 31. 1.
[7]) *T. B. Sanh.* 108b.
[8]) *Gen. R.* 30. 4.
[9]) *Gen. R.* 30. 5; cf. *Cant. R.* 2. 15. 2 for other comments on the righteousness of Noah.
[10]) *Gen. R.* 30. 6; cf. Philo, *Abr.* 31; *QG.* i. 97.
[11]) *Gen. R.* 30. 8.
[12]) *Est. R.* 6. 3.

in agreement with R. Samuel b. Naḥman (PA. 3), [1]) contended that it
implied that he saw a new world. Others take it that he was prepared
for the task, or destined for salvation, [2]) while the rabbis say, by
comparison of other occurrences, that it implies that he fed and
sustained the inmates of the ark. [3])

"Wholehearted," according to Bar Ḥuṭah (PA. 4 (?)), implied
that he lived a multiple of seven years (350) after the flood. [4]) Others
implied from it that he was a perfect physical specimen. [5])

That he is called "a man" (איש), Gen. 6:9, implied that he warned •
others. [6]) Noah was the one herald in his generation, said R. Abba
(BA. 4). [7]) He spoke to them words as hard as fiery flints. [8]) "Ye good
for nothings, ye forsake Him whose voice breaks cedars and worship
a dry log." [9]) "Repent, for if not, the Holy One, blessed be He, will
bring a deluge upon you, and cause your bodies to float upon the
water like gourds... Moreover ye shall be taken as a curse for all
future generations."[10]) "Woe to ye foolish ones, tomorrow a flood
will come, so repent."[11])

The dimensions prescribed for the ark were considered by Bar
Ḥuṭah (PA. 4 (?)) to set forth those proportions to be used by a
ship builder in boat building.[12]) The door in the side, according
to R. Isaac (PA. 3), teaches that a chamber of ten cubits square should
have a door at the side.[13])

The קנים are chambers.[14]) The details of the general plan for
the ark were differently understood. R. Judah (T. 4) contended that
there were 330 compartments, each ten cubits square, arranged in
four rows, separated by two corridors four cubits wide, and then there
was a gangway around the outside of a cubit's width. The ark tapered
inward and the upper story had only three rows of compartments.[15])

---

1) *Est. R.* 6. 3; *Gen. R.* 30. 8.
2) *Ex. R.* 2. 4.
3) *Gen. R.* 30. 8.
4) *Gen. R.* 30. 8.
5) *T. B. Zeb.* 116a.
6) *Gen. R.* 30. 7; cf. *Ruth R.*, Proem 3, for other homilies on "איש".
7) *Gen. R.* 30. 7.
8) *T. B. Sanh.* 108b.
9) *Gen. R.* 31. 3.
10) *T. B. Sanh.* 108a.
11) *Eccl. R.* 9. 15. § 1.
12) *Gen. R.* 31. 10.
13) *Gen. R.* 31. 11.
14) *Gen. R.* 31. 9; cf. Rashi and Ibn Ezra (*EBI.* II, 11).
15) *Gen. R.* 31. 11.

One assumes that he thought that there was a flat top above.

R. Nehemiah (T. 4) insisted that there were 900 compartments, each six cubits square, arranged in six rows, with three corridors of four cubits width, and then a gangway of two cubits width at the outside. The ark had straight sides, and then had a sloping roof of a cubit's height, exclusive of the thirty cubits.[1])

The lower floor was for garbage. Noah and the clean animals inhabited the second, while the unclean were on the third. A sort of trap door enabled him to shovel garbage down. [2]) Others differ and insist that the top floor was for garbage and the bottom for unclean animals. [3]) One tanna suggests that man was on top, and that the animals were in the middle. [4]) That the unclean animals were on the same floor with man is proved by R. Jeremiah (PA. 4) from מאתו, Gen. 8:8. [5])

"Gopher wood" was understood to be some sort of cedar by R. Nathan (T. 5). [6]) R. Adda (BA. 3-4) in the name of the scholars of R. Shila (BA. 1), proposed that it was מבליגה. A variant rendering of the same passage eliminates the name of R. Adda and has Rab (BA. 1)

---

[1]) *Gen. R.* 31. 11. The view of Origen, which is later also held by Jerome, that the ark began being thirty cubits broad and gradually narrowed to one (*C. Celsum* iv. 41 (*GCS.* 2. 314); *Hom. in Gen.* ii. 1 (*GCS.* 29. 23); Jerome, *Dial. adv. Luciferianos* 22 (*PL.* 23. 185)), would show some affinities to the ideas of R. Judah and R. Nehemiah without exactly corresponding with either of them. Origen also thought that the top of the ark was only one cubit long. Ibn Ezra diminished the 30 cubits of the ark to a top one cubit long and one-sixth of a cubit wide, while Shadal proposed an ark with a sharp line one cubit long and no width at all so that the water would run off (*EBI.* II, 13).

[2]) *Gen. R.* 31. 11. Origen has received the tradition from his Jewish teachers that the garbage was in the hold of the ark, *Hom. in Gen.* ii. 1 (*GCS.* 29. 24-25). The early Syrian fathers suggest that no refuse was thrown off by the inhabitants of the ark because of the slender food allowance; otherwise the foul smell would have been oppressive; see A. Levene, *op. cit.*, p. 82. Ambrose supposes that garbage was thrown outside at the door, *De offic.* i. 78 (*PL.* 16. 46).

[3]) *Gen. R.* 31. 11.

[4]) *T. B. Sanh.* 108b.

[5]) *T. B. Sanh.* 108b. Origen has the garbage in the hold. That level immediately above was to store food. Then came the three levels with wild animals, then more tame ones, and finally man at the top, *Hom. in Gen.* ii. 1 (*GCS.* 29. 25); cf. *Num. Hom.* 21. 2 (*GCS.* 30. 201). Hippolytus, with no reference at all to the garbage, puts the fierce, wild, and dangerous beasts on the lower story, separated by stakes. The middle contains the birds, while the upper (though the text is not specific) was for Noah and his family; see *Arabic Frag. to Pent.* ii (*GCS.* I. 2. 88); this arrangement agrees with the Arabic ms. cited by Frazer, *Folklore in the O.T.*, I, 145-146; and with *PRE.* 23. Augustine, *C. Faustum* 12. 16 (*CSEL.* 25. 346), divides the lower spaces into two or three chambers.

[6]) *Gen. R.* 31. 8.

to propose that gopher is אדרא. Others use the term גולמיש. [1])
These seem to be names for types of cedar. [2]) The rabbis noticed
the difference in the caulking of Noah's ark both inside and out with
pitch and that of Moses which had slime inside. This was to keep
the water out and at the same time to remove the babe Moses from
the odor of pitch. [3])

The צהר is assumed by R. Abba b. Kahana (PA. 3) to be a sort of
skylight. [4]) This same idea seems also to be the view of R. Ahiyya b.
Zeirah (A. 4) who held that the heavenly bodies did not function
during the flood, so precious stones were needed in addition to the
skylight. [5]) With these there would be a tacit identification of צהר
and *ḥalon* of Gen. 8:6. [6]) To the contrary, R. Phinehas (PA. 5) in
the name of R. Levi (PA. 3) explains it as a gem which was bright
at night and dim in the day. [7]) The same would seem to be the view
of R. Joḥanan (PA. 2). [8]) This view is arrived at by the supposed
correspondence between צהר and צהרים (noon). [9])

In the view of some, the ark built itself. This is attained by reading
תעשה as *niphʿal* rather than *ḳal*.[10]) But elsewhere Noah built it as
God commanded.[11])

---

[1]) *T. B. Sanh.* 108b; cf. *Tanḥuma Bᵊreshith* (*EBI.* II, 11, § 34).

[2]) Ibn Ezra comments that גפר is "the name of a light wood upon the surface
of the water." Rashi said the ark was made of גופר so that brimstone גפרית
would not destroy it. Abrabanel comments, "resinous wood that does not rot
in water and rides lightly upon the water." Shadal and Ranhaw insist that גפר
comes from the sap of the tree which is כפר. Cassuto insists that it belongs to
the pine family; see *EBI.* II, 11.

[3]) *Gen. R.* 31. 9; *T. B. Sotah* 12a; *Ex. R.* 1. 21.

[4]) *Gen. R.* 31. 11. Ibn Ezra and Radak (*EBI.* II, 12) identify it with a window.

[5]) *J. Pes.* 1. 1 (*T.S.* 6. 181).

[6]) *Gen. R.* 33. 5.

[7]) *Gen. R.* 31. 11; cf. *PRE.* 23 where R. Meir says that a pearl was suspended
in the ark for this purpose.

[8]) *T. B. Sanh.* 108b.

[9]) Jerome comments on the fact that there is a problem of equating *colligens*,
which he evidently obtained from the LXX, with *meridanum* which he understood
the Hebrew to imply. He evidently assumed that צהר comes from צהרים
(noonday). He then notes Symmachus' reading and concludes that the fundamental idea is *fenestra*, "window" (*Quaest. Heb. in Gen.* 6. 16 (*PL.* 23. 998)); cf. M.
Rahmer, *op. cit.*, p. 24.

Differing entirely are the early Syrian fathers who take the word to refer to
things that project from the ark like a porch, and sundries are placed on them
Gabriel calls it the wood which is placed in the middle of the ship for crossing
from one side to the other; see A. Levene, *op. cit.*, p. 82.

[10]) *Gen. R.* 31. 11.

[11]) *Gen. R.* 31. 14; cf. Augustine, *De Catech.* 22. 29 (*PL.* 40. 338); Lactantius,
Div. inst. ii. 13 (*CSEL.* 19. 160); Julius Africanus, *Chron.* 4 (*PG.* 10. 68). "How

When completed and loaded, the ark drew eleven cubits of water.
This is calculated from the estimate that the water diminished one
cubit in four days after the flood. [1])

The position of R. Abba b. Kahana (PA. 3) over what was eaten in
the ark is unclear. First he is reported to have taught that most
of the food taken into the ark was pressed figs which all ate, in which
explanation he agrees with teaching set forth in R. Nehemiah's (T. 4)
name. But immediately he is placed opposite R. Levi (PA. 3), with
R. Abba b. Kahana insisting that branches were taken for elephants,
חצובות for the deer, and glass for the ostriches; that is, food suitable
for each type was taken.[2]) R. Levi (PA. 3) contended that there were vine,
fig, and olive shoots also taken for future plantings. Both are interpreting the verse "for thee and for them." [3]) R. Ḥana b. Bizna's
(BA. 3) story of the pomegranate worm which the chameleon ate
would imply more than figs to eat. [4])

The animals gathered themselves to the ark. [5]) That only perfect,

---

wise was Noah who built the whole of the ark," exclaims Ambrose, *De offic.* i.
121 (*PL.* 16. 63).

[1]) *Gen. R.* 33. 7.

[2]) *Gen. R.* 31. 14; and Sforno (*EBI.* II, 16).

[3]) *Gen. R.* 31. 14. The reading is based on a proposed emendation of the text
with the name being reversed, see *EBI.* II, 17, n. 2. Philo avoids the problem
under discussion by having the destruction affect only the face of the earth,
QG. ii. 15. Ps.-Clem., *Recog.* i. 29 (*PG.* 1. 1224) speaks of the seeds he had shut
up with him.

[4]) *T. B. Sanh.* 108b. Radak and Ibn Ezra assume that carnivorous animals may
have eaten fodder (*EBI.* II, 16). Christian sources tend toward the view of a
variety of food. Origen, *Hom. in Gen.* ii. 1 (*GCS.* 29. 25), supposes that each animal
ate that which was natural to it. Carnivorous animals were fed meat which was
supplied from the numbers of suitable animals. The early Syrian fathers are not
specific on the point, but do insist that food was so scarce that there was no refuse;
see A. Levene, *op. cit.*, p. 82. Hippolytus, *Arabic Frag. to Pent.* II. Gen. 7. 6 (*GCS.*
1. 2. 89), includes in the original command of God victuals of wheat ground,
kneaded with water, and dried. The women of Noah's family were diligent and
spent a great deal of time in preparing just the right amount. Theodoretus,
Quaest. in Gen. vi. 51 (*PG.* 80. 153 D), argues that the food was fodder and seeds.
Augustine, *Civ. Dei*, 15. 27 (*CSEL.* 40. 2. 121 f.), supposes that during this period
the carnivorous animals may have eaten vegetables, fruit, figs, and chestnuts, or
that it would not have been impossible for God to keep them alive without food
of a proper sort.

[5]) *Gen. R.* 32. 8. Cf. Philo, *Mos.* ii. 61; *PRE.* 23; *T. B. Zeb.* 116a;
Sefer Hayashar, Noah (*EBI.* II, 31); and Ibn Ezra (*EBI.* II, 16). This idea
was known to Ephraem; see L. Ginzberg, *Die Haggada bei den Kirchenvätern*,
pp. 80-81; for the text of Ephraem see R. M. Tonneau, *S. Ephr. Syr. in Gen. et
Ex. Comm.* (*CSCO.* 72), p. 47. It is further repeated by Augustine: "Noah did
not have to catch the animals. He merely let them in as they came by. They

young animals were taken in can be deduced from "with thee" which means "perfect like thee"; while "to keep seed alive" eliminates the old, the castrates, and those torn (טרפה) or defective in limbs. [1] R. Samuel b. Naḥman (PA. 3) in R. Jonathan's (PA. 2) name taught that from "man and wife" and "clean" one could deduce that only those animals that had mated after their kind were taken in. As Noah led them by the ark, it rejected those that had been involved in sin. [2] Another test proposed was: if the male pursued after the female, they were accepted, but if the female pursued after the male, they were rejected. [3] Still again, those who crouched were taken in. [4]

It is insisted that fourteen is the total of clean birds, for one would be short a mate if only seven were meant. [5] But Resh Laḳish (PA. 2) assumed that there were only two unclean birds. [6] R. Eleazar (PA. 3) said in R. Jose's (c. 150) name that "birds of every wing" excluded from the ark those that were moulting or unfit for sacrifice by the Noahides. [7] God ordered that there be more clean than unclean animals because he desired that sacrifices be made of them. [8] A divergent view is that God wished to decrease the number of unclean animals and at the same time to increase the number of clean. That a total of 366 species each of cattle, of reptiles, and of birds were

---

came by God's will and not by man's work." *Civ. Dei* 15. 27 (*CSEL*. 40. 2. 121); cf. Theodoretus, *Quaest. in Gen.* 44 (*PG*. 80. 97 B).

PRE. 23 has angels collect the animals to preserve them; cf. *supra*, p. 28. Ramban has the unclean animals come themselves, but Noah has to assemble the clean ones (*EBI*. II, 21).

Hippolytus has Noah bring them all together, *Arabic Frag. to Pent.* 1 (*GCS*. 1. 2. 88).

[1] *T. B. Zeb.* 116a; *Abodah Zarah* 6a; 51a.

[2] *T. B. Sanh.* 108b; *Zeb.* 116a.

[3] *Gen. R.* 31. 13. This question is not dealt with very clearly in the church fathers we have investigated. Pope Damasus wonders how God could give a charge to Noah concerning unclean animals when He had made everything good; see Jerome, *Ep.* 35. 2 (*CSEL*. 54. 266). Jerome remarks that the eating of the unclean was already forbidden, otherwise "unclean" is an unnecessary word, but he does not enlarge on when it was forbidden; *Adv. Jovinianum* ii. 15 (*PL*. 23. 320 A). Julius Africanus has the "firstlings of every living creature" taken in; *Chron.* 4 (*PG*. 10. 68).

[4] *Sefer Hayashar*, Noah (*EBI*. II, 31).

[5] *Gen. R.* 32. 4; cf. Ibn Ezra (*EBI*. II, 21).

[6] *T. B. Sanh.* 108b.

[7] *Gen. R.* 32. 8.

[8] *Gen. R.* 34. 9; *Ex. R.* 50. 2; cf. Rashi (*EBI*. II, 46); Jerome, *Ep.* 123. 11 (*CSEL*. 56. 85); *Adv. Jovin.* 1. 16 (*PL*. 23. 247); Theodoretus, *Quaest. in Gen.* 59 (*PG*. 80. 153); see L. Ginzberg, *Die Haggada bei den Kirchenvätern* (Berlin: S. Calvary and Co., 1900), p. 78.

taken is arrived at by adding the total number of rooms presumed
to be on each floor. [1]

Unusual inhabitants of the ark included the spirits of those not
yet born, according to R. Hoshaya (PA. 1). [2] In *Midrash Tehillim* [3]
falsehood comes for shelter in the ark, but is refused because he has
no mate. He goes away and forms an alliance with misfortune on
condition that she get what he earns, and then they are accepted into
the ark. Following the flood she forces him to keep his bargain.

R. Judah (T. 4) and R. Nehemiah (T. 4) differed over whether the
ראם, an unusually large animal, went into the ark. Judah thought
that only its whelps were taken in, while R. Nehemiah insisted that
it was only tied to the ark and plowed furrows in the water. Those
who said Palestine was exempt from the flood said that it stayed there.
In the Talmud this discussion is between R. Jannai (T. 4) and Rabbah
b. bar Ḥanah (BA. 4). R. Joḥanan (PA. 2) suggests that only the head
of the animal was in the ark. The waters were cooled at the edge of
the ark so that he could survive. [4]

Og and Sihon, because of their enormous size, survived outside
the ark. [5] The water came only to their ankles. [6]

Opinions differed over the entrance of Noah into the ark. R.
Joḥanan (PA. 2) had said that he only entered when the water reached
his ankles. [7] Others emphasized that he only entered when commanded to do so, which was the appropriate season to enter. [8] Still others
stressed the importance of the entrance into the ark in "the self-same
day" as a challenge to the people of the time who threatened to
demolish the ark if Noah attempted to enter it.[9] Or it was to invite the
objector to speak out lest they should later say, had we known
what he was doing, we would have prevented his entrance into the
ark.[10]

---

[1] *PRE.* 23. One edition reads "thirty-two" species of birds.

[2] *Gen. R.* 31. 13.

[3] *EBI.* II, 26-27, § 22.

[4] *Gen. R.* 31. 13; *T. B. Zeb.* 113b.

[5] *T. B. Niddah* 61a; *T. B. Zeb.* 113b.

[6] *Deut. R.* 11. 10; cf. *PRE.* 23 where Og sat under the eaves of the ark; cf.
also *T. Ps.-Jon.*, Gen. 14:13; Deut. 2:11; 3:11.

[7] *Gen. R.* 32. 6; cf. Rashi and Abrabanel (*EBI.* II. 23). This is in marked contrast with those authorities where Noah was in the ark for seven days before the
flood: cf. *PRE.* 23; Radak (*EBI.* II, 23); and Ephraem Syrus, *Comm. in Gen.*
6:10 (*CSCO.* 72. 47-48).

[8] *Eccl. R.* 3. 1; 10. 4. § 1; see also *Torah Shelemah* 8:64.

[9] *Sifre, Debarim* 337 (*EBI.* II, 26, § 20).

[10] *Gen. R.* 32. 8.

God made a covenant with Noah before the flood, Gen. 6:18, so that the produce taken in would not rot or change its characteristics. [1]) Without it, Noah could not have successfully made the ark, or kept out the giants and animals. [2])

The seven days in the ark prior to the flood lent itself to numerous interpretations. Corresponding to the time one mourns for a dead relative, God mourned for His world seven days before He destroyed it. [3]) These were seven extra days of grace to the wicked generation.[4]) During this time God gave them a taste of the world to come so that they could know the good from which they withheld themselves. He caused the sun to rise in the west and set in the east as a warning, yet they did not repent. [5]) Rab (BA. 1) said they were the days of mourning for Methuselah. [6])

R. Levi (PA. 3) said God shut Noah in as a king might do who had declared a general execution and who wished to protect a friend. [7]) Those animals that were not taken into the ark remained about the ark seven days. When the flood finally broke, 700,000 of the men who had remained impenitent until this time implored Noah to grant them protection. Upon his refusal, they attempted to take the ark by storm, but the wild beasts set on them and they were killed. [8])

The forty days of rain correspond with the sin after the forty days Moses was on the mountain, according to R. Simeon b. Yoḥai (T. 4), and with the sin which defaces the embryo which is forty days in taking shape, according to R. Joḥanan (PA. 2). [9])

Whether the planets ceased to function during the flood was de-

---

[1]) *Gen. R.* 31. 12; cf. Ps.-Philo, *Bib. Ant.* iii. 4, where the covenant is to destroy the earth.

[2]) *Gen. R.* 31. 12.

[3]) *Gen. R.* 32. 7; cf. *T. B. Sanh.* 108b.

[4]) *T. B. Sanh.* 108b; *ARN.* 32; cf. *T. Ps.-Jon.*, Gen. 7:4, and Philo, *QG.* ii. 13. The idea of an extra period of grace is taken up by Ephraem Syrus, *Comm. in Gen.* 6:11 (*CSCO.* 72. 48); cf. L. Ginzberg, *Die Haggada bei den Kirchenvätern* (Berlin: S. Calvary and Co., 1900), p. 79.

[5]) *T. B. Sanh.* 108b; *ARN.* 32.

[6]) *T. B. Sanh.* 108b; *ARN.* 32; *Gen. R.* 32. 7; 3. 6. LXX figures would demand that Methuselah survive the flood 14 years. In the MT. his death corresponds with the flood year. Cf. Augustine, *Civ. Dei* 15. 10-11 (*CSEL.* 40. 2. 76-79).

[7]) *Gen. R.* 32. 8; cf. *Ex. R.* 29. 7 for a different homily.

[8]) *Sefer Hayashar*, Noah (EBI. II, 32); *Gen. R.* 32. 14 ("Ktav" edit.). Ephraem surmised that God closed the ark lest the wanton ones should break the door in; cited in L. Ginzberg, *Die Haggada bei den Kirchenvätern*, p. 81; cf. *Legends of the Jews*, V, 178, n. 25.

[9]) *Gen. R.* 32. 5. This Midrash may have been known to Ephraem; see L. Ginzberg, *Die Haggada bei den Kirchenvätern*, pp. 79-80.

bated with R. Johanan (PA. 2) and R. Joshua insisting that theλ
ceased. R. Elieser insisted that they did function. R. Jonathan (PA. 1)
contended that they functioned, but could not be seen. [1]

Water not only had its destructive power, but those of the flood
were boiling hot as a fitting punishment for the inflamed sensuous
behaviour of the sinners. R. Johanan (PA. 2) taught, drawing the
idea from the phrase "through his heat were they consumed," that
God boiled every drop in Gehenna before he brought it down on
them. [2] R. Ḥisda (BA. 3) attained the same concept through an
analogy of Gen. 8:1 and Est. 7:10 where שכך occurs. "The waters
cooled down" (A.V. "abated"), he translated. [3] The great hot fountains at Biram, the gulf of Gaddor, and the caravan spring of Paneas
were not stopped up when the flood came to an end. [4]

R. Berekiah (PA. 5), making an analogy dependent on the word
"great," said in R. Johanan's (PA. 2) name that the generation of
the flood was punished by fire as were the people of Sodom. [5]

R. Judah (T. 4) insisted that the water of the flood was not on a
level, but was only fifteen cubits deep at any given point. R. Nehemiah
(T. 4) said it was fifteen cubits over the mountains and immeasurable
over the plains. [6] But as high as the flood was, R. Eleazar of Modiʻim
(T. 2) insisted that it did not compare with the depth of the manna
in the wilderness. Concerning the former, "windows of heaven"
is used, while "doors," Ps. 78:23, refer to the latter. In rabbinic
thought, this is four times greater. [7]

That the water extended down into Samaria is reflected in the controversy of R. Jonathan (PA. 1) with the Samaritan who insisted
that Mt. Gerizim was not covered. A donkey driver refuted the
Samaritan with the phrase "all the high mountains were covered." [8]
Resh Laḳish (PA. 2) and R. Johanan (PA. 2) differ over whether the

---

[1] *Gen. R.* 34. 11; cf. 25. 2; cf. Radak (*EBI.* II, 51). Philo, *Abr.* 43, contends
that they functioned, but could not be seen. Cf. also *Bk. of Adam and Eve*, iii. 9.
Gaius of Rome makes the specific point that they were not done away; see R.
Grant, *Second Cent. Christ.* (London: SPCK., 1946), pp. 105-106.

[2] *Lev. R.* 7. 6; *Eccl. R.* 9. 4. § 1; cf. *Gen. R.* 28. 8 where the same is used to
prove that He will do this to them at the resurrection.

[3] *T. B. Rosh Hashana* 12a; *Zeb.* 113b; *Sanh.* 108b; *PRE.* 22.

[4] *T. B. Sanh.* 108a; cf. *Gen. R.* 33. 4.

[5] *Gen. R.* 49. 5.

[6] *Gen. R.* 32 11; cf. *T. B. Yoma* 76a.

[7] *Mekilta Vayassaʻ* 4. 82-89; *Ex. R.* 25. 7.

[8] *Deut. R.* 3. 6; *Cant. R.* 4. 4. § 5.

land of Israel was included, for R. Johanan insisted that it was not. [1])
R. Levi (PA. 3) agreed appealing to Ez. 22:23, "a land . . . not
rained upon in the day of indignation." [2]) Some authorities insisted
that the flood did not reach as high as the Garden of Eden. [3])

Though man had not been created first, it is deduced from the
order of mention that he came first in punishment, [4]) for he had
been the first to sin. [5]) Various figures are used to express the com-
pleteness of the destruction. R. Huna (BA. 2) and R. Jeremiah (c.
320), in R. Kahana's (PA. 2) name, insist that even the three hand-
breadths of the earth's surface which the plow turns were washed
away. R. Levi (PA. 3), in R. Johanan's (PA. 2) name, derived from
Job 14:19 that the nether millstone was dissolved. [6]) R. Judah b.
R. Simon (PA. 4) said the dust of Adam was dissolved, but this
the congregation refused. [7]) R. Simeon b. Jehozadak (A. 1) said
the nut of the spinal column from which God will cause men to
blossom forth in the future was dissolved. [8]) The world had been
brought back to the state it knew before the creation of man. [9])
R. Judah b. R. Simon (PA. 4) found in Gen. 1:2 an allusion to the
flood and to the spirit of God coming over the waters at its end.[10])

Cain, who had been kept in suspense about his destiny up to this
time, was swept away, according to R. Samuel [11]) and according to R.
Levi (PA. 3), the latter of whom was teaching in the name of Resh
Lakish (PA. 2) and interpreting היקום in the sense of "rebellion."[12])
R. Berekiah (PA. 4, 5) interpreted היקום in the sense familiar to us:

---

[1]) *T. B. Zeb.* 113b.

[2]) *Gen. R.* 33. 6; *PRE.* 23.

[3]) *Gen. R.* 33. 6; *Lev. R.* 31. 10; *Cant. R.* 1. 15. § 4; 4. 1. § 2; cf. *PRE.* 23
and Nachmonides, Gen. 8:11. Some Syrian fathers shared this view, among
whom was Mar Ephrem who said it only reached the outer confines of Paradise.
Rabban, on the other hand, insisted that Paradise was covered; see A. Levene,
op. cit., p. 83; cf. D. Gerson, *Die Commentarien des Ephraem Syrus im Verhältniss
zur jüdischen Exegese* (Breslau: Schletter'schen Buchhandlung, 1868), p. 12. The
viewpoint that it was covered is likely represented by III *Bar.* 4:10.

[4]) *T. B. Berakoth* 61a; *'Erubin* 18a.

[5]) *Mekilta, Pisha* 7. 36 ff.; *Num. R.* 9. 18.

[6]) *Gen. R.* 28. 3; 31. 7; *Est. R.* 6. 3; *Lev. R.* 31. 10.

[7]) *Gen. R.* 28. 3; R. Judah's view is directly opposed to *Bk. of Adam and Eve*
iii. 7 where the body of Adam is taken into the ark.

[8]) *Gen. R.* 28. 3.

[9]) *Lam. R.* 1. 17. § 52; cf. *Gen. R.* 5. 1; 28. 2.

[10]) *Gen. R.* 2. 3.

[11]) *Eccl. R.* 6. 3. § 1.

[12]) *Gen. R.* 32. 5; 22. 12; *Eccl. R.* 6. 3. § 1; *Ex. R.* 31. 17, and some mss. of
T. Benj. 7. 4.

"whatever exists," (קיומיה). [1]) R. Abin (I: 355; II: 370) took it to be the human race which upholds the world. R. Eliezer said it meant money which gives standing to its owner's feet. [2])

That even Noah suffered some, coughing blood on account of the cold, is deduced from the particle אך of Gen. 7:23. [3]) In addition the lion struck him while in the ark, leaving him unfit to serve in the priesthood. Other authorities taught that the blow came when the lion was leaving the ark. [4])

Fish, however, were not included in the destruction, since Scripture says "on dry land," said R. Ḥisda (BA. 3). [5]) Some insist they would have been gathered into the ark, but they fled to the Mediterranean. [6])

The dead who perished in the flood sank or were emptied out in Babylon, according to R. Joḥanan (PA. 2) and R. Simeon b. Lakish (PA. 2). The former argues on the word צולה, Is. 44:27, and צללו (to sink), and the latter argues on שנער and ששם נערו (empty out). [7])

Life in the ark was without doubt a trying experience. That cohabitation of male and female was forbidden was taught by R. Judah b. R. Simon (c. 320) and R. Ḥanan in the name of R. Samuel b. R. Isaac (PA. 3), [8]) and by R. Joḥanan (PA. 2). [9]) This is reached by observing that the wives are not mentioned in the immediate connection with their husbands in Gen. 6:18, but are in Gen. 8:16. Three culprits in the lack of continence were Ham, the raven, and the dog, each of which received an appropriate punishment.[10]) *Sefer Hayashar*

---

[1]) *Gen. R.* 32. 5; cf. *Eccl. R.* 6. 3. § 1.

[2]) *Eccl. R.* 6. 3. § 1. R. Eliezer is punning on the verb קום.

[3]) *Gen. R.* 32. 11.

[4]) *Gen. R.* 30. 6; cf. *Lev. R.* 20. 1; *Tanḥ. B.* I, 38; see L. Ginzberg, *Legends of the Jews* (Phila.: Jew. Pub. Soc., 1955), V, 182.

[5]) *T. B. Zeb.* 113b; *Sanh.* 108a; cf. Augustine, *Civ. Dei* 15. 27 (*CSEL.* 40. 2. 121), who exempts both fish and water birds.

[6]) *Gen. R.* 32. 11.

[7]) *Lam. R.*, Proem 23; *Eccl. R.* 12. 7. § 1; *T. B. Sabbath* 113b; *Zeb.* 113a, b.

[8]) *Gen. R.* 31. 12; 34. 7; *J. Taan.* 1. 6 (*T.S.* 6. 200); *EBI.* II, 15; cf. II, 44, 45); *PRE.* 23; cf. Rashi (*EBI.* II, 43); and Philo, *QG.* ii. 49.

[9]) *T. B. Sanh.* 108b.

[10]) *T. B. Sanh.* 108b; *J. Taan.* 1. 6, where the statement is attributed to R. Ḥiyya b. Ba; and *Gen. R.* 36. 7. This ascetic note had a certain appeal to ascetic tendencies in the church and is commented on by a number of church fathers: Origen, *Selecta in Gen.* 53 (*PG.* 12. 105); Julius Africanus, *Chron.* 4 (*PG.* 10. 68); Hippolytus, *Arabic Frag. to Pent.* II, Gen. 7:6 (*GCS.* I. 2. 88); John of Damascus, *De fide orth.* iv. 24 (*PG.* 94. 1208 C); see also L. Ginzberg, *Die Haggada bei den Kirchenvätern*, pp. 81-83, and the Arabic ms. cited by J. G. Frazer, *Folklore in the O.T.*, I, 146; cf. also *Bk. of Adam and Eve* iii. 8; Hilary, *Tract. myst.* i. 13 (*SC.* 19.

(*EBI.* II, 32) speaks of the lions' roaring and the wolves' howling as each animal vented its agony through its own proper means. Noah and his sons thought death was near and cried to God. [1]) There was also the "stench of the lions" to endure. [2])

R. Ḥana b. Bizna (BA. 3) said the animals had to be fed at the times they normally ate, whether day or night. Noah did not know what to feed the chameleon until one day he let a worm drop from a pomegranate which it ate. After that he grew worms for it. The lion had a fever and so required little food. The phoenix made no demands, not wishing to bother Noah. He in return prayed that it not die. [3]) In caring for them all, Noah was the Lord's herdsman. [4]) For twelve months he was so busy he could not sleep. [5])

All sources agree that the flood covered twelve months. [6]) However, the point of beginning was heatedly debated. R. Judah (T. 4) insisted that the year of the flood was not included in Noah's total years, while R. Nehemiah (T. 4) insisted that it is counted in the total chronological scheme of the world. [7]) While one source states that the exact day of the beginning is not given, [8]) R. Eliezer (T. 1st-2nd cent.) insisted that the flood began in *Marḥeshwan* and then decreased until *Ab*, and finally dried up in *Tishri*. [9]) R. Joshua (T. 1st-2nd cent.) said it began on the seventeenth of *Iyar*. The rabbis favored Eliezer, but the Talmud admits that some follow Joshua.[10]) The

---

101). It served Cyril of Jerusalem, *Procatechesis* 14 (*PG.* 33. 355 A), as an argument that men and women should not sit together in the church. The *Apoc. of Paul* 50 expands this ascetic period to cover Noah's behaviour during the entire period while the ark was being built.

[1]) Origen, *Hom. in Gen.* ii. 1 (*GCS.* 29. 27) knows a tradition that the animals were kept silent. Ephraem Syrus, *Nisibene Hymns* i. 10 (*NPNF.* ser. ii. 13. 168), said: "Noah stood between the terrible waves that were without and the destroying mouths that were within. The waves tossed him and the mouths dismayed him."

[2]) *PRE.* 23.

[3]) *T. B. Sanh.* 108b; cf. *Gen. R.* 29. 4.

[4]) *Lev. R.* 1. 9.

[5]) *T. B. Sanh.* 108b; *Tanḥ. B.*, Noah 31; *Midrash Ps.* on 37:1.

[6]) *Lam. R.* 1. 12. § 40; *Gen. R.* 28. 8; 30. 6; 33. 7; 34. 1; *Num. R.* 10. 2; this is the opinion of R. Akiba in *M. Eduyoth* 2. 10.

[7]) *Gen. R.* 32. 6; *T. B. Rosh Hashana* 11b-12a.

[8]) *Num. R.* 1. 5.

[9]) *Gen. R.* 33. 7; 22. 4; this is the view of *T. Ps.-Jon.*, Gen. 7:11; Josephus, *Ant.* i. 3. 3; and *PRE.* 23. *Seder Olam* 4 has the 40 days end in *Kislev* in harmony with this view; the 150 days end on the first of *Sivan*. The ark rested on the Mt. on the 17th of *Sivan*. The earth was finally dry in the month of *Marḥeshwan*.

[10]) *T. B. Rosh Hashana* 11b-12a; cf. Philo, *QG.* ii. 17, 47, and Shadal (*EBI.* II, 31). The Syrian Fathers have the flood begin in the summer so that no one

fact that the earth was not dry until the 27th day of the second month, though Noah went into the ark on the 17th, is explained to be due to the fact that the solar year is eleven days longer than the lunar year. [1]

The ark came to rest on Ararat which is the mountain range of Cordyene. [2] When Noah was ready to send the raven forth, according to R. Judan (PA. 4) in the name of R. Judah b. R. Simon (PA. 4), the raven argued back (deduced from a supposed relation of ושוב with השיב), that God hated him since only a few unclean animals were taken into the ark. Noah also hated him, for if he sent him out and an accident should occur, there would be one less species. He also suggested that perhaps Noah was lewdly interested in the female raven. Noah replied with a *kal we-ḥomer* that he had been continent in the ark. [3] Elsewhere he had insisted that the raven was good for nothing, but God had commanded him to take the raven back because it was needed to feed Elijah. [4] In *Pirke de R. Eliezer* the raven never returns to the ark, but feeds on dead bodies. [5]

R. Judah b. Naḥman (PA. 3) in the name of Resh Laḳish (PA. 2) said the dove would not have returned had she found a place of rest. [6] She was a symbol of Israel who would find no resting place in exile. R. Jose b. R. Ḥanina (PA. 2) insisted on the basis of "yet another" (Gen. 8:12 ff.) that there was a total of three periods of seven days involved in the post-flood episodes.[7] The source from whence the dove obtained the olive branch brought controversy. R. Abba bar Kahana (BA. 4) insisted she brought it from the young shoots of the land of Israel. R. Levi (PA. 3) contended for the Mt. of Olives which had not been submerged. R. Birai (PA. 4-5) said she brought it from the Garden of Eden.[8] טרף (E.V. "torn"), according to R. Eleazar

---

will think that it was accidental; see A. Levene, *op. cit.*, p. 188. Hippolytus, *Arabic Frag. to Pent.*, Gen. 8:1 (*GCS.* 1. 2. 90), spells the name "*Ijar*," but Ephraem spells it "*yar*"; see *Comm. in Gen.* 6: 12 (*CSCO.* 72. 48); cf. L. Ginzberg, *Die Haggada bei den Kirchenvätern* (Berlin: S. Calvary and Co., 1900), p. 80.

[1]) *Gen. R.* 33. 7.
[2]) *Gen. R.* 33. 4.
[3]) *Gen. R.* 33. 5; *J. Taan.* 1. 6; *T. B. Sanh.* 108b ascribes the view to Resh Laḳish.
[4]) *Gen. R.* 33. 5; Shadal has the raven go forth from the ark for good; while Rashi has it flying around the ark but not going on its errand because of its anxiety for its mate; see *EBI.* II, 38.
[5]) This is a common assumption: *PRE.* 23; Augustine, *C. Faustum* 12. 20 (*CSEL.* 25. 348); Sulpicius Severus, *Chron.* i. 3 (*CSEL.* I. 5).
[6]) *Gen. R.* 33. 6.
[7]) *Gen. R.* 36. 6.
[8]) *Gen. R.* 33. 6; cf. Philo, *QG.* ii. 42, 47. R. Levi's view is repeated in *T. Ps.-*

(PA. 3), making an analogy with הטריפני, Prov. 30:8, implies that it was for food. The dove preferred bitter food from God to the sweetest food from man. [1]) Another, basing an analogy upon the same expression in Gen. 37:33, insisted that טרף implies that Noah upbraided the dove for not having left the olive to grow into a great tree. [2])

It was just the moment of the exit from the ark which is represented in the mosaic floor panel of the Jerash Synagogue discovered in 1928 by the joint expedition of Yale University and the British School of Archaeology, Jerusalem. The surviving rectangular panel displays the heads of two men over which is written in Greek: "Shem and Japheth." A dove with a twig in its beak sits above them. There are also three long rows of fowl, beasts, cattle, and creeping things. The panel is too fragmentary to support any dogmatic interpretation. The synagogue was built apparently in the first half of the fifth century. It is also reported that the Jewish tombs in Palestine use the artistic representation of Noah. [3])

Noah remained in the ark until commanded to go out. He said, I entered with permission of God, and I will go out by permission. [4]) Another interpretation emphasizes that he would not go out until God swore that there would be no more flood. [5]) The rabbis arrived at the idea that Noah did not immediately begin conjugal relationships by a comparison of Gen. 8:16 with 8:17. R. Judah (T. 4) took this to be a fault for which he was punished in the episode with Ham. R. Nehemiah (T. 4) interpreted it to his credit since God spoke to him again in Gen. 9:8, a thing He only does for a righteous man. [6])

Jon., Gen. 8:11. Theophrastus asserts that the olive puts shoots under water; see A. Dillmann, *Genesis* (Edinburgh: T. and T. Clark, 1897), I, 286. Strabo says that the olive is found in Armenia; see A. Heidel, *The Gilgamesh Epic* (Chicago: U. Press, 1954), p. 252. The medieval commentator Ramban suggested that the trees were not uprooted by the flood (*EBI.* II, 40). This is evidently the view earlier expressed by Sulpicius Severus when he stated that the olive leaf was a sign that the tops of trees could now be seen, *Chron.* 1. 3 (*CSEL.* 1. 5).

[1]) *T. B. Sanh.* 108b; *Erub.* 18b; *Lev. R.* 31. 10; *Cant. R.* 1. 15. § 4; 4. 1. § 2; *PRE.* 23.

[2]) *Gen. R.* 33. 6.

[3]) E. L. Sukenik, *Ancient Synagogues in Palestine and Greece* (Schweich Lectures, 1930; London: Humphrey Milford, 1934), pp. 35-37; E. R. Goodenough, *Jewish Symbols in the Greco-Roman Period* (N. Y.: Pantheon Books, 1953), I, 259-260; 99, n. 271.

[4]) *Gen. R.* 34. 4; *Eccl. R.* 10. 4. § 1.

[5]) *Gen. R.* 34. 6.

[6]) *Gen. R.* 35. 1.

Noah arrived at the obligation to build an altar, Gen. 8:20, by a process of deduction. Surely God had commanded more clean animals than unclean animals to be preserved because he desired sacrifice. [1] *Aboth R. Nathan* § 1, on the other hand, has Noah to offer a bullock whose horns extend beyond his hoofs. R. Eliezer b. Jacob (T. 1) insisted that the offering was made on the great altar in Jerusalem. [2] Noah, when offering his sacrifice, put on the high priestly garments that had been given to Adam following his sin and handed down to the firstborn in each generation. Noah in turn passed them on to Shem who, though not the firstborn, was the progenitor of the patriarchs. [3] Other sources assert that Noah was unfit to serve in the priesthood because of his wound from the lion and that it was really Shem who made the offering. [4]

Despite the sacrifice's not being so pleasing to God as those later to be offered by Israel, [5] the blessing of God (Gen. 9:1) came as a reward for the sacrifice. [6] The righteous, unlike the wicked, give orders to their hearts; hence God spoke to his heart saying He would not again curse the earth. That curse sent forth in the days of Adam would suffice. [7] The fact that God repeated the promise that water would come no more, once in Gen. 9:11 and once in 9:15, makes it a binding oath according to the view of Raba (BA. 4). [8]

The bow in the clouds was in response to Noah's lack of faith which demanded a further sign despite all those which he had enjoyed

---

[1] *Gen. R.* 34. 9; *Ex. R.* 50. 2; cf. Rashi (*EBI.* II, 46); *Bk. of Adam and Eve* iii. 11 has the Word of God to instruct Noah to offer clean animals.

[2] *Gen. R.* 34. 9. Miscellaneous references to the building of the altar are found in *Num. R.* 10. 1 and *Cant. R.* 5. 15. § 1.

[3] *Num. R.* 4. 8.

[4] *Lev. R.* 20. 1; *Eccl. R.* 9. 2. § 1; *Gen. R.* 30. 6; *Tan. Noah* 9 (*EBI.* II, 31). This controversy has left no echoes in pre-rabbinic or Christian literature which discuss the sacrifice: *Jub.* 6:2-3; Philo, *QG.* ii. 50; Josephus, *Ant.* i. 3. 7; Ps.-Philo, *Bib. Ant.* iii. 6-8; Jerome, *Ep.* 123. 11 (*CSEL.* 56. 85); Augustine, *Civ. Dei* 15. 16 (*CSEL.* 40. 2. 95).

[5] *Lev. R.* 7. 4.

[6] *Gen. R.* 34. 12. Later Midrash considers that the blessing was a requirement for reproduction; see *Midrash HaGadhol*; *Midrash Agada*, Gen. 9:1; *PRE.* 23. In a comparable form the idea appears in Hippolytus who sees in the spoken word power which enabled Noah's sons to produce seventy-two children, *Elenchos* x. 31 (*GCS.* 26. 287); cf. Aphraates, *Hom.* 18. 2 (*TU.* III. 3. 291); Salvian the Presbyter, *De gubern. Dei* i. 35 (*CSEL.* 8. 17).

[7] *Gen. R.* 34. 10.

[8] *T. B. Shebuʿoth* 36a. Miscellaneous appeals to the covenant made with Noah that there would be no more flood are to be found in: *Cant. R.* 1. 14. § 3; 2. 15. § 1; *Gen. R.* 44. 5; *Ex. R.* 1. 9, 18; 22. 1; *Lam. R.* 5. 21. § 1; *Mekilta, Amalek* 3. 14; *T. B. Baba Bathra* 74a; *Moʿed Ḳaṭan* 25b.

in the ark. [1]) The rabbis understood that the rainbow as a sign of the covenant was only needful in a wicked generation. Based on the resemblance of קשתי and קישותי they saw in it a faint resemblance of God. [2]) The covenant made, said R. Judan (PA. 4) in R. Aḥa's (PA. 4) name, is not eternal, but is only for the time the earth remains; or it is as long as day and night endure, said R. Huna (BA. 2) in the name of R. Aḥa (PA. 4). [3])

Already in the latter part of Isaiah this oath is appealed to as an example of an unchanging promise of God: "As I swore that the waters of Noah should no more go over the earth." The real problem is, what if men should prove wicked again? In such a case God would destroy only that part of mankind. The promise did not exclude the possibility of local floods. [4]) Some rabbis considered that the promise of God had been abused by the wicked. The Egyptians thought of drowning the Israelites because they knew God would not punish them with a flood for doing it. [5]) But the promise did not prevent there being a flood in one land. In this case, however, the Egyptians fell into the sea as a fitting punishment. [6])

A bit of Jewish and Christian polemic is evident in the treatment of the covenant with Noah. Aphraates sets forth the history of the world in a series of successive covenants. Adam's covenant is replaced by Noah's, then Noah's by Abraham's, and on to the New Covenant. [7]) The rabbis reply with an Haggadah in which Abraham protests to God that a later man might arise and Abraham's covenant have to give way as Noah's had done. God promises that righteous men and protectors of Abraham's covenant will be raised up. [8]) Thus the rabbis both affirm the eternal validity of the law and deny the efficacy of the atoning death of Jesus.

R. Aḥa (PA. 4) interpreted the statements of the blessing, Gen. 8:22, to be hardships: bearing children and burying them, fever and

---

[1]) *Ex. R.* 9. 1.
[2]) *Gen. R.* 35. 3; cf. Bahya (*EBI.* II, 63).
[3]) *Gen. R.* 34. 11.
[4]) Philo, *QG.* ii. 63, 54.
[5]) *Ex. R.* 1. 18.
[6]) *Ex. R.* 1. 9; 22. 1; *Cant. R.* 2. 15. § 1. For other homilies on the passage of Isaiah, see *Gen. R.* 34. 6; *Lev. R.* 10. 1; *Lam. R.* 5. 22. § 1; *T. B. Sanh.* 99a; *Soṭah* 11a; *Shebuʿoth* 36a; *Mekilta, Bahodesh* 5. 55 ff.; *PRE.* 23.
[7]) Aphraates, *Hom.* 11. 11; see M. Simon, *Verus Israel* (Paris: E. de Boccard, 1948), p. 101.
[8]) *Cant. R.* 1. 14. § 3; *Gen. R.* 44. 5; *T. B. Megilla* 31b; *Taʿanith* 27b.

ague, and degradation of birds. ¹) The statement of Gen. 9:1 is considered to be a commandment to procreate in which both men and women are included, but with special obligation upon man. ²) Others said that only the dread and fear of man came upon the animals. Dominion over them which had been given to Adam, Gen. 1:28 f., did not come. ³)

Flesh had not been permitted to Adam, according to R. Jose b. R. Abin (A. 5) in R. Johanan's name (PA. 2), but to the children of Noah it is permitted. ⁴) On the other hand others insisted that from the beginning of the world all that was edible was permitted. ⁵) According to R. Ḥanania b. Gamaliel (T. 3), Gen. 9:4 prohibits blood drawn from a living animal. ⁶)

Heterogeneous breeding and emasculation is forbidden by the words "after their families" of Gen. 8:19. ⁷)

Suicide is prohibited by the decree against shedding blood, ⁸) but the particle *ak* provided that one could take his own life as Saul did (I Sam. 31:4), or be a martyr as were the three Hebrew children. ⁹) The beasts of whose hand blood will be required are the kingdoms of Dan. 2 and 7. R. Levi (PA. 3), by reading אדום instead of אדם,

---

¹) *Gen. R.* 34. 11.

²) *PZ. Noah* (*EBI.* II, 52, § 2); Ps.-Philo, *Bib. Ant.* iii. 11; *Or. Sib.* 1. 315-325 and *Bk. of Adam and Eve* iii. 12 give the force of a commandment to the statement. Rashi (*EBI.* II, 59) attempts to harmonize the idea of command and blessing by attaching significance to the repetition in the text. Verse one is a blessing. Verse seven is a command.

³) *Gen. R.* 34. 12. In Christian discussion of this matter, it is pointed out that the fear was limited to animals. Man is not to be feared by man, nor should he wish that man fear him; see Gregory the Great, *Regulae Pastoralis* ii. 6 (*PL.* 77. 34). Another argued that man proved unworthy of this part of the blessing. His sin undermined his authority and dissipated the fear of the animals. God is not obligated to carry out a promise when man is unworthy; see Chrysostom, *In Matt.*, *hom.* 64. 1 (*PG.* 58. 610). The present attitude of animals towards man is a constant reminder of his ancient sin; see Chrysostom, *De statuis hom.* 8. 1 (*PG.* 49. 97).

⁴) *Gen. R.* 34. 13.

⁵) *Tanhuma, Lev.*, end of *Schemini*, as cited by L. Ginzberg, *Die Haggada bei den Kirchenvätern* (Berlin: S. Calvary and Co., 1900), pp. 83-84; cf. *Gen. R.* 16. 6; Justin M., *Dial.* 20; Clement of A., *Paed.* ii. 1. 16 (*CSEL.* 12. 165); and Aphraates, *Hom.* 15. 4 (*TU.* III. 3. 261).

⁶) *T. B. Sanh.* 56b, 59a; cf. Rashi and Sforno (*EBI.* II, 54); *T. Ps.-Jon.*, Gen. 9:4.

⁷) *Gen. R.* 34. 8.

⁸) *T. B. Baba Kama* 91b.

⁹) *Gen. R.* 34. 13.

understood it to be required of Edom by which he meant Rome. The "man's brother," then, refers to Israel. [1]

Shedding of blood impairs the image of God since man is made in it. R. Ḥanina (c. 225) understood that the ruling of one judge was sufficient to condemn a man for murder from the singular איש, "man," Gen. 9:6. Murder through the hand of an agent is condemned. Slaughter of the embryo and strangling were prohibited by באדם, understood as "within man," taking the ב as locative instead of instrumental. R. Levi (PA. 3) punned on כשיבא אדם to deduce that his blood would be shed when man comes. [2] If not punished, he will be slain at the final judgment. [3]

To shed blood is to impair God's image, said R. Akiba (T. 3). The close proximity of mention of God's image and the command to be fruitful and multiply suggested that to fail to procreate was the equivalent of bloodshed. [4] It was a special blessing from God that He made known that man was in His image. [5]

There seems to be little speculation in the early sources over what became of the ark. One passage assumes that Sennacherib could find a plank from it. [6]

We encounter an altogether different evaluation of Noah when we turn to the vine growing episode. The rabbis rendered Gen. 9:20 "and Noah the husbandman was degraded (ויתחלל) and debased (חולין)." They found no good in Cain, Noah, and Uzziah, all of whom had a passion for agriculture. [7] R. Joḥanan (PA. 2) called attention to the fact that וי occurs fourteen times in the passage, which he proceeded to compare to וי (woe). [8] R. Abba b. Kahana (PA. 3) insisted that he got his vine shoot from those he had taken with him in the ark. [9] R. Ḥiyya b. Ba (T. 5) contended that the planting, drinking, and humiliation all took place in one day. His drunk-

---

[1]) *Gen. R.* 34. 13; cf. Ibn Ezra and Radak who more literally interpret that God will order another animal to kill the animal that kills a man (*EBI.* II. 56).

[2]) *Gen. R.* 34. 14; *T. B. Sanh.* 57b.

[3]) *Gen. R.* 34. 14; cf. *T. Ps.-Jon.,* Gen. 9. 6.

[4]) *Gen. R.* 34. 14.

[5]) *M. Aboth* 3. 15.

[6]) *T. B. Sanh.* 96a.

[7]) *Gen. R.* 22. 3; 36. 3; cf. Rashi and Sforno (*EBI.* II, 67). Philo, *Plant.* 140, took the passage to mean "begin"; cf. *Jer. Targum,* Gen. 9:20.

[8]) *Gen. R.* 36. 4; the view is that of ʿUbar the Galilean in *T. B. Sanh.* 70a.

[9]) *Gen. R.* 36. 3; cf. Rashi (*EBI.* II, 68); Philo, *QG.* ii. 15, exempts seeds under the ground from the destructiveness of the flood. Sforno (*EBI.* II, 30) exempts even those plants above the ground.

enness is roundly denounced by all, even to saying that he caused
exile for himself and his descendants. [1]) "Wine caused a division
between Noah and his sons in the matter of slavery," they say. [2])
A third of the world was cursed. [3]) He should have learned from
Adam whose transgression was also caused by wine. Solomon,
later, admits that he should have learned from Noah. [4]) Drunkenness
is compared to idolatry. [5])

The rabbis tend to interpret "his tent," Gen. 9:21, as his wife's
tent. [6])

Though Shem is frequently mentioned first in the lists of the sons
of Noah, R. Nehemiah (T. 4) in the name of R. Eliezer b. Jose the
Galilean (T. 4) insisted that Japheth was the eldest son. [7]) Noah is
said to have begotten a son when he was 500 years old, and to have
come out of the ark at the age of 600. Two years later Shem begat
Arpachshad (Gen. 11:10), a fact which would demand that he be begotten when Noah was 502 years old. [8]) Gen. 10:21 is rendered,
"Shem . . . the brother of Japheth the elder." [9]) Several reasons are given
for the order of names. The boys are enumerated in the order of wisdom; [10]) Shem was more righteous; was born circumcised; God
is called the God of Shem; Shem was minister in the high priesthood;
and the temple was built in his territory. Bar Ḥuṭa (PA. 4 (?)) taught
that the flood had been postponed 338 years, which is the numerical
value of Shem's name.[11]) The patriarchs were descended from him.[12])

---

[1]) *Gen. R.* 36. 4; cf. *Midrash Mishle* 30. 2 (*EBI.* II, 5, § 16).
[2]) *Lev. R.* 12. 1.
[3]) *Num. R.* 10. 2.
[4]) *T. B. Sanh.* 70a-b.
[5]) *Midrash Hagadol* (*EBI.* II, 69, § 55).
[6]) *Gen. R.* 36. 4. This episode is also made into an affair with his wife by *Bk.
of Adam and Eve* iii. 13 and by Jerome, *Ep.* 22. 8 (*CSEL.* 54. 155), who says,
"self indulgence culminated in lust."
[7]) *Gen. R.* 26. 2. Arguing from the fact that Shem begat Arpachshad at the age
of one hundred, two years after the flood, it was deduced that Noah must have
been 502 at the time of Shem's birth. Therefore the son begotten when Noah
was 500 must have been Japheth; see *T. B. Sanh.* 69b; *Sefer Hayashar*, Noah
(*EBI.* II, 18); RaMBaN (*EBI.* II, 6). Philo, *QG.* ii. 79, knew the tradition that
Japheth was the oldest but personally thought it made little difference.
[8]) *T. B. Sanh.* 69b; *Gen. R.* 37. 7.
[9]) *Num. R.* 4. 8. The early Syrian church fathers agree that Japheth is the eldest,
see A. Levene, *op. cit.*, p. 84, but say that Shem was made eldest because of his
familiarity with God and because Christ was destined to arise from him.
[10]) *T. B. Sanh.* 69b.
[11]) *Gen. R.* 26. 3.
[12]) *Num. R.* 4. 8; cf. Rashi (*EBI.* I, 180).

Ham is called the youngest son in the sense of being the worthless son. [1])

The crime of Ham is variously interpreted. Some go no further than his ridiculing his father's attempt at begetting a fourth son. [2]) But the general trend is toward either sexual abuse, for which Rab (BA. 1) contends, or toward emasculation of his father, which was the position of Samuel (BA. 2-3). [3]) This is probably implied in the phrase "a disqualifying blemish" which Noah is said to receive. [4]) The rabbis decide that both indignities were perpetrated. [5]) This Haggadah is not in agreement with that which had the lion to attack Noah. [6]) It is to be remembered that some rabbis believed that Ham had not been continent in the ark. [7])

Shem and Japheth, in contrast, even covered their faces with their hands and walked backward to cover their father, giving him due respect.

R. Judan (PA. 4) suggested that they used their prayer cloaks, while R. Huna (BA. 2) thought it was their breeches that made the covering. [8])

The curse on Canaan for Ham's sin caused considerable perplexity. Ham, having previously (Gen. 9:1) been blessed, could not now be cursed, said R. Judah (T. 4). [9]) R. Nehemiah (T. 4) argued that it was Canaan who had first seen Noah's shame and reported it to the others.[10]) R. Huna (BA. 2) in R. Joseph's name, seeing an example

[1]) *Gen. R.* 36. 7; cf. *T. Ps.-Jon.*, Gen. 9:24; Rashi (*EBI.* II, 71). This Haggadah was known to the Syrian Fathers who say, "Ham was called because of his sin, small" (A. Levene, *op. cit.*, p. 84).

[2]) *Gen. R.* 36. 5. Ridicule without explaining a basis is found in the phrases "making sport," *PRE.* 23; and "derisively jeering," Radak (*EBI.* II, 70).

[3]) *T. B. Sanh.* 70a; *Num. R.* 10. 2; *Gen. R.* 36. 3. Cf. expressions which insist that Noah had only three sons: "to teach that he had no other son," *Midrash Hagadol*, Noah (*EBI.* II, 6, § 21); and "only these three constituted his generations," Ramban and Tur (*EBI.* II, 6). Cf. also Theophilus, *Ad Autol.* iii. 18-19 (*ANF.* II, 116-117) where Noah is called Eunuchos.

[4]) *Num. R.* 10. 2.

[5]) *T. B. Sanh.* 70a; *Gen. R.* 36. 3, 7; cf. *PRE.* 23 and Rashi where deed is Canaan's.

[6]) *Gen. R.* 30. 6; *Lev. R.* 20. 1.

[7]) *T. B. Sanh.* 108b; *Gen. R.* 36. 7.

[8]) *Gen. R.* 36. 6.

[9]) *Gen. R.* 36. 7. Justin knew this Haggadah; see *supra*, p. 114.

[10]) *Gen. R.* 36. 7; cf. 36. 2. Others who would have Canaan to be the culprit include Philo, *LA.* ii. 62; *PRE.* 23; Rashi (*EBI.* II, 69); Theodoretus, see L. Ginzberg, *Die Haggada bei den Kirchenvätern* (Berlin: S. Calvary and Co., 1900), p. 86; Ambrose, *Ep.* 37. 6 (*PL.* 16. 1131); Ephraem Syrus, *Comm. in Gen.* 7: 3 (*CSCO.* 72. 51-52); see D. Gerson, *Die commentarien des Ephraem Syrus im Ver-*

of measure for measure punishment said, "Since you have prevented me from having a fourth son, I will curse your fourth son." [1]) Another teacher explains that Noah really meant to curse Ham. [2])

What the curse on Canaan involved was explained by R. Huna (PA. 3-4) in R. Joseph's (BA. 3) name, as referring to the fact that his seed would be ugly and dark-skinned. R. Hiyya (B-P. 3) and R. Levi (c. 200) take this consequence to have come through the failure of Ham to be continent in the ark. [3]) God's curse did not deprive him of his livelihood, said R. Jose (c. 150). [4]) A general curse on the slave is premised upon this verse. [5])

That greatness was conferred upon Shem is implied in the phrase, "Blessed be the Lord, the God of Shem," for ordinarily God's name is not spoken in connection with an individual until after that individual dies. [6]) *Midrash Agada* interprets that in the future Israel was to arise from Shem and was to receive the Law and declare the unity of God. [7])

Whether the "he" who dwells in the tents of Shem of Gen. 9:27 referred to God or to Japheth was disputed. R. Judah (T. 4), following the opinion of R. Samuel b. Gamaliel (T. 4), and Bar Kappara (T. 5), taking it to be Japheth, thought it meant that Greek could be used in the synagogue. [8]) R. Judan proved by it that a translation could be used. [9]) R. Simeon b. Lakish and *T. Ps. -Jonathan*, as we have earlier seen, insisted that it pointed to the admission of proselytes to the houses of study.[10]) Others took the antecedent of "he" to be the *Shekinah* which would be in the tents of Shem. R. Eleazar (PA-BA. 3)

---

hältniss zur jüdischen Exegese (Breslau: Schlechter'schen Buchhandlung, 1868), p. 27.

[1]) *Gen. R.* 36. 7; cf. *T. Ps.-Jon.*, Gen. 9: 24-25.

[2]) *Num. R.* 10. 2; miscellaneous references to the curse are to be found in *T. B. Horayoth* 13a; *Sanh.* 91a; *Mekilta, Pisha* 12. 46; and *Lev. R.* 12. 1.

[3]) *Gen. R.* 36. 7; *T. B. Sanh.* 108b; *J. Ta'an.* 1. 6 (*EBI.* II, 45, § 40); *Midrash Hagadol*, Gen. 9:27. *PRE.* 23 does not identify these people with the negro. Their habitation is the "coast of the sea" which could either be the Egyptian or Palestinian coast.

[4]) *T. B. Yoma* 75a.

[5]) *T. B. Horoyoth* 13a.

[6]) *Midrash Hagadol*, Noah (*EBI.* II, 74).

[7]) *Midrash Agada*, Gen. 9 (*EBI.* II, 74).

[8]) *Gen. R.* 36. 8; *Deut. R.* 1. 1; cf. *T. B. Megilla* 9b where R. Johanan asks why R. Simeon took this position.

[9]) *Gen. R.* 36. 8.

[10]) *Gen. R.* 36. 12 ("Ktav" edition); *T. Ps.-Jon.*, Gen. 9:27. This Haggadah was known to Jerome; see L. Ginzberg, *Die Haggada bei den Kirchenvätern* (Berlin: S. Calvary and Co., 1900), pp. 87-88.

understood by the "tents" the schools of study of law. [1]) Resh
Lakish (PA. 2) used the passage to prove that the *Shekina* was not
in the second temple, since it had been built by the authority of the
Persians, for although God enlarged Japheth, the Divine Presence
rests only in the tents of Shem. [2])

Following the flood, the world was reconstructed from one man [3])
and became seventy nations. [4]) Noah had been appointed, according
to R. Berekiah (PA. 5), a prototype of those saved from calamity. [5])

This chapter has shown that the figure of Noah in rabbinic literature
is a creation of a multitude of thinkers spread out over more centuries
than the writers treated in any other section of this study. The
haggadic method of interpretation represents a departure from the
simple meaning of the text, but in quite a different way from the
allegory of Philo or the typology of the later church fathers. In
haggadic interpretation a verse has its simple meaning (*peshaṭ*) which
it never loses, [6]) but this does not hinder its being expounded in
other senses, for a biblical verse is subject to many interpretations. [7])
These derived meanings are the *derash*. The biblical verse serves as
the stimulus for the *derash*. Once the stimulus is present, the *derash*
need have no other connection with the *peshaṭ*.

The rabbis considered that the words of Torah may be poor (or
deficient) in one place, but rich in another; hence biblical details
far removed from an episode may describe that episode. [8]) The
rabbis were aware that their *derash* was a development of the actual
wording of Scripture, but they do not in every instance distinguish
between the simple meaning and the haggadic interpretation. [9])

---

[1]) *T. B. Makkoth* 23b.
[2]) *T. B. Yoma* 9b-10a.
[3]) *Lev. R.* 5. 1.
[4]) *Num. R.* 14. 12.
[5]) *Est. R.*, Proem 10.
[6]) *T. B. Shabbath* 63a; *Yeb.* 11b; 24a.
[7]) *T. B. Sanh.* 34a.
[8]) *J. Rosh Hashana* 58d.
[9]) I am indebted for elements in this summary to M. Kadushin, *The Rabbinic
Mind* (N. Y.: Jewish Theological Seminary, 1952), pp. 98-130.

CHAPTER SEVEN

THE FLOOD AND LATER
CHRISTIAN SPIRITUAL EXEGESIS

Though there are many parallels in the interpretations of the flood between the rabbis and the church fathers, it is in the spiritual interpretation that they went their separate ways. We have earlier seen how typology of the flood had its rise in the O.T. and is developed further in the N.T., especially in the Epistle to the Hebrews and in I Peter. From these beginnings, its flowering in Christian exegesis is to be expected. Furthermore, its limited use in connection with flood materials in second century writers is only a prelude to its full-blown exploitation by later writers. Not only is the christological and eschatological typology continued, but an ecclesiastical and soteriological typology develops.[1]

Though no uniformity of opinion or terminology concerning the senses is to be found, later Christian exegesis espouses the multiple sense of Scripture. Clement of Alexandria [2] and Origen [3] found Scripture to have three senses, while Eucherius [4] found four.[5] One immediately discovers in dealing with the flood that the line between typology and the other spiritual senses is not always clear.

All will agree that the typological interpretation was pursued to absurdity. Every episode and detail of the O.T. contained some hidden allusion to gospel fact. The typologist was working in a very subjective realm in which he was only limited by his ingenuity. The same fact might typify to him a series of things. Having given one interpretation, there was no reason why he should not immediately turn around and give an alternate. The typologist did not realize that he was reading his own ideas into Scripture, but felt rather that God had some such meaning in mind in having the episode recorded. To fail to acknowledge this was to be like Ham who laughed at his father's

---

[1] The writer hereby acknowledges a heavy indebtedness in this section to J. Daniélou, *Sacramentum Futuri* (Paris: Beauchesne et ses Fils, 1950), pp. 55-94.

[2] Clement of A., *Strom.* i. 28 (*GCS*. 15. 110).

[3] Origen, *De Princ.* iv. 2. 4-6 (*GCS*. 22. 312-318).

[4] Eucherius, *Liber Formularum spiritualis intelligentiae*, praef. (*PL*. 50. 727 f.).

[5] See R. P. C. Hanson, *Allegory and Event* (London: SCM. Press. 1959), pp. 1-161.

shame.[1]) Augustine argued that no man in his senses could deny that there is some meaning in addition to the naked facts.[2])

What is certain to all men of faith is, first that these things were not done without some prefiguring of what was to come, and second, that they are to be referred only to Christ and his church which is the City of God, concerning which from the beginning there has been no lack of prophecy which we now see completely fulfilled. [3])

It is in keeping with such traditions that Chrysostom asserts: "The story of the deluge was a sacrament (μυστήριον) and its details a figure (τύπος) of things to come." [4])

It will be observed that typology presupposes the actual literal event of Scripture. It then attempts to interpret the purpose of that event. There is no single system of exegesis of the flood that can be neatly summarized. Augustine in his reply to Faustus worked out more details than are now extant in other sources, but he readily admitted that others might take the symbols in different ways. He did not feel that this was undesirable. "All explanations need not be the same," he said. He did insist, however, that none be proposed that were incompatible with the Catholic faith.[5])

We shall now consider one by one the important items in the spiritual exegesis of the flood.

A. ידון

The church fathers used the LXX and followed it in the reading of καταμένειν for ידין,[6]) but instead of referring the verse to information concerning the world to come as the rabbis did, they read it in the light of Paul's contrast between the flesh and spirit. God's spirit dwells in the righteous man. Since the flood generation was wicked, it is obvious that God's spirit could not be in them. Origen quoted the verse and commented: "It is clearly shown that the Spirit of God is taken away from all who are unworthy." [7]) The early Syrian fathers understood God to be declaring that he would remove His providence which enabled them to live in the world. After equating

---

[1]) Asiatic elder cited by Irenaeus, *Adv. haer.* iv. 31.1.
[2]) Augustine, *Civ. Dei* 15. 27 (*CSEL.* 40. 2. 119).
[3]) Augustine, *Civ. Dei* 16. 2 (*CSEL.* 40. 2. 127; Eng. tr. *F. of Ch.* 14, 489).
[4]) J. Chrysostom, *De Laz. concio* 6 (*PG.* 48. 1037).
[5]) Augustine, *Civ. Dei* 15. 26 (*CSEL.* 40. 2. 118).
[6]) Ps.-Clement, *First Ep. Concerning Virginity* 8.
[7]) Origen, *De Princ.* i. 3. 7 (*GCS.* 22. 58); *C. Celsum* vii. 38 (*GCS.* 3. 188).

providence and spirit, seven other possible meanings for spirit are suggested: desire, soul, angels, devils, the spirit itself, grace, and air.[1])

Ambrose follows the same line laid down by Origen: "Wherefore God shows that the grace of the spirit is turned away by carnal impurity and the pollution of grave sin." [2]) This interpretation is given without essential change by Tertullian, Chrysostom, Jerome, and Augustine.[3])

Tertullian, in arguing with opponents who disparaged the flesh, made the point that those who use the passage from Genesis to preclude the resurrection of the flesh should also consider Joel's promise of an outpouring of the Spirit. The resurrection is not precluded by God's threat.[4])

B. NOAH

Noah for the later church is chiefly a type of Christ. We have earlier traced the line of thought originating with Philo where Noah is τέλος of one race and ἀρχή of another. This concept continues in the later church to be one of the main links of typology, though the specific details are not worked out in every case. Tertullian speaks of the beginning, counted in Adam and recounted in Noah, from which point he then moves on to Christ, whom he sees as τέλος. [5]) In the third century liturgy God is invoked as He who "rescued Noah from the flood (making an end and a beginning)."[6]) The *Recognitions of Clement* know Noah as the "colonizer of the world" and as one "preserved for the continuance of the race." [7]) The *Homilies* know him as "the second beginning of life." [8]) He is known to Origen as the founder of the new universe [9]) and the progenitor of those born after

---

[1]) A. Levene, *The Early Syrian Fathers on Genesis* (London: Taylor's Foreign Press, 1951), pp. 81, 178-179.

[2]) Ambrose, *De myst.* 10 (*CSEL.* 73. 92).

[3]) Tertullian, *De monog.* 1. 6 (*CSEL.* 76. 45); Chrysostom, *In Ep. I Tim.* c. 5, hom. 13. 4 (*PG.* 62. 569); *In Ep. ad Rom.* hom. 13. 7 (*PG.* 60. 517); Jerome, *Adv. Jovinianum* i. 22 (*PL.* 23. 251); *Contra Ioannem Hierosol.* 28 (*PL.* 23. 397); *Ep.* 79. 9 (*CSEL.* 55. 98); Augustine, *Civ. Dei* 15. 23 (*CSEL.* 40. 2. 112); *De Trinitate* 13. 12. 16 (*PL.* 42. 1026).

[4]) Tertullian, *De res. carn.* 10 (*CSEL.* 47. 38); cf. the rabbinic argument over the resurrection, *supra*, pp. 129-130.

[5]) Tertullian, *De monog.* 5. 5 (*CSEL.* 76. 52).

[6]) Text cited in R. P. C. Hanson, *op. cit.*, p. 18.

[7]) Ps.-Clem., *Recog.* i. 29; iv. 12 (*PG.* 1. 1224, 1320).

[8]) Ps.-Clem., *Hom.* viii. 17 (*GCS.* 42. 128).

[9]) Origen, *Hom. in Ez.* iv. 8 (*GCS.* 33. 369).

the deluge.[1]) He is the "end of the foregoing generations and the beginning of those that were to come." [2]) Ambrose knew him as the "survivor of past generations and the author of one to come." [3]) He sealed up that which was past and began that which was.[4]) The seeds of the new world were in the ark.[5]) Noah was the father of all who came after,[6]) a kind of second root of the human race.[7]) Just how vigorous this τέλος motif was in the church is realized when one remembers that Augustine takes all the Psalms in which τέλος occurs in the title as referring to Christ.[8])

The concept of δίκαιος, which also is to be traced back to Philo, is likewise important. It is not surprising that the church fathers would magnify the righteousness of Noah in view of their tendency to see in him a type of Christ. We have seen how Justin asserted that Noah, though uncircumcised, was well pleasing to God.[9]) Ambrose saw in him a wise, just, brave, and temperate man who used moderation.[10]) Praise of him is lavish on the part of all. Africanus spoke of his pleasing God "on account of his righteousness."[11]) Hippolytus said, "He was a most religious and Godloving man."[12]) Lactantius likewise called him "a most worthy example of righteousness."[13]) Eusebius argued that the entire flood episode demonstrated his righteousness.[14]) He was more pleasing to God than the entire ten generations before him.[15])

It is only Origen and Jerome who repeat the Midrash already known to Philo that Noah was righteous only in his generation.[16]) Augustine,

---

[1]) Origen, *C. Celsum* iv. 41 (*GCS*. 2. 315).
[2]) *Const. Apost.* viii. 12. 22 (Funk, p. 502).
[3]) Ambrose, *De offic.* i. 121 (*PL*. 16. 63).
[4]) Ephraem Syrus, *Adv. Scrut. Rhythms* 49. 1.
[5]) Gregory of Nazianzus, *Oratio* 28. 18; 43. 70 (*PG*. 36. 49 A; 592 B).
[6]) Aphraates, *Hom.* 13. 4; 18. 2 (*TU*. III. 3. 201, 291); Chrysostom, *In Ep. I Cor. hom.* 34. 4 (*PG*. 61. 291).
[7]) Jerome, *Adv. Jovin.* i. 17 (*PL*. 23. 247).
[8]) G. H. Gilbert, *Interp. of the Bible* (N. Y.: Macmillan Co., 1908), p. 130.
[9]) Justin M., *Dial.* 92. 2; see A. H. Goldfahn, "Justinus Martyr und die Agada," *Monatschrift für Geschichte und Wissenschaft des Judentums*, XXII (1873), 262.
[10]) Ambrose, *De offic.* i. 121 (*PL*. 16. 63-64).
[11]) Julius Africanus, *Chron.* 4 (*PL*. 10. 68).
[12]) Hippolytus, *Elenchos* x. 30 (*GCS*. 26. 268).
[13]) Lactantius, *Div. inst.* ii. 13 (*CSEL*. 19. 160).
[14]) Eusebius, *Praep. Evang.* vii. 8. 16 (*GCS*. 43. 1. 372).
[15]) Aphraates, *Hom.* 18. 3 (*TU*. III. 3. 292).
[16]) Origen, *Num. Hom.* 9. 1 (*GCS*. 30. 56); Jerome, *Quaest. Heb. in Gen.* 6:9 (*PL*. 23. 997); cf. L. Ginzberg, *Die Haggada bei den Kirchenvätern* (Berlin: S.

on the other hand, explained that "in his generation" meant that he was as perfect as any could be in this life, though not to be compared with the perfection of the angels of God.[1]) He wanted it understood that he was far from denying Noah's righteousness despite the fact that Noah lived prior to the time of Sarah who in his system prefigured the church.[2]) The relevance of Noah as δίκαιος to typology had been made plain much earlier by Origen who spoke of "our Noah who is alone truly just and perfect, our Lord Jesus Christ." [3])

The third concept borrowed from Philo is that of ἀνάπαυσις. It is this concept which makes even more clear the connection seen by Christians between Noah and Christ, for the crucial point is derived from Lamech's prediction of ἀνάπαυσις at the birth of Noah (Gen. 5:29). It is here that Origen supplies us with a key insight into the rationale of typology which is lacking in Justin and Irenaeus. Though they knew the concept, Origen explains that Noah did not fulfill the requirements of ἀνάπαυσις since his generation was destroyed by the flood. It was only the spiritual Noah who gives rest as the invitation of the Gospel, "Come ... I will give you rest" (Mt. 11:28-29), implies.[4]) Origen makes clear that an O.T. prophecy which does not seem to find its literal application to the O.T. character is to be considered as realized in the N.T. when some circumstance can be found to connect it to the N.T. figure. In this case ἀνάπαυσις used in each location furnishes that connection. This line of thought is further clearly expounded by Hilary: "It is the Christ who brings rest to souls." [5]) Playing upon the same word, Asterius points to the fact that Christ put an end (ἔπαυσεν) to the flood of impurity.[6]) While for both Justin and Irenaeus the rest is that of the millennium,[7]) Gregory of Elvira points to the "rest" of saints in the kingdom of the age to come.[8])

The idea of Christ as the antitype of Noah can be traced in the works of Cyril of Jerusalem who speaks of the "true Noah" [9]) and

---

Calvary and Co., 1900), p. 78; M. Rahmer, *Die hebräischen Traditionen in den Werken des Hieronymus* (Breslau: Schletter'schen Buchhandlung, 1861), pp. 23-24.

[1]) Augustine, *Civ. Dei* 15. 26 (*CSEL*. 40. 2. 116).
[2]) Augustine, *Cont. duas ep. Pelag.* iii. 8 (*CSEL*. 60. 494).
[3]) Origen, *Hom. in Gen.* ii. 3 (*GCS*. 29. 30).
[4]) Origen, *Hom. in Gen.* ii. 3, 5 (*GCS*. 29. 31, 34).
[5]) Hilary, *Tract. myst.* i. 12, 13 (*SC*. 19. 96-100).
[6]) Asterius, *On Ps. vi.* hom. xx (*PG*. 40. 448 C).
[7]) Justin M., *Dial.* 138. 2-3; 81. 3; cf. Iren., *Adv. haer.* v. 30. 4.
[8]) Gregory of Elvira, *De Arca Noe* in *Rev. Ben.*, 26 (1909), 6.
[9]) Cyril of Jerusalem, *Catech.* 17. 10 (*PG*. 33. 981 A).

in the system of Ephraem Syrus who speaks of how Noah, affording rest in the stead of him who was afar off, longed to see the one of whom he was the type.[1]) It is further used by Cyril of Alexandria [2]) and by Augustine.[3])

On the other hand, Augustine, in another place, completely departs from this christological typology and takes an entirely different tack when he has Noah, Daniel, and Job to prefigure three classes of men to be delivered from impending wrath. In this case Noah represents the righteous leaders of the nations by reason of his government of the ark.[4])

C. THE ARK

There are forty-one paintings in the catacombs and thirty-three representations on sarcophaguses of Noah and his ark.[5]) The earliest of these representations showed the ark as a box with a lid, fitting well the wording of the *Sibylline Oracles* in which "God fitted the key to the lid" and Noah "lifts the lid that was joined with skillful stays." [6]) The oldest picture is that of the catacomb of Domitilla in which, though it is badly deteriorated, one can still make out the dove flying toward the cover of the ark.[7]) The catacomb of Peter and Marcellinus shows Noah in a box with no lid, his arms outspread and the dove bringing back the olive branch.[8]) A sarcophagus of the third century, which chiefly treats the story of Jonah, has Noah at one side floating in his box.[9]) There is also a coin from Apamea in Phrygia, thought to show Jewish influence, about the middle of the third century which shows Noah and his wife with their heads emerging from the ark, pushing back the lid. A dove sits on the lid and another flies in with an olive leaf in its claws. The box floats in the water. Noah in Greek spelling is written across the box.[10]) Despite the popularity of Noah as a theme in art, there is no effort to present the ark in true

---

[1]) Ephraem Syrus, *Hymns on the Nativity* 1 (*NPNF.* ser. ii. 13. 225).
[2]) Cyril of Alexandria, *Glaphyra* ii. 5 (*PG.* 69. 65 B-C).
[3]) Augustine, *In Ioannis Evang.* Tr. 9. 11 (*PL.* 35. 1464).
[4]) Augustine, *De remiss. pecat.* ii. 10. 12 (*CSEL.* 60. 83).
[5]) J. Fink, *Noe der Gerechte in der Früchristlichen Kunst* (Munster/Köln: Böhlau-Verlag, 1955), pp. 39, 44-45.
[6]) *Or. Sib.* i. 252, 275-276.
[7]) H. Leclercq, "Arche," *Dictionnarie d'Archéologie Chrétienne* I, 2, col. 2709 ff.
[8]) J. Finegan, *Light from the Ancient Past* (Princeton: U. Press, 1946), fig. 168.
[9]) *Ibid.*, fig. 173, pp. 394-395.
[10]) E. R. Goodenough, *Jewish Symbols in the Greco-Roman Period* (N. Y.: Pantheon Books, 1953), II, 119-120.

perspective in the historical sense in the paintings. Goodenough argues that theological motivation in which the ark has been allegorized as a sarcophagus has influenced the choice of the box;[1]) however, the texts give little specific support to this theory. It is not until toward the end of the fourth century that an attempt is made to show the ark from the side, depicted as a boat.[2])

A clear distinction is to be made between illustrative use of the O.T. and typology strictly speaking. In an illustrative way Nisibis, in Ephraem's hymn, while in peril of siege compares herself to the ark in the flood.[3])

Whereas the ark may to Asterius typify the sepulchre of Christ,[4]) and whereas in Justin the wood of the ark is the cross,[5]) in later typology the ark and every detail of its construction frequently signifies something in the church.[6]) Here christological typology has given place to ecclesiastical typology. Though Jerome claims that Peter expounds this type,[7]) it is actually a post-biblical development that makes its appearance in the second century. God saves the race of Adam by the type of the ark.[8]) Closely related is the popular figure of speech in which the church is spoken of as a ship.[9]) That there was no animal to be the type of the idolater in the ark could be used by Tertullian to argue that none should be in the church.[10]) For Cyprian, the fact that there was only one ark demonstrated that there was only one church,[11]) for the church is the ark of safety. All outside will perish.

---

[1]) *Ibid.*, fig. 173, pp. 394-395.
[2]) H. Leclercq, *op. cit.*, col. 2712-2713.
[3]) Ephraem Syrus, *Nisibene Hymn* 1 (*NPNF*. ser. ii. 13. 167-168).
[4]) Asterius, *On Ps.* 6, hom. xx (*PG*. 40. 488 C).
[5]) Justin M., *Dial.* 138.
[6]) Tertullian, *De baptismo* 8 (*CSEL*. 20. 207-208); Origen, *Hom. in Gen.* ii. 5 (*GCS*. 29. 34); Ephraem Syrus, *Adv. Scrut. Rhythms* 49. 1-3; J. Chrysostom, *De Laz. concio* 6 (*PG*. 48. 1037-1038); Gregory of Elvira, *De Arca Noe* in *Rev. Ben.*, 26 (1909), 6; Ambrose, *Ex. in Luke* ii. 92; iii. 48 (*CSEL*. 32. 4. 95; 135-136); Jerome, *Ep.* 123. 11 (*CSEL*. 56. 84-85); *Dial. adv. Luciferianos* 22 (*PL*. 23. 185); *Adv. Jovin.* i. 17 (*PL*. 23. 247); Augustine, *Civ. Dei* 15. 27 (*CSEL*. 40. 2. 122); *In Ps.* 128. 2 (*PL*. 37. 1689); *C. Faustum* 33. 13 (*CSEL*. 25. 772); Didymus, *De Trin.* 2 (*PG*. 39. 696 A-B).
[7]) Jerome, *Ep.* 123. 11 (*CSEL*. 56. 84-85); *Adv. Jovin.* i. 17 (*PL*. 23. 247); *Dial. adv. Luciferianos* 22 (*PL*. 23. 185).
[8]) "Arcae typum," Iren., *Adv. haer.* iv. 36. 4. For the textual problem, see W. W. Harvey, *Sancti Irenaei* II, 279.
[9]) Hippolytus, *De antichr.* 59 (*GCS*. 1. 2. 39).
[10]) Tertullian, *De idol.* 24 (*CSEL*. 20. 58).
[11]) Cyprian, *Ep.* 74. 11 (*CSEL*. 3. 2. 808); cf. Ps.-Cyprian, *Ad Novatianum* 2, 5 (*CSEL*. 3. 3. 54-55; 56).

If one could have been saved out of the ark of Noah, he could be saved out of the church.[1]) On the basis that male and female were separated in the ark, Cyril of Jerusalem could argue that men and women should not sit together in the church.[2]) Hilary insisted that it taught continence when in the catecumenate of the church.[3]) Jerome could argue that there should be monogamy since Noah's sons had in the ark only one wife each.[4]) For him, it was the Roman Church in particular that was the ark of safety: "This is the ark of Noah, and he who is not in it shall perish when the flood prevails." [5]) Augustine repeatedly alludes to this typology, making it even a part of his first catechetical training.[6])

Many trends are observable in Christian exegesis. One stream continues the spirit and form of Philo's allegorical exegesis in which the dimensions of the ark are made to be the same proportions as the ideal human figure or made to signify matters of the soul.[7]) Still another seeks cosmological secrets, as when the three stories of the ark represent sky, earth, and the abyss.[8])

Also following Philo [9]) is the effort, which seems to have been popular in the school of Alexandria, of expounding the symbolism of the measures of the ark. Clement of Alexandria finds three hundred to be sixfold when considered as six times fifty, and to be tenfold when thought of as ten times thirty. The three hundred is the symbol of the Lord's cross, likely because of the resemblance between the shape of the Greek letter *tau*, which is the gematrical value of three hundred, and that of the cross.[10]) Fifty is the symbol of hope and of the remission given at Pentecost; and the thirty represents the thirty years of the

---

[1]) Cyprian, *De Unit. Eccl.* 6 (*CSEL.* 3. 1. 214); cf. Firmilian in the ep. preserved by Cyprian, *Ep.* 75. 15 (*CSEL.* 3. 2. 820).

[2]) Cyril of Jerusalem, *Procatechesis* 14 (*PG.* 33. 355 A).

[3]) Hilary, *Tract. myst.* i. 13 (*SC.* 19. 102).

[4]) Jerome, *Ep.* 123. 11 (*CSEL.* 56. 85).

[5]) Jerome, *Ep.* 15. 2 (*CSEL.* 54. 63-64); cf. also Gregory of Elvira, *De Arca Noe* in *Rev. Ben.*, 26 (1909), 6-7.

[6]) Augustine, *Civ. Dei* 15. 26 (*CSEL.* 40. 2. 118); 18. 38 (*CSEL.* 40. 2. 328); *In Ps.* 128. 2 (*PG.* 37. 1689); *De catech.* 27. 53 (*PL.* 40. 343); *In Ioannis Evang.* Tr. 6. 3 (*PL.* 35. 1426).

[7]) Philo, *QG.* ii. 5; Origen, *Hom. in Gen.* ii. 6 (*GCS.* 29. 36-39); Ambrose, *De Noe* vi. 13-14 (*CSEL.* 32. 422-423); *De offic.* i. 77-78 (*PL.* 16. 50); *Hexaemeron* vi. 9. 72 (*CSEL.* 32. 258-259); Augustine, *Civ. Dei* 15. 26 (*CSEL.* 40. 2. 116-117); *C. Faustum* 12. 14 (*CSEL.* 25. 344).

[8]) Origen, *Hom. in Gen.* ii. 5 (*GCS.* 29. 35-36).

[9]) Philo, *QG.* ii. 5.

[10]) See *Ep. Barn.* 9. 8; Tertullian, *Adv. Marc.* iii. 22 (*CSEL.* 47. 416).

Lord's life. Clement also knows some who think the thirty should be twelve, which he equates with the twelve apostles.[1] The mystery of the "measures" maintains itself in the church until the time of Augustine.[2] Origen, by connecting the height of the ark with Paul's "breadth, length, depth and height" (Eph. 3:18), arrives at the fact that God announces through Moses "great mysteries." [3] Moses shows the resurrection of those who are brought back by Christ from death. Origen proceeds to show that three hundred is a combination of one hundred and of three. One hundred indicates fullness, representing the totality of spiritual creation as is indicated in the Lord's parable of one hundred sheep. Because the totality descends from the Father, Son, and Holy Spirit and receives length of life—immortality—it is multiplied by three. Fifty is dedicated to redemption and remission of sins. Thirty has the same sacrament as three hundred. Finally, the one cubit at the top of the ark implies one God, one Saviour, one faith, and one baptism.[4] Augustine declares that the fifty cubits represent the fifty days from the resurrection of Jesus to Pentecost; the thirty cubits are the thirty years of Jesus' life; and the three hundred cubits when broken down into six units of fifty cubits represent the six periods of the world.[5] Each of these scholars, like the earlier Gnostics,[6] has developed the "measures" in keeping with his own thought and presuppositions.

Still another trend expounded details in an ecclesiastical typology. "They are all symbols of something in the church." [7] The thirty cubits' height, narrowing to one cubit, represents the different grades in the church, ending in deacons, presbyters, and bishops. The many rooms prefigure the many mansions in heaven.[8] The three stories in the ark prefigure various stages of spiritual development represented in the church; [9] or the three virtues praised by Paul:

---

[1] Clement of A., *Strom.* vi. 11. 86 (*GCS.* 15. 474-475).

[2] J. Daniélou, *Sacramentum Futuri*, p. 86, includes Hippolytus among the writers who thus speculate, but Hippolytus' allegory is on the ark of the covenant and not on Noah's ark; see Hippolytus, *Comm. in Daniel* 4. 24 (*GCS.* 1. 1. 244).

[3] Application of this symbolism to the ark is also to be found in Cyril of Alexandria, *Glaphyra* ii. 5 (*PG.* 69. 65 C), cited in J. Daniélou, *Sacramentum Futuri*, p. 91.

[4] Origen, *Hom. in Gen.* ii. 5 (*GCS.* 29. 35).

[5] Augustine, *C. Faustum* 12. 14 (*CSEL.* 25. 344).

[6] See Irenaeus, *Adv. haer.* i. 18. 4.

[7] Augustine, *Civ. Dei* 15. 26 (*CSEL.* 40. 2. 117).

[8] Origen, *Hom. in Gen.* ii. 5 (*GCS.* 29. 36); Jerome, *Dial. adv. Luciferianos* 22 (*PL.* 23. 185); cf. *Adv. Jovin.* 1. 17 (*PL.* 23. 247).

[9] Origen, *Hom. in Gen.* ii. 3 (*GCS.* 29. 31).

faith, hope, and charity; or they might represent chaste marriage, chaste widowhood, and on the higher level, virginal purity; or again they might represent the repeopling of the earth from the three sons of Noah.[1])

The door in the side of the ark symbolizes the wound in the side of the crucified one through which the blood issued, by means of which the believers enter the church.[2]) Elsewhere Augustine makes the door merely the sacraments by which one enters the church.[3])

The "squared beams"[4]) of the ark represent the doctors, teachers, and zealous persons who admonish persons in the church and safeguard them from heretics and gentiles without.[5]) They may represent the stability of the holy life showing that in whatever way the Christian may fall, he stands erect;[6]) or again they may represent the city of the Apocalypse which is foursquare[7]) or the Christian prepared unto every good work.[8])

The pitch of the ark signifies that one should be pure in heart as well as clean externally.[9]) Or under other conditions it may signify the compact union of the forbearance of love which keeps the brotherly connection from being broken.[10])

The inclusion of all types of animals in the ark signifies the opportunity for all nations and races in the church[11]) or symbolizes the

---

[1]) Augustine, *Civ. Dei* 15. 26 (*CSEL*. 40. 2. 118).

[2]) *Ibid.*, 15. 26 (*CSEL*. 40. 2. 117); *In Ioannis Evang.* Tr. 120. 2 (*PL*. 35. 1953).

[3]) Augustine, *C. Faustum* 12. 16 (*CSEL*. 25. 345-346).

[4]) Those who use the LXX, from Philo on, of necessity base their interpretations and allegories on its reading and do not reflect that they are aware of its failure to render correctly the Hebrew; see Philo, *QG*. ii. 2; Victorinus, *Comm. in Apoc.* 21. 3 (*CSEL*. 49. 149); Origen, *Hom. in Gen.* ii. 1 (*GCS*. 29. 24); Augustine, *Civ. Dei* 15. 26 (*CSEL*. 40. 2. 117); *In Ps.* 86. 3 (*PL*. 37. 1103). Origen (*loc. cit.*) comments that the ark was of square wood so that one could join the boards more easily and prevent infiltration of waters. The early Syrian fathers comment, "Gopher is a very stout wood. Some say that it is acacia wood. Mar Abba and Gabriel of Katar say that teak is gopher"; see A. Levene, *op. cit.*, pp. 81-82. Jerome, unlike the above mentioned writers, notes the divergence between Greek and Hebrew and translates עֲצֵי־גֹפֶר with "bituminata"; see *Quaest. Heb. in Gen.* 6. 14 (*PL*. 23. 998).

[5]) Origen, *Hom. in Gen.* ii. 4 (*GCS*. 29. 32).

[6]) Augustine, *Civ. Dei* 15. 26 (*CSEL*. 40. 2. 117); *In Ps.* 86. 3 (*PL*. 37. 1103).

[7]) Victorinus, *Comm. in Apoc.* 21. 3 (*CSEL*. 49. 149).

[8]) Augustine, *C. Faustum* 12. 14 (*CSEL*. 25. 343-344).

[9]) Origen, *Hom. in Gen.* 2. 4 (*CSEL*. 29. 33).

[10]) Augustine, *C. Faustum* 12. 14 (*CSEL*. 25. 344-345).

[11]) Origen, *Hom. in Gen.* 2. 5 (*GCS*. 29. 36); Augustine, *In Ioannis Evang.* Tr. 9. 11 (*PL*. 34. 1464); *C. Faustum* 12. 15 (*CSEL*. 25. 345); *Civ. Dei* 15, 26 (*CSEL*. 40. 2. 118); Jerome, *Dial. adv. Luciferianos* 22 (*PL*. 23. 185).

manifold character of the church.[1]) Cyril of Jerusalem saw it prefiguring the rulers of the world being guided by churchmen.[2]) At various
times, there were some like Callistus who attempted to prove from
the varieties of animals that all sorts of moral types were excusable in
the church and that discipline by the church was unnecessary. Callistus' opponent, Hippolytus, felt that this was a very serious error.[3])
The view must have shown itself repeatedly, for Augustine felt called
upon to give rebuttal to those who so contended and to make it quite
clear that the church had the impure in it[4]) not because of corruption
of doctrine, but because the faithful needed to practice tolerance.[5])

Following the line of argument already met under other circumstances in the *Letter of Aristeas*, Philo, Barnabas, Justin, Novatian, and
Tertullian insist that the unclean animals illustrate characteristics that
men should not develop.[6]) Augustine said the domestic animals
represent holy laymen and ministers; the beasts of the fields are men
who rejoice in the works of the flesh.[7])

The fact that there were more clean than unclean animals does not
imply that the good are more numerous than the bad, but that the
good maintain the unity of the spirit, and that the spirit has a seven-
fold working. The bad are in twos because of their being easily divided
and because of their tendency to schism.[8])

We have earlier seen how the Gnostics saw in the eight saved in
the ark a picture of their Ogdoad.[9]) Justin, on the other hand, saw
prefigured the eighth day of the week on which Christ appeared when
he arose from the dead.[10]) Asterius further develops this type, which
to him is the figure of all men who are saved, showing the resurrection
in advance.[11]) Still another current represented by Gregory of Elvira
develops it to symbolize seven churches which in his system will be
liberated by Christ to receive glory of the age to come.[12])

---

[1]) Jerome, *Adv. Jovin.* i. 17 (*PL.* 23. 247).
[2]) Cyril of Jerusalem, *Catech.* 17. 10 (*PG.* 33. 981).
[3]) Hippolytus, *Elenchos* ix. 12. 23 (*GCS.* 26. 250).
[4]) Augustine, *In Ioannis Evang.* Tr. 6. 3 (*PL.* 35. 1426).
[5]) Augustine, *De fide et oper.* 49 (*PL.* 40. 228).
[6]) Novatian, *De cibis judaicis* 2 (*PL.* 3. 956); Tertullian, *De idol.* 24 (*CSEL.* 20. 58).
[7]) Augustine, *In Ps.* 8. 13 (*PL.* 36. 115; *NPNF.* 3. 31).
[8]) Augustine, *C. Faustum* 12. 15 (*CSEL.* 25. 345).
[9]) See Irenaeus, *Adv. haer.* i. 18. 3.
[10]) Justin M., *Dial.* 138; cf. Augustine, *C. Faustum* 12. 15 (*CSEL.* 25. 345); for other uses of the eight, see Jerome, *Dial. adv. Luciferianos* 22 (*PL.* 23. 185).
[11]) Asterius, *On Ps.* vi. hom. xx (*PG.* 40. 448 B-D).
[12]) Gregory of Elvira, *De Noe et Arca* in *Rev. Bén.*, 26 (1909), 7. Gregory doubtless

D. The Wood

The wood out of which the ark was made fitted naturally into the sort of interpretation that made a type of the cross out of every mention of wood in the O.T. Why this should be is made clearer if one remembers the comparison made by Justin where the mast of a ship is said to be like the cross.[1]) This typology is more ancient than that which made the ark the church and maintained itself after the other arose. From the time of Justin, the "mystery of the wood" becomes a commonplace.[2]) "You see the water, you see the wood, you see the dove, and do you doubt the mystery? . . . The wood is that on which the Lord Jesus was fastened when he suffered for us." [3])

E. The Waters of the Flood

The flood which the ark as the church rides out is described by a series of figures. When used as a symbol of persecution it continues the symbolism based on the O.T. itself, especially in the book of Isaiah, which we have seen in the first chapter of this study. We have also seen it in IV *Maccabees* where the endurance of the mother of seven sons is compared to the endurance of the ark in the flood.[4]) This figure is taken up by a bishop in the third century to describe the persecutions of Decius of his own day. Those who poured forth from all sides for the desolation of the church were, in the symbolism, the cataracts that broke forth. The connecting link with the flood comes from the Apocalypse where waters are said to be peoples, nations and kingdoms (Rev. 7:15).[5])

The line of allegory begun by Philo is continued by Ambrose who makes the flood to be a flood of passions.[6]) For others it may be a deluge of impiety. Gregory of Nazianzus, in extolling the greatness of Basil, compared the victory of the ark over the flood to Basil's escape from the flood of impiety. Basil had made his city an ark of safety

---

deals with seven because of the biblical phrase: "Noah. . . with seven other persons" (II Pet. 2: 5).

[1]) Justin M., *Apol.* i. 55.

[2]) Justin M., *Dial.* 138; Cyril of Jerusalem, *Catech.* 13. 20; 17. 10 (*PG.* 33. 797, 981); Augustine, *Civ. Dei* 15. 26 (*CSEL.* 40. 2. 116); *De Catech.* 19. 32; 20. 34 (*PL.* 40. 334, 335); *In Ioannis Evang.* Tr. 9. 11 (*PL.* 35. 1464); Firmicus Maternus, *De errore prof. relig.* 27 (*CSEL.* 2. 121).

[3]) Ambrose, *De myst.* 10-11 (*CSEL.* 73. 93).

[4]) IV *Macc.* 15: 31-32.

[5]) Ps.-Cyprian, *Ad Novatianum* 5 (*CSEL.* 3. 3. 56).

[6]) Ambrose, *De Noe* 9 (*CSEL.* 32. 432); cf. Philo, *QG.* ii. 18.

which lightly sailed over the heretics.[1]) To still others, the deluge may
be, as it was to Asterius, the deluge of impurity.[2]) Comparable to this
are Jerome's and Augustine's comparisons of the peril of the church in
the world to that of the ark in the flood.[3]) These items, as well as that
of persecution, belong in the category of illustrative uses of the flood
rather than in that of typology.

Following the lead of I Pet. 3:21, however, the mainstream of the
church transformed the destructive waters of the deluge into the
saving waters of baptism. Beginning with Justin Martyr, repeated
comparisons are made between the purified world after the flood and
the convert emerging from the fount of baptism purified of sins. Like
Noah, Christ is the beginning of a new race which is regenerated by
Him through water.[4]) This symbol plays a particularly important part
in Cyprian's argument for the unity of the church. He speaks of the
flood as "that baptism of the world" [5]) and says, "He who was not
in the ark of Noah could not be saved by water, so neither can he
appear to be saved by baptism who has not been baptized in
the church." [6]) The symbol is taken up by Ambrose and specifically
defined: "You see the water, you see the dove, and do you hesitate
as to the mystery? The water then is that in which the flesh is dipped
that all carnal sin may be washed away." Ambrose saw "the outer
man" being destroyed by baptism as "all flesh" was destroyed by the
flood.[7]) In certain circles any occurrence of water in the O.T. suggested
baptism. Such is seen in John of Damascus who finds the first baptism
in the flood and then moves on to the second in the Red Sea.[8]) The
flood-baptism symbolism is obviously traditional and can be further
traced without essential addition in the thought of Tertullian, Cyril of
Jerusalem, Jerome, and Augustine.[9]) Augustine, in an intricate cal-

---

[1]) Gregory of Nazianzus, *Oratio* 43. 70 (*PG*. 36. 591 B).
[2]) Asterius, *On Ps.* vi. hom. xx (*PG*. 40. 448 C).
[3]) Jerome, *Dial. adv. Luciferianos* 22 (*PL*. 23. 185); Augustine, *Civ. Dei* 15. 26
(*CSEL*. 40. 2. 117); *In Ioannis Evang.* Tr. 6. 3 (*PL*. 33. 1426); cf. Hippolytus,
De antichr. 59 (*GCS*. 1. 2. 39): "The sea is the world."
[4]) Justin M., *Dial.* 138.
[5]) Cyprian, *Ep.* 69. 2 (*CSEL*. 3. 2. 751).
[6]) Cyprian, *Ep.* 74. 11 (*CSEL*. 3. 2. 809); cf. *Ep.* 75. 15 (*CSEL*. 3. 2. 820).
[7]) Ambrose, *De myst.* 10-11 (*CSEL*. 73. 93); *De offic.* 3. 108 (*PL*. 16. 175);
De sacramentis ii. 1, 2 (*CSEL*. 73. 25 f.).
[8]) John of Damascus, *De fide orth.* iv. 9 (*PG*. 94. 1124 A).
[9]) Tertullian, *De bapt.* 8 (*CSEL*. 20. 207-208); Cyril of Jerusalem, *Catech.*
3. 5; 17. 10 (*PG*. 33. 433, 981); Jerome, *Ep.* 10. 1 (*CSEL*. 54. 35); *Ep.* 69. 6
(*CSEL*. 54. 689-690); *Dial. adv. Luciferianos* 22 (*PL*. 23. 185); Augustine, *De*

culation from the fifteen cubits which he breaks down into seven and eight with seven pointing to the rest of the seventh day and eight to the resurrection, finds an allusion to baptism: "Thus the sacrament of baptism, like the waters of Noah, rises above all the wisdom of the proud." It is easy to see that both ἀνάπαυσις and the *ogdoad* which we have earlier considered lie in the background of Augustine's thought.

Second in importance only to baptism in the symbolism of the flood is the flood of fire.[1] This eschatological typology, as we have earlier seen, has its roots in and already begins to develop in the O.T. That God will judge the world in fire is amply attested in both canonical and non-canonical literature.[2] The destruction will involve both the heavens and the earth.[3]

The flood of fire finds definite expression in Philo who explained the failure of men before the time of Moses to keep the Sabbath on the basis that the repeated destructions by water and fire kept the generations from receiving the proper sequence of events until the time of Moses. [4] Considerable light is cast on this passage by the report in Josephus that Adam had predicted that the world would be destroyed twice, once by fire and another time by water. Adam instructed his descendants to build two pillars, one of stone and one of brick, and to inscribe upon them the discoveries made up until that time. They would in this way escape either sort of destruction.[5] It is to be noticed that the destruction of fire is mentioned first. It is expected in the days of the Sethites. The passage is extant almost verbatim in the *Life of Adam and Eve*[6] in which place it is even more

---

catech. 20. 34 (*PL.* 40. 335); *In Ioannis Evang.* Tr. 7. 3 (*PL.* 35. 1439); cf. Didymus of Alex., *De Trinitate* ii. 122a (*PG.* 39. 696 A).

[1] See L. Ginzberg, "*Mabul shel Esh*," in S. A. Horodezky, *Hagoren, Abhandlungen über die Wissenschaft des Judentums* (Berdischew: Scheftel, 1911), VIII, 35-51; S. Rappaport, *Agada und Exegese bei Flavius Josephus* (Wien: Alex. Kohut Memorial Foundation, 1930), pp. 90-93; W. Bousset and H. Gressmann, *Die Religion des Judentums im Späthellenistischen Zeitalter* (Tübingen: J. C. B. Mohr, 1926), p. 493.

[2] Is. 66:15; Dan. 7:9, 10; I Cor. 3:13; II Thess. 1:7-8. For the Apocrypha see I *Enoch* 1:6; 10:12-14; *Test. of Levi* 3:2; *Jub.* 36:10, 11. Threats of a coming fire are frequent in the *Sibylline Oracles*: 3:71-76; 4:130-135, 162-178; 5:270-279.

[3] Ps. 102:26; II Pet. 3:10; Rev. 21:1; Mt. 5:18; cf. II *Enoch* 65:6-10; and the river of fire in I *QH.* iii. 28-36.

[4] Philo, *Mos.* ii. 263.

[5] See Josephus, *Ant.* i. 2. 3; for reports of finding such stones, see *Jub.* 8. 3; II *Enoch* 33:12; see S Rappaport, *Agada und Exegese bei Flavius Josephus* (Wien: Alex. Kohut Memorial Foundation, 1930), p. 91.

[6] *Vita Adae et Evae* 49. 3.

obvious that the speaker is not certain which will come first. While this document is a Christian book of the fourth or fifth century, evidently it here preserves an early tradition already known to Josephus as belonging to the Adam literature.

We have already seen how the rabbis were well acquainted with the concept of a "flood of fire," but, unlike the earlier sources just mentioned, in rabbinic literature the flood of water definitely precedes that of fire. The discussions usually assume that God's oath to Noah that there would be no more flood merely meant "the flood of water." R. Eliezer of Modium (c. 135) tells how the kings of the nations retort to Balaam who has just assured them that God will bring no more flood: "Perhaps He may not bring a flood of water, but He may bring a flood of fire." [1]) R. 'Azariah (PA. 4-5) on the authority of R. Aḥa (c. 320) had Abraham argue with God, attempting to prove that a flood of fire is not permitted by the oath.[2]) The same argument is set forth by R. Judah (PA. 3-4) in R. 'Azariah's name: "Why wilt thou with subtilty evade the oath?" asks Abraham.[3]) In these cases the flood of fire is to punish godless men rather than to destroy heaven and earth.[4]) One may even consider the destruction of Sodom as a flood of fire.[5])

The church fathers, following the lead of II Pet. 3 and Mt. 24, develop this symbolism taken over from Judaism in their own way. In these N.T. passages the careless days of the antediluvians and the days preceding the coming of the Son of Man are compared. Scoffers who do not believe that the world will be destroyed are reminded that as the ancient world was destroyed by a flood, so the present world is stored up for fire; but the doom is delayed by God's mercy that men may repent. The church found here the major themes of its flood typology: a calamity to destroy the sinful world, a delay due to the mercy of God which corresponds to the present age, and the building of the ark—the church—in which some would escape to the rest given by the spiritual Noah.

The apologists were confronted with the relationship of the flood of fire to the ἐκπύρωσις of Stoicism. Justin admits the similarity and admits that the Sibyl and Hystaspes had said that there would

---

[1]) Mekilta, *Amalek* iii. 14; *Baḥodesh* v. 55 ff.
[2]) *Gen. R.* 49. 9; 39. 6.
[3]) *Lev. R.* 10. 1.
[4]) H. L. Strack und Paul Billerbeck, *Kommentar zum Neuen Testament aus Talmud und Midrasch* (München: C. H. Beck, 1928), III, 773.
[5]) *Tos. Taʿanit* 3. 1; cf. Philo, *Abr.* 133, 138.

be a dissolution of things by God, but he argues that the wicked demons led the heathen to such doctrines. The Christian ἐκπύρωσις is not a mere transformation as was that of the Stoics. [1]) Justin, himself, believed that the fire of judgment would descend and utterly dissolve all things just as formerly the waters of the flood left no one. [2]) It was from this destruction that the ark—the church—would deliver one. [3]) Clement of Alexandria saw in the ἐκπύρωσις of the Stoics evidence that pagans were acquainted with the idea of purification by fire and of resurrection. He further noticed that Plato taught that the earth at certain periods was purified by fire and water. Clement thought the philosophers had borrowed these ideas from Moses and the prophets without understanding prophetic allegory. [4]) When, however, it is remembered that Clement saw the details of the shape of the ark as a symbol of those who were purified and tested by fire, [5]) it is obvious that Clement has really combined concepts of the Greek and biblical flood.

Celsus ridiculed what he described as the general view of Christians of his day—that there would be a conflagration—and attempted to trace the source of the belief to the cycles of conflagrations and floods, the last of which took place in the time of Phaethon and of Deucalion respectively. The cycle, says Celsus, demands that a conflagration be next. Origen replied to the argument by appealing to the prediction of Adam in Josephus, which we have already noticed, and then denied that Christians believe in cycles or that there is evidence that there have been cycles. He found further support for the possibility of fire in Deut. 4:24 and Mal. 3:2 where God is described as "fire." Origen makes no appeal to II Peter, for the idea there expressed did not fit well with his belief that the final fire should be understood figuratively. It would consume wood, hay, and stubble, he argued, referring to I Cor. 3. These are to be taken figuratively for the works of men. The final fire is a fire for refining. [6]) Elsewhere he interprets the redundant phrase "flood of waters" to be a deliberate contrast

---

[1]) Justin M., *Apol.* i. 20.
[2]) Justin M., *Apol.* ii. 7. 2.
[3]) Justin M., *Dial.* 138.
[4]) Clement of A., *Strom.* v. 1. 9-10 (*GCS.* 15. 332).
[5]) Clement of A., *Strom.* vi. 11. 86 (*GCS.* 15. 475).
[6]) Origen, *C. Celsum* i. 19; iv. 11-13 (*GCS.* 2. 70; 281-283); *Hom. in Gen.* 2. 3 (*GCS.* 29. 30); cf. *Hom. in Ex.* 7. 8 (*GCS.* 29. 216-217); Lactantius, *Div. inst.* ii. 10 (*CSEL.* 19. 151).

with "flood of fire." [1]) How closely eschatological ideas are inter-
woven in various symbols is seen when it is remembered that Origen
declared that in the waters of baptism we are raised with Christ, but
in the baptism of fire we are made like his glorious body. [2])

Origen's spiritual fire by no means represents the predominant
view. Certain Gnostics of the Valentinian school believed in a cycle
of world events at the culmination of which fire that lies hidden in
the world would blaze forth and burn and destroy all matter; however,
in this system matter would then have no further existence. [3]) Irenaeus
struggles against this extreme as he argues that the world will only
be transformed rather than annihilated, for it is merely the "fashion
of the world" which passes away.[4]) Because of the wickedness of
the antichrist, who is prefigured in the 600 years of the life of Noah
plus the 66 cubits of Nebuchadnezzar's image, a cataclysm of fire
would come upon the earth. [5])

Evidence for the large role played in eschatological typology by
the flood of fire can be traced from the second century on. A Roman
presbyter late in the second century argued that things would be
at the end of the world as they had been at the flood. [6]) Ps.-Melito
departed from the usual pattern by having a flood of wind in addition
to those of water and fire. The last would burn the wicked, but
the just would be delivered as they had been in the ark. [7]) After
Tertullian makes his comparison between the flood and baptism,
he declares that the world has returned to sin, "and so it is destined to
fire." [8]) Victorinus makes clear that the covenant with Noah did not
preclude fire.[9]) Ephraem specifically makes the deluge "the figure
($\tau \acute{u} \pi o \varsigma$) of the inextinguishable fire" which will cover all as the water
covered the mountains.[10]) Gregory of Elvira states that when the Lord
"comes to judge the world in the flames of fire, he will put an end to
the rebellious angels and to the crimes of the world in order to give

---

[1]) Origen, *Selecta in Gen.* 54-55 (*PG.* 12. 106); cf. *Hom. in Ez.* iv. 8 (*GCS.* 33. 369-370).
[2]) Origen, *Com. in Matt.* 15. 23 (*GCS.* 40. 418).
[3]) See Irenaeus, *Adv. haer.* i. 7. 1.
[4]) *Ibid.*, v. 36. 1.
[5]) *Ibid.*, v. 29. 2.
[6]) See R. M. Grant, *Second Cent. Christianity* (London: SPCK., 1946), pp. 105-106.
[7]) Ps.-Melito, *Apol.* in W. Cureton, *Speciligium Syriacum*, p. 50, line 33 ff.
[8]) Tertullian, *De bapt.* 8 (*CSEL.* 20. 208).
[9]) Victorinus, *Comm. in Apoc.* iv. 3 (*CSEL.* 49. 48).
[10]) Cited in J. Daniélou, *Sacramentum Futuri*, p. 73.

to his saints rest in the kingdom of God." [1]) Chrysostom places the two floods in juxtaposition and warns of the "deluge of Hell." [2]) Jerome warns that those not in the ark—the church—will perish when the flood prevails.[3]) It is quite obvious that the symbolism is a tradition within the church which eventually passes into the medieval hymn *Dies irae dies illa*. The present age is the period of delay for repentance.[4]) The only really debatable element seems to have been the extent of the destruction. Augustine, like many before him, thought the conflagration need be no more destructive than the flood had been. A transformation would take place but the saints would escape from it.[5]) In the flood God had given men a pattern of future judgment and foreannounced the deliverance of the holy by the mystery of the wood.[6])

F. The Raven

The typology of the sending forth of the raven presents two currents in the church, one of which expounded soteriological secrets, and the other ecclesiastical. The former of these followed the symbolism of Philo in which Noah was expelling whatever residue of folly there might be in the mind.[7]) The action illustrates the expelling of sin from the life "which goes forth and does not return." [8]) Jerome explained that "the unclean bird, the devil," or "the foul bird of wickedness" was expelled by baptism.[9]) Those who sought ecclesiastical typology saw the raven as a type of impure men and of apostates who are sent forth from the church and cannot return. A presbyter of the third century, in order to make his point, linked the raven with the command: "Everything leprous and impure, cast abroad outside the camp." [10]) The tradition is further developed by Gregory of Elvira [11]) and by Augustine who found in the raven a type of men who are defiled with impure desire and are eager for things

---

[1]) Gregory of Elvira, *De Arca Noe* in *Rev. Bén.*, 26 (1909), 6.
[2]) Chrysostom, *In Ep. I Thess.* c. 4, hom. 8. 2 (*PG.* 62. 442).
[3]) Jerome, *Ep.* 15. 2 (*CSEL.* 54. 64).
[4]) Ambrose, *De Noe* 13. 42 (*CSEL.* 32. 440).
[5]) Augustine, *Civ. Dei* 20. 18, 24 (*CSEL.* 40. 2. 468-470, 493).
[6]) Augustine, *De catech.* 19. 32 (*PL.* 40. 334).
[7]) Philo, *QG.* ii. 35.
[8]) Ambrose, *De myst.* 11 (*CSEL.* 73. 93).
[9]) Jerome, *Dial. adv. Luciferianos* 22 (*PL.* 23. 185); *Ep.* 69. 6 (*CSEL.* 54. 690).
[10]) Ps.-Cyprian, *Ad Novatianum* 2 (*CSEL.* 3. 3. 55).
[11]) Gregory of Elvira, *De Arca Noe* in *Rev. Bén.*, 26 (1909), 9.

outside the church.[1]) The raven may also be a type of the procrastinator.[2])

G. The Dove

Water, wood, and the dove are actually the major themes of the church's typology. In a passage we have already alluded to several times, Ambrose said:

> You see the water, you see the wood, you see the dove, and do you hesitate as to the mystery... The dove is that in the form of which the Holy Spirit descended, as you have read in the N.T., who inspires in you peace of soul and tranquility of mind. [3])

Unlike some types, the dove is not a further development of biblical trends, but as Ambrose makes clear, the fact that the Holy Spirit is said to have descended upon Jesus in the form of a dove at his baptism made it quite normal that the typologist should have the dove of Noah prefigure the Holy Spirit in the church. It can be traced from the time of Tertullian:

> To our flesh as it emerges from the fount, after its old sins, flies the dove of the Holy Spirit bringing us the peace of God, sent out from the heavens, where is the church the typified ark. [4])

Without essential change, it is repeated by Hippolytus, Gregory of Nazianzus, the anonymous bishop in the middle of the third century, Jerome, Chrysostom, Ephraem Syrus, John of Damascus, and Didymus.[5]) A very important link in the chain of typology, unexpressed though present in the minds of other writers, is furnished by Cyril of Jerusalem as he expounds the flood as a type of the baptism of Christ, which in turn is a type of that of the Christian.[6]) Thus one

---

[1]) Augustine, *C. Faustum* 12. 20 (*CSEL.* 25. 348); *In Ioannis Evang.* Tr. 6. 3 (*PL.* 35. 1426).

[2]) The idea is drawn from the raven's cry, "cras, cras," which is interpreted "Tomorrow, tomorrow," Augustine, *In Ps.* 102. 16 (*PL.* 37. 1330).

[3]) Ambrose, *De Myst.* 10-11 (*CSEL.* 73. 93); cf. *Ep.* 51. 21 (*PL.* 16. 1166).

[4]) Tertullian, *De bapt.* 8 (*CSEL.* 20. 207-208).

[5]) Hippolytus, *Sermo in Sancta Theophania* 7 (*GCS.* 1. 2. 261); Gregory of Nazianzus, *Orat.* 39. 16 (*PG.* 36. 353); Ps.-Cyprian, *Ad Novatianum* 3 (*CSEL.* 3. 3. 55-56); Jerome, *Ep.* 69. 6 (*CSEL.* 54. 690); *Dial. adv. Luciferianos* 22 (*PL.* 23. 185); Chrysostom, *In Matt. hom.* 12. 3 (*PG.* 57. 205); *De Laz. concio* 6 (*PG.* 48. 1037); Ephraem Syrus, *Adv. Scrut. Rhythms* 49. 2; John of Damascus, *De fide orth.* iv. 9 (*PG.* 94. 1125 B); Didymus, *De Trin.* ii. 122a (*PG.* 39. 696 A).

[6]) Cyril of Jerusalem, *Catech.* 17. 10 (*PG.* 33. 981).

moves from the dove at Jesus' baptism to the Holy Spirit coming to each Christian.

The olive branch as a symbol of peace is well-known in antiquity.[1]) It is this symbol that grasped the attention of Christian interpreters. "The coming of the dove signifies the Holy Spirit and the reconciliation from on high. The olive is a symbol of peace." [2]) A favorite theme for early Christian art, as we have seen, was the flood. That particular moment when the dove returned with the olive branch— the moment of the hope of new life—is often shown. This is the scene in the catacombs of Domitilla, of Peter and Marcelinus, and on the coin of Apamea.[3])

Another segment of the church expounded from the dove an ecclesiastical typology. To the bishop in the middle of the third century, with Zech. 3:1-2 as his point of departure, in addition to the Holy Spirit the dove represented the man in the church who, though he fell into error, did not find rest out of the church, and so he hastened to return to it. The twofold sending out of the dove presented two stages in persecution. In the first—that of Decius— some had lapsed, but in the second they had remained steadfast. In this picture the dove becomes an important element in the argument for lenient treatment of the lapsed.[4]) Augustine also makes the doves of the ark to be the faithful in the church.[5]) As the dove found no rest, so the saints could not expect to find rest in this world.[6]) On other occasions Augustine can see the bringing of the olive branch to imply that though some might find baptism outside the church, they might come with their fruit—charity—after all into the one communion.[7]) Augustine's symbolism is actually a parallel development to the rabbinic symbolism where the dove represents Israel

[1]) II *Macc.* 14:4; Dionysius Halicar. i. 20; Virgil, *Aeneid* viii. 116; Livy, 24. 30 and 29. 16; cited in A. Dillmann, *Genesis* (Edinburgh: T. and T. Clark, 1897), I, 287.

[2]) Didymus, *De Trin.* ii. 122a (*PG.* 39. 696 A); cf. Tertullian, *De bapt.* 8 (*CSEL.* 20. 207-208); Ps.-Cyprian, *Ad Novatianum* 6 (*CSEL.* 3. 3. 57); Jerome, *Ep.* 69. 6 (*CSEL.* 54. 690); Augustine, *De doct. Christ.* 2. 16 [24] (*PL.* 34. 47); Methodius, *Convivium decem virginum* 10. 2 (*GCS.* 27. 124); John of Damascus, *De fide orth.* iv. 9 (*PG.* 94. 1125 B); Ambrose, *Ex. in Lk.* ii. 92 (*CSEL.* 32. 4. 95).

[3]) See *supra*, pp. 161-162.

[4]) Ps.-Cyprian, *Ad Novatianum* 3 (*CSEL.* 3. 3. 53-56); cf. J. Fink, *op. cit.*, pp. 59 ff., for a strong argument that this is the major motif of "Noah the Just" in art.

[5]) Augustine, *In Ioannis Evang.* Tr. 6. 3 (*PL.* 35. 1426).

[6]) Augustine, *C. Faustum* 12. 20 (*CSEL.* 25. 348).

[7]) *Ibid.*, 12. 20 (*CSEL.* 25. 349); *In Ioannis Evang.* Tr. 7. 3 (*PL.* 35. 1439).

that finds no rest in the exile and returns to Palestine.[1]) In the church at an earlier period, one had found the three trips of the dove to symbolize the Trinity.[2])

Still a third current found a christological typology in the dove: Christ who finds no rest among the Jews is symbolized. After his rejection he found a resting place among the Gentiles when they received the Gospel.[3]) Hilary found symbolized here some facts of the Gospel. The second return of the dove represents the return of the seventy disciples (Lk. 10:1) who returned with the news [fruit] that the unclean spirits were subject to them. The dove's failure to find rest illustrates that the Holy Spirit did not come upon them. Hilary assumes that they later forsook the Lord and that there is no rest to the disciple who does so. The third trip of the dove represents the Spirit's abiding with the believer, since the Holy Spirit always remains in the soul of the faithful.[4])

H. The Exit from the Ark

The symbolism of the exit from the ark is developed by the church in two ways, each of which has to do with eschatology. The first finds it a picture of the resurrection. Chrysostom lists God's shutting Noah in the ark in a series of O.T. miracles in which "God schooled us little by little" toward belief in the resurrection.[5]) Asterius compared Christ's stay in the sepulchre to Noah's stay in the ark.[6]) The fact that men and women went into the ark separately implies that the flesh lusteth against the spirit and the spirit against the flesh. Their going out together implies that in the resurrection the body will be united to the spirit in perfect harmony, undisturbed by the wants and passions of mortality.[7]) The second current of typology is to be seen in Jerome who used the coming out of the ark as a figure of the coming judgment when the storehouses of the church will be opened and the Lord will bring forth vessels of wrath.[8])

---

[1]) *Gen. R.* 33. 6; cf. *Lam. R.* 1. 3. § 29.
[2]) Ps.-Cyprian, *Ad Novatianum* 3 (*CSEL.* 3. 3. 56).
[3]) *Bk. of Adam and Eve* iii. 10.
[4]) Hilary, *Tract. myst.* i. 14 (*SC.* 19. 102-104).
[5]) J. Chrysostom, *In Ep. ad Col.* c. ii, hom. 5.4 (*PG.* 62. 336); cf. *De Laz. concio* vi (*PG.* 48. 1037).
[6]) Asterius, *On Ps.* vi, hom. xx (*PG.* 40. 448 C).
[7]) Augustine, *C. Faustum* 12. 21 (*CSEL.* 25. 350).
[8]) Jerome, *Dial. adv. Luciferianos* 22 (*PL.* 23. 186).

I. Noah's Drunkenness and Nakedness

The interest of the church fathers in moral values to be found in Genesis is clearly seen in their treatment of Noah's drunkenness which becomes a classic example of the evils of drinking. Clement of Alexandria called it "the spectacle of transgression of ignorance." [1] "How great is the power of wine . . . just men have succumbed. Wine made him naked which the waters of the deluge could not," commented Ambrose.[2] "One hour's debauch made Noah uncover his nakedness which through sixty years of sobriety he had kept covered," admonished Jerome.[3]

At the same time, there is a certain contrary tendency which attempts to excuse Noah. Such is seen in the 38th *Ode of Solomon* [4] as well as when Peter, in the Clementines, insists that Noah was not a transgressor and promises a later explanation that is not forthcoming.[5] Ambrose emphasizes that Noah was not ashamed of his nakedness, for he was filled with joy and spiritual gladness.[6] Origen and Jerome say that he lived in a rude age of the world and perhaps did not know the power of the wine.[7]

That Jesus had spoken of his approaching death as "drinking the cup," that he used the cup in the last supper,[8] and that his clothes were taken from him in the crucifixion laid the foundation for seeing in Noah's drunkenness a type of the passion of Jesus. This likeness was already observed by Cyprian [9] and Hilary.[10] It served Jerome as a bit of anti-Jewish polemic when he pointed out that as Noah planted a vineyard, Christ planted the church and suffered. He then identified Ham's attitude with the Jewish attitude toward the cross; while

---

[1] Clement of A., *Paed.* ii. 6. 51; cf. ii. 2. 34 (*GCS.* 12. 188, 177).

[2] Ambrose, *De virginibus* i. 8. 53 (*PL.* 16. 214); *Ep.* 68. 27 (*PL.* 16. 1248).

[3] Jerome, *Ep.* 69. 9 (*CSEL.* 54. 696). Equally serious denunciations are to be found in Origen, *De orat.* 29. 18 (*GCS.* 3. 392); Methodius, *Conv. decem virginium* 10. 2 (*GCS.* 27. 124); Basil, *On Renunciation of the World* (*F. of Ch.* ix, p. 25); Chrysostom, *In Acta Apostolorum*, hom. 27. 3 (*PG.* 60. 208); Ephraem Syrus, *Nisibene Hymns* 57. 6-7; *Hymns on the Nativity* 3 (*NPNF.*, ser. ii. 13. 210, 232); Augustine, *De pecc. rem.* ii. 10. 12 (*CSEL.* 60. 84).

[4] See J. R. Harris, "Two Flood-Hymns of the Early Church," *Expositor*, 8. 2 (1911), 407.

[5] Ps.-Clem., *Hom.* ii. 52 (*GCS.* 42. 55).

[6] Ambrose, *Ep.* 58. 12 (*PL.* 16. 1231).

[7] Origen, *Selecta in Gen.* 62-63 (*PG.* 12. 109); Jerome, *Ep.* 22. 8 (*CSEL.* 54. 155).

[8] III *Baruch* 5:15 has Noah plant the vine because Jesus was to use it.

[9] Cyprian, *Ep.* 63. 6 (*CSEL.* 3. 2. 702).

[10] Hilary, *Tract. myst.* i. 15 (*SC.* 19. 104).

Shem and Japheth symbolized the Gentiles who honor Jesus.[1]) The figure is further enlarged by Augustine. That the nakedness was in the house typified the treatment Jesus received from his own nation. That the two sons went backward symbolized the turning a back to the "sins of the Jews" which one does when he reverences the passion.[2])

J. HAM

The typological treatment of the sons of Noah shows various currents as do other items in the flood narrative. One of these repeats the trend already seen in Philo in which the three sons represent the good, the bad, and the indifferent.[3])

The moral interest in Ham's action expressed itself by drawing a warning against the exposure of the body. Ham was one who was wanton in looking on his father and laughing at his pathetic condition.[4]) By his action he showed a lack of filial devotion.[5]) There are certain tendencies to make Ham an archsinner. It was he who had learned enchantments from the daughters of Cain. These he inscribed on plates of metal and stone that they might survive the flood. After the flood he found them and revived these practices.[6]) The Gnostic, Isadore, claimed that the people of his day called Ham Zoroaster as the first founder of magic.[7]) He also taught that the Greek philosopher Pherecydes had taken his theological allegories from the prophecy of Ham.[8]) Some of the church fathers saw in Noah's curse the origin of slavery.[9]) Aphraates explained Esau's subjection to Jacob on the basis that Esau had married a daughter of Canaan and thus

---

[1]) Jerome, *Dial. adv. Luciferianos* 22 (*PL.* 23. 185).

[2]) Augustine, *Civ. Dei* 16. 2 (*CSEL.* 40. 2. 125-126); *C. Faustum* 12. 23 (*CSEL.* 25. 351).

[3]) Ambrose, *De Noe* 2 (*CSEL.* 32. 414).

[4]) Ambrose, *De virginibus* i. 8. 53 (*PL.* 16. 214); *De offic.* i. 79 (*PL.* 16. 51); Chrysostom, *In Matt.* hom. 6. 6 (*PG.* 57. 69); Gregory the Great, *Ep.* 45 (*PL.* 77. 1157 C).

[5]) Vincent of Lerins, *Commonitorium* 7 (*PL.* 50. 647).

[6]) John Cassian, *Collatio* VIII. 21 (*CSEL.* 13. 2. 240). Allusions to Ham's sin without explanation are found in: Ps.-Clem., *Recog.* i. 30 (*PG.* 1. 1224); Lactantius, *Div. inst.* ii. 13 (*CSEL.* 19. 161); Augustine, *Civ. Dei* 16. 1 (*CSEL.* 40. 2. 123); *Ep.* 78. 8 (*CSEL.* 32. 2. 343).

[7]) Ps.-Clem., *Recog.* iv. 27 (*PG.* 1. 1326).

[8]) Clement of A., *Strom.* vi. 6. 53 (*GCS.* 15. 459).

[9]) Basil, *De spir. sanct.* 20 (*PL.* 32. 161 B); Augustine, *Civ. Dei* 19. 15 (*CSEL.* 40. 2. 400).

came under the curse.[1]) Chrysostom considered the curse fulfilled in the enslaving of the Gibeonites who were Canaan's descendants.[2])

Still another trend found the three sons of Noah to be types of those under the Law, of those justified by grace, and of the pagans who are mockers of the death of the Saviour and the nude body of God.[3])

As the mocker of his father, Ham is also an excellent type of the mockers and heretics in the church. Vincent of Lerins spoke of them "treading in the footsteps of their father Ham" to bring shame upon the memory of each holy man and spread an evil report of what ought to be buried in silence.[4]) Taking up the suggestion made by Philo that Ham means "hot," Augustine makes Ham a symbol of the sort of heretical heat which is kindled by the blaze of bigotry by which the passions of heretics disturb the peace of the faithful.[5]) Elsewhere Ham represents the Jewish people who saw the nakedness in that they consented to Christ's death.[6])

K. SHEM

Shem and Japheth are roundly praised in this literature for their filial devotion and modesty in covering Noah rather than looking upon him. The blessing came upon them for their act.[7]) Basing his interpretation upon a supposed etymology of Shem, "renowned," Augustine makes Shem a type of Christ, for he is more "renowned" than any other since his name is spread throughout the world.[8]) Augustine, however, can also make Shem and Japheth represent the Jew and Gentile who have believed in Christ. They cover the nakedness in honoring the death of Jesus; their backs are turned, for the church celebrates the passion of Christ not as something in the future, but as something already accomplished.[9])

---

[1]) Aphraates, *Hom.* iii. 9 (*TU*. 3. 3. 50).
[2]) J. Chrysostom, *In Matt.* hom. 8. 3 (*PG*. 57. 86).
[3]) Hilary, *Tract. myst.* i. 15 (*SC*. 19. 104).
[4]) Vincent of Lerins, *Commonitorium* 7 (*PL*. 50. 647).
[5]) Augustine, *Civ. Dei* 16. 2 (*CSEL*. 40. 2. 124); cf. Ambrose, *De Noe* 32 (*CSEL*. 32. 494).
[6]) Augustine, *C. Faustum* 12. 23 (*CSEL*. 25. 351); Jerome, *Dial. adv. Luciferianos* 22 (*PL*. 23. 185).
[7]) Clement of A., *Paed.* ii. 2. 34; ii. 6. 51 (*GCS*. 12. 177, 188); Ambrose, *De virginibus* i. 8. 53 (*PL*. 16. 214); *De offic.* i. 79 (*PL*. 16. 51); *Ep*. 37. 6 (*PL*. 16. 1131).
[8]) Augustine, *Civ. Dei* 16. 2 (*CSEL*. 40. 2. 125).
[9]) Augustine, *C. Faustum* 12. 23 (*CSEL*. 25. 351); *Civ. Dei* 16. 2 (*CSEL*. 40. 2. 125).

L. JAPHETH

The church fathers take the blessings of Noah almost entirely in a christological sense. "Shem and Japheth, being gracious, looked for the gracious Son, who should come and set free Canaan from the servitude of sin," says Ephraem.[1]) Japheth, since his name, according to Augustine, means "width," signifies the churches in which widely scattered peoples find a home.[2]) All the world is occupied by the church among the Gentiles.[3]) The "dwelling in the tents of Shem" prophesies the admission of Gentiles into the church.[4])

This extended survey of spiritual exegesis has demonstrated clearly that the treatment of the flood is a product of the *Sitz im Leben* of the interpreter. Christian allegory and typology develop some trends observable in biblical and Jewish literature; however, both in the quantity of typology and in the choice of those things prefigured by the type and allegory, Christian treatment of the flood manifests its own individuality.

---

[1]) Ephraem Syrus, *Hymns on the Nativity*, Hymn I (*NPNF.*, ser. ii. 13. 224).
[2]) Augustine, *Civ. Dei* 16. 2 (*CSEL*. 40. 2. 124).
[3]) Augustine, *C. Faustum* 12. 24 (*CSEL*. 25. 352).
[4]) Irenaeus, *Demonst.* 21; cf. Justin M., *Dial.* 139; Hilary, *Tract. myst.* i. 16 (*SC*. 19. 104); Augustine, *C. Faustum* 12. 24 (*CSEL*. 25. 352).

CONCLUSION

In the course of this study we have surveyed the interpretation of the flood story through the various Jewish and Christian writings of the early period. The sources have been taken individually without a thoroughgoing effort at a synthesis. In this manner a sort of anthology on the flood has been assembled in order to set forth in the clearest way what each writer has to contribute. It is too much to hope that the topic has been exhausted, but an effort has been made to omit no significant reference in the literature of the period covered. Few biblical themes occupy more space.

From the study it is obvious that certain problems inherent in the narrative of Genesis perplexed the ancients as much as they do students of our own day. The most striking of these is that of the identity of the בני־האלהים, the צהר, the עצי־גפר, and the curse on Canaan. The particular solution for these problems comes out of the *Sitz im Leben* of the individual expositor.

In the larger problem of the interrelation of the methods of biblical interpretation used in the non-canonical literature, in Christianity, and in the writings of the rabbis, while recognizing the precariousness of forming a judgment from a survey of such a limited literature as here has been treated, some conclusions are perhaps possible.

There are some motifs held in common by Philo and the rabbis that pass on into Christian writings after the time of Justin. An example would be that Noah is the beginner of a new race. Philo also lays the foundation for Christian allegory in motifs where he is not paralleled in rabbinic literature. Examples would be that the sending out of the raven represents sin going out of the man and that the sons of Noah represent the good, the bad, and the indifferent.

Those Christian writers who are definitely known to have had contact with Jewish teachers, Justin, Origen, Ephraem, Aphraates, and Jerome, have used some Haggadah which we assume they obtained from these teachers. Examples of these can be seen in the idea that the 100 years is a time given the flood generation for repentance; that "rest" is an etymology for Noah; that Noah was only righteous "in his generation"; that the clean animals were destined for sacrifice; and that Noah did not have to work to assemble the animals. Some of these and similar elements are then repeated by later writers who did not have such direct contact with Jewish teachers.

A counter influence of Christian exegesis in Jewish writing is even more elusive. These elements are more in the nature of replies to Christian positions than in the nature of direct borrowing of ideas. There are ample points at which Jew and Christian differ, but these points are often not the view unanimously held by Christians. On the other hand, closer examination of the opinions of the rabbis may reveal that it is only to a divergent view that a teacher is replying and not to a Christian position at all. It would seem likely, however, that some of the emphasis upon God alone being the author of the flood could be called forth by the counter contention that the *Logos* played a part in it. The emphasis on the earth's being repeopled after the flood by Noah's three sons and the emphasis on Ham's sin preventing a fourth son may counter the story of additional children after the flood. A position first found in Christian writing and then later taken up by a Jewish interpreter may be seen in the explanation of the בני האלהים as sons of Seth.

But after all of these are noted, there is a gulf between the type of exegesis practiced by Jew and Christian. The church is more reserved in allegory than was Philo. It has less to do with the haggadic material than the rabbis. It in turn devoted itself to finding types that would be rejected both by Philo and by the rabbis. The interpreters are parallel only in matters that are so obvious that it is unnecessary to try to claim an interrelation between them, or parallel only in such superficialities as we have just mentioned above. In the early period each was going its own way even in areas where there need not be heated theological conflict.

APPENDICES

APPENDIX A

INDEX OF SCRIPTURE PASSAGES ON THE FLOOD IN THE WORKS OF PHILO [1])

Genesis 5.

    28. *De Posteritate Caini* 48.
    29. *Quod Deterius Potiori insidiari solet* 120-123.
        Quaestiones et Solutiones in Genesin i. 87.
    32. *Quaestiones et Solutiones in Genesin* i. 88; cf. ii. 71.

Genesis 6.

    1. *Quaestiones et Solutiones in Genesin* i. 89.
      De Gigantibus 1.
    2. *De Gigantibus* 6.
    3. *Quaestiones et Solutiones in Genesin* i. 91.
      De Gigantibus 19, 55.
    4. *Quaestiones et Solutiones in Genesin* i. 92.
      De Gigantibus 58.
      Quod Deus immutabilis sit 1.
    5. *De Confusione Linguarum* 24.
      Quod Deus immutabilis sit 20.
    6. *Quaestiones et Solutiones in Genesin* i. 93.
      QG., Gk. Frag. i. 93.
      Quod Deus immutabilis sit 20, 33.
    7. *Quaestiones et Solutiones in Genesin* i. 94-95.
    7. *QG.*, Gk. Frag. i. 94.
      Quod Deus immutabilis sit 20, 51, 70.
    8. *Quaestiones et Solutiones in Genesin* i. 96.
      Legum Allegoriae iii. 77-78.
      Quod Deus immutabilis sit 70, 86, 104, 109.
    9. *Quaestiones et Solutiones in Genesin* i. 97.
      Quod Deus immutabilis sit 117.
      De Abrahamo 31.
    11. *Quaestiones et Solutiones in Genesin* i. 98.
      Quod Deus immutabilis sit 122.
    12. *Quaestiones et Solutiones in Genesin* i. 99.
      Quod Deus immutabilis sit 140 ff.
    13. *Quaestiones et Solutiones in Genesin* i. 100.
    14. *Quaestiones et Solutiones in Genesin* ii. 1, 2, 3, 4.
      De Confusione Linguarum 105.
    15. *Quaestiones et Solutiones in Genesin* ii. 5.
    16. *Quaestiones et Solutiones in Genesin* ii. 6-7.
    17. *Quaestiones et Solutiones in Genesin* ii. 8-9.
    18. *Quaestiones et Solutiones in Genesin* ii. 10.

---

[1]) Philo's works are cited according to the Loeb edition.

Genesis 7.

1. *Quaestiones et Solutiones in Genesin* ii. 11.
2. *Quaestiones et Solutiones in Genesin* ii. 12.
   Quod Deterius Potiori insidiari solet 170.
4. *Quaestiones et Solutiones in Genesin* ii. 13, 14, 15.
5. *Quaestiones et Solutiones in Genesin* ii. 16.
10. *Quaestiones et Solutiones in Genesin* ii. 13.
11. *Quaestiones et Solutiones in Genesin* ii. 17, 18.
    De Abrahamo 40-47.
11. *De Confusione Linguarum* 23.
    De Fuga et Inventione 192.
16. *Quaestiones et Solutiones in Genesin* ii. 18.
18. *Quaestiones et Solutiones in Genesin* ii. 20.
20. *Quaestiones et Solutiones in Genesin* ii. 21.
21. *Quaestiones et Solutiones in Genesin* ii. 22.
22. *Quaestiones et Solutiones in Genesin* ii. 23.
23. *Quaestiones et Solutiones in Genesin* ii. 24, 25.

Genesis 8.

1. *Quaestiones et Solutiones in Genesin* ii. 26-28.
2. *Ibid.,* ii. 29.
3. *Ibid.,* ii. 30.
4. *Ibid.,* ii. 31.
5. *Ibid.,* ii. 32.
6. *Ibid.,* ii. 33, 34.
7. *Ibid.,* ii. 34, 36, 37.
8. *Ibid.,* ii. 38.
9. *Ibid.,* ii. 40.
10. *Ibid.,* ii. 41.
11. *Ibid.,* ii. 42, 43.
12. *Ibid.,* ii. 44.
13. *Ibid.,* ii. 45, 46.
14. *Ibid.,* ii. 47.
15. *Ibid.,* ii. 48.
18. *Ibid.,* ii. 49.
20. *Ibid.,* ii. 50-51, 52.
21. *Ibid.,* ii. 53, 54.
22. *Ibid.,* ii. 55.

Genesis 9.

1. *Ibid.,* ii. 56.
3. *Ibid.,* ii. 57, 58.
4. *Ibid.,* ii. 59.
   QG., Gk. Frag. ii. 59.
5. *Quaestiones et Solutiones in Genesin* ii. 60.
6. *Ibid.,* ii. 61.
   QG., Gk. Frag. ii. 62.
   De Somniis i. 74.
   Quaestiones et Solutiones in Genesin ii. 62.
11. *Ibid.,* ii. 63.
    De Somniis ii. 223-224.
13. *Quaestiones et Solutiones in Genesin* ii. 64.
18. *Ibid.,* ii. 65.

Genesis 9 continued.

    Quod Deterius Potiori insidiari solet 105.
    De Agricultura 1, 125, 181.
    De Ebrietate (General theme of drunkenness and says little about Noah).
21. *Quaestiones et Solutiones in Genesin* ii. 68, 69.
    Legum Allegoriae ii. 60.
22. *Quaestiones et Solutiones in Genesin* ii. 70, 71.
23. *Ibid.*, ii. 72.
24. *Ibid.*, ii. 73.
    De Sobrietate 1, 51 ff.
    Quis Rerum Divinarum Heres 260.
    De Virtutibus 201 ff.
25. *Quaestiones et Solutiones in Genesin* ii. 74.
25. *De Sobrietate* 32, 51.
26. *Quaestiones et Solutiones in Genesin* ii. 75.
    De Sobrietate 53-58.
27. *Quaestiones et Solutiones in Genesin* ii. 76, 77.
    De Sobrietate 59-60.
28. *Quaestiones et Solutiones in Genesin* ii. 78.

Genesis 10.

1. *Quaestiones et Solutiones in Genesin* ii. 79.

Genesis 11.

10. *De Mutatione Nominum* 189.

APPENDIX B

THE NOAH COMMANDMENTS

"Sons of Noah" in rabbinic literature in the narrow sense refers to Shem, Ham, and Japheth, but in the wider and more technical sense designates both all people before the revelation at Sinai and the non-observer of the Law of Moses since Sinai. The "Noah commandments" are a series of laws thought to be binding upon both Israelite and non-Israelite as the basic requirements of social progress. [1]) As the law was finally codified by Maimonides, there are seven items: prohibition of idolatry, of blasphemy, of murder, of adultery, of robbery, of eating a limb from a living animal, and the command to establish courts. [2]) These are to be enforced under pain of death. [3]) The one who publicly accepts them is a "resident alien (*ger toshab*)," and if he properly observes them he will have a share in the world to come. [4])

In the formative period, the first to the third centuries, the idea of "Noah commandments" was in a fluid state and the number not definitely defined. In addition to the seven later accepted, R. Ḥanania b. Gamaliel (T. 3) included blood drawn from a living animal; R. Ḥidka (c. 120) included emasculation; R. Simeon (c. 120), sorcery; R. Jose (T. 2), all that is mentioned in Deut. 18: 10 ff.; and R. Eleazar (T.), hybridization of animals and trees. [5]) A Tanna of the school of Manasseh gave a list of idolatry, murder, adultery, robbery, flesh cut from a living animal, emasculation, and forbidden mixtures. [6]) 'Ulla (PA. c. 280) had extended the number to thirty, though he admitted that only three were kept: the sons of Noah did not draw up *kethubah* documents for males; they did not weigh flesh of the dead in the market; and they respected the Torah. [7])

---

[1]) J. Hamburger, "Noachiden," *Real-Encyclopädie für Bibel und Talmud* (Strelitz: J. Hamburger, 1883), II, 663-866; E. L. Dietrich, "Die 'Religion Noahs,' ihre Herkunft und ihre Bedeutung," *Z. f. Religions-u. Geistesgeschichte*, I (1948), 301-315.

[2]) Maimonides, *The Book of Judges* V. 9. 1; cf. *Gen. R.* 34. 8.

[3]) *T. B. Sanh.* 56a; *Abodah Zarah* 71b.

[4]) *T. B. Abodah Zarah* 64b; Maimonides, *The Book of Judges* V. 8. 11.

[5]) *T. B. Sanh.* 56b.

[6]) *T. B. Sanh.* 56b.

[7]) *T. B. Ḥullin* 92a-b.

The criteria by which the number seven is arrived at is set forth by R. Jose b. Ḥanina (PA. 2); of all the pre-Mosaic legislation, only that repeated at Sinai is included in the list.[1]) The rule has its difficulties when circumcision is considered, but the rabbis exempt it from the seven on the basis that there is another reason for its inclusion, namely, to permit it to be carried out on the Sabbath. [2])

Six of these commandments had previously been made known to Adam [3]) though they were transgressed by the antediluvians. [4]) Noah added the prohibition of eating a limb of a living animal. [5])

Only two of the precepts are actually mentioned in Gen. 9: abstinence from blood and the prohibition of murder. Rabbinic exegesis supplied a scriptural basis for all from certain phrases in Genesis. Courts are provided by "he commanded," Gen. 2:16, compared with the same phrase in Gen. 18:19 where it occurs in proximity to justice and judgment. "The Lord," Gen. 2:16, prohibits blasphemy on analogy with the occurrence of the same phrase in Lev. 24:16. "God," Gen. 2:16, compared with the same phrase in Ex. 20:3, prohibits idolatry. "The man," Gen. 2:16, compared with Gen. 9:6 forbids bloodshed. "Saying," Gen. 2:16, compared with Jer. 3:1, prohibits adultery. Prohibition of robbery follows from the fact that it was needful to give man permission to eat of the trees of the garden. Flesh from a living animal is prohibited by "Thou mayest freely eat," which implies food that is ready to be eaten. [6])

These rules as finally stated are a theoretical formulation. To what extent the intercourse of Jews and Gentiles was regulated by them in historic Palestine cannot now be determined.

We have already seen that in the *Bk. of Jubilees* 7 a series of postdiluvian commandments, ordinances, and judgments are made known by Noah. Since the author believed that the just kept the Law before it was revealed from Sinai, the concept of a "Noah commandment" as such is out of the question for him. [7]) But some overlapping with the specific commandments of the later concept can

---

[1]) *T. B. Sanh.* 59a.

[2]) *T. B. Sanh.* 59a-b.

[3]) *Cant. R.* 1. 2. § 5; *Ex. R.* 30. 9; *Deut. R.* 2. 25; *Num. R.* 14. 12; *Gen. R.* 16. 6; *T. B. Sanh.* 56b, 59a.

[4]) *Gen. R.* 24. 5; *Mekilta, Baḥodesh* 5. 82, 90.

[5]) *Cant. R.* 1. 2. § 5; *Ex. R.* 30. 9; *Gen. R.* 16. 6; *T. B. Sanh.* 56a, 59a.

[6]) *T. B. Sanh.* 56b.

[7]) C. Albeck, *Das Buch der Jubiläen und die Halacha* (Berlin: Hochschule für die Wissenschaft des Judentums, 1930), pp. 34-35.

be seen: (1) Do justice. (2) Cover the shame of your flesh. (3) Bless your creator. (4) Honor father and mother. (5) Love your neighbor. (6) Guard yourselves from fornication, uncleanness, and iniquity. (7) Spill no blood. (8) Eat no blood. (9) Cover blood when slaughtering. (10) Eat no fruit of a tree during its first three years. (11) Account the fourth-year fruit holy and offer its firstfruits. (12) Make a release in the seventh (5th?) year. [1]) Numbers 1, 3, 6, 7, and 8 find a correspondence in the rabbinic list.

A similar correspondence can be seen in the list of obligations set forth by the Sibyl: one must refrain from idolatry, murder, robbery, and adultery; but along with these prohibitions in the same context are made obligatory the duty of blessing God before eating and the prohibition of sodomy which do not parallel the Noah laws. [2]) The duty to form courts of justice might be seen in the phrase, "rendering justice one to another, on from age to age." [3])

The Apostolic Letter (Acts 15:20; 21:25) bound upon Gentile Christians four items: abstinence from pollution of idols, from unchastity, from things strangled, and from blood. Codex D, Irenaeus, and Tertullian leave out "things strangled" and add "all that you would not that men do unto you, do not unto them." [4]) Efforts to categorize these exclusively either as moral laws or as food laws fail to fit the evidence exactly. [5]) There is no evidence that the rabbinic definition of "Noah commandments" is as early as Acts. Despite the overlapping, the fact that each of the four items could easily be supported from the Law makes it unnecessary to connect the Apostolic Letter and the Noah laws.

The concept of a natural law universally binding on men prior to the revelation from Sinai, though not specifically connected with Noah, is to be found in Philo, [6]) and then later in Irenaeus, [7]) Tertullian, [8]) and John Cassian. [9]) In Philo's case five of these laws, if one count

---

[1]) *Jubilees* 7:20, 28, 31, 36-37.

[2]) *Or. Sib.* iv. 24-44.

[3]) *Or. Sib.* i. 317-323.

[4]) Irenaeus, *Adv. haer.* iii. 12. 14; Tertullian, *De pudicitia* 12 (*CSEL.* 20. 241-242).

[5]) F. J. Foakes Jackson and K. Lake, *The Beginnings of Christianity* (London: Macmillan, 1933), V, 205-209.

[6]) H. A. Wolfson, *Philo* (Cambridge: Harvard U. Press, 1948), II, 183-187. For an evaluation of Wolfson's argument, see *supra*, p. 55.

[7]) Irenaeus, *Adv. haer.* iv. 15-17.

[8]) Tertullian, *Adv. Jud.* 2 (*CSEL.* 70. 256-258).

[9]) John Cassian, *Collatio VIII.* 23 (*CSEL.* 13. 242).

the prohibition of hybridization which is in some rabbinic lists, coincide with the "Noah laws." The eating of blood and the prohibition of murder are the only two items which Philo specifically connects with Noah; however, we have earlier shown that there are major differences between the concepts of Philo and the rabbis on this matter. [1]) Irenaeus' natural law is identified with the ten commandments and not connected with Noah at all. Tertullian does not enlarge upon his unwritten natural law.

We have seen individual items in the "Noah Laws" list occurring elsewhere, but the fact that there is some biblical basis for them precludes tracing an influence from the rabbis on apocryphal and Christian sources in the matter or vice versa.

---

[1]) Philo, *QG*. ii. 59, 60; see *supra*, p. 55.

APPENDIX C

THE CHRONOLOGY OF THE FLOOD

While the flood lasted one year, [1]) the details of the chronology of the episode are a problem of particular complexity. The account in the MT. hinges around five points: (1) The beginning of the flood in the second month, the seventeenth day of the six hundredth year of Noah's life (Gen. 7:11). (2) The ark rests on the mountains on the seventeenth of the seventh month (Gen. 8:4). (3) The mountain tops are visible on the first of the tenth month (Gen. 8:5). (4) The waters are dry on the first of the first month in the six hundred and first year of Noah's life (Gen. 8:13). (5) The exit from the ark is on the twenty-seventh of the second month (Gen. 8:14). This makes the stay in the ark last for one year and ten days.

The LXX differs by ten days on the first two dates, giving each as the twenty-seventh rather than the seventeenth. The mountains are visible on the first of the eleventh month. The result is that in the LXX the stay in the ark is exactly one calendar year. The Vulgate, while agreeing with the MT. on the beginning and ending dates, agrees with the LXX on the second date (Gen. 8:4) and also has the mountains appear on the first of the eleventh month which is one month's difference from the MT.

Both Augustine [2]) and Hippolytus [3]) follow the LXX except that in the latter source there is confusion on the second figure: "The ark . . . neared Mt. Kardu on the first day of the tenth month and that is the second month Kanun." Aphraates gives the length of time found in MT. without giving a detailed chronology. [4])

Philo differs from each of these. The flood begins on the twenty-seventh of the seventh month. The ark rests on the twenty-seventh of the month, seven months later, which is the fall equinox. Philo could agree with the LXX on this latter date if the LXX thought the flood started in the spring. There are, however, actually only five complete months between the points he gives, so he must have count-

---

[1]) I *Enoch* 106:15; Origen, *Hom. in Gen.* ii. 1, 2 (*GCS*. 29. 24, 28).
[2]) Augustine, *C. Faustum* 12. 18 f. (*CSEL*. 25. 346 f.).
[3]) Hippolytus, *Arabic Frag. to Pent.*, Gen. 8:1 (*GCS*. 1. 2. 90).
[4]) Aphraates, *Hom.* 13. 4, 23 (*TU*. 3. 3, 201, 394-395).

ed the partial months at the beginning and at the end. He agrees
with the MT. on the date upon which the mountains are seen. But
he compresses the drying of the earth and the exit from the ark into
one date, the twenty-seventh of the seventh month, despite the
fact they are separated by twenty-seven days in the MT. and in the
LXX. [1])

The *Book of Jubilees* adds additional dates. The water prevailed
five months (*Jub.* 5:27). The fountains were closed on the new moon of
the fourth month (*Jub.* 5:29). The abysses were opened on the new
moon of the seventh month (*Jub.* 5:29). Of the points mentioned
above, *Jubilees* agrees with the MT. on the start of the flood (*Jub.*
5:23). The resting of the ark is not dated. The drying of the earth
is on the seventeenth of the second month rather than the first (*Jub.*
5:31). The exit from the ark is on the twenty-seventh of the second
month as in the MT. (*Jub.* 5:32).

The *Sibylline Oracles* (I. 231) has a unique chronology in which
Noah is upon the water for two hundred and one days. Other specific
dates are not given. This system is not in agreement with any other
system included in this study.

The *Book of Adam and Eve* (iii. 9-11) names the months rather than
giving their numerical order. The entrance into the ark is on the
twenty-seventh of *Gembot*; the ark rests on the twenty-seventh of
Tkarnt; the mountains appear on the first of the eleventh month.
The earth is dry on the second of *Barmudeh*, and the exit comes in
the next month, the twenty-seventh of *Gembot* which is on Sunday.
Despite the variants, this dating is obviously dependent on the LXX.
It differs from it on the date of the drying of the earth. But even more
noticeable is the fact that this event is in the 607th year of Noah's
life.

The idea that the flood lasted one year is harmonized in some
sources with the figures given in the MT. by the expedient that the
months are counted by a lunar count, while the year is a solar year.[2])
The early Syrian church fathers considered that these extra eleven

---

[1]) Philo, *QG.* ii. 17, 29, 31, 33, 45, 47.
[2]) *Gen. R.* 33. 7; Rashi (*EBI.* II, 43); reference to a year without an effort to
harmonize is made in *Sefer Hayashar*, Noah (*EBI.* II, 32); see also D. Gerson,
Die Comm. des Ephraem Syrus im Verhältniss zur jüdischen Exegese (Breslau: Schletter'-
schen Buchhandlung, 1868), p. 32; and Augustine, *Civ. Dei* 15. 14 (*CSEL.* 40.
2. 86-89).

days were an extra penalty for the sins of the flood generation. [1])
Equally interesting with the question of the duration of the flood is
the question of whether the year is counted from the spring or the
fall. R. Joshua (T. 1st or 2nd cent.) and certain sages of the Gentile
world are said to teach that it began in the dry season, the month
of *Iyar*. [2]) This is also the view of Philo who has the flood come at
the spring equinox which made it more severe since everything was
then in bloom or giving birth. [3]) Somewhat corresponding to this
view is that of the Syrian fathers that the flood began in the summer
so that no one would think it accidental. [4]) Hippolytus spells the
name of the month *"Ijar,"* [5]) while Ephraem spells it *"yar."* [6])

Rabbi Eliezer (T. 1st or 2nd cent.) insisted that the flood began
in *Marḥeshwan* and finally dried up in *Tishri*. [7]) This means it began
in the fall which is the rainy season in Palestine. This is the view of
T. Ps.-Jonathan [8]) and Josephus. [9]) The rabbis favored Eliezer's
argument,[10]) but the Midrash admits that the day of the beginning
is not revealed.[11])

It is obvious from these figures that the *Sitz* of the expositor has
played a major role in his chronological calculations.

---

[1]) A. Levene, *The Early Syrian Fathers on Genesis* (London: Taylor's Foreign
Press, 1951), p. 83.

[2]) *T. B. Rosh Hashana* 11b, 12a.

[3]) Philo, *QG.* ii. 17, 45, 47; cf. also Shadal (*EBI.* II, 31).

[4]) A. Levene, *op. cit.*, p. 188.

[5]) Hippolytus, *Arabic Frag. to Pent.*, Gen. 8:1 (*GCS*. 1. 2. 90).

[6]) Ephraem Syrus, *Comm. in Gen.* 6: 12 (*CSCO*. 72. 48); cf. L. Ginzberg,
Die Haggada bei den Kirchenvätern (Berlin: S. Calvary and Co., 1900), p. 80.

[7]) *T. B. Rosh Hashana* 11b-12a; *Gen. R.* 33. 7.

[8]) *T. Ps.-Jonathan*, Gen. 7:11.

[9]) Josephus, *Ant.* i. 3. 3.

[10]) *Gen. R.* 33. 7; *T. B. Rosh Hashana* 11b-12a.

[11]) *Num. R.* 1. 5.

BIBLIOGRAPHY

Aland, K., and Cross, F. L., *Studia Patristica*. 2 vols. (*TU.*, 63). Berlin: Akademie Verlag, 1957.

Albeck, C., *Das Buch der Jubiläen und die Halacha*. Berlin: Hochschule für die Wissenschaft des Judentums, 1930.

Allen, D. C., *The Legend of Noah*. Urbana: U. Ill. Press, 1949.

Arndt, W. F., and Gingrich, F. W., *A Greek-English Lexicon of the N.T.* Chicago: U. of Chicago Press, 1957.

Avigad, Nahman, and Yadin, Yigael, *A Genesis Apocryphon*. Jerusalem: Magnes Press of the Hebrew University, 1956.

Barclay, W., *A N.T. Wordbook*. London: SCM. Press, 1955.

Bardenhewer, O., *Patrology*. St. Louis: B. Herder, 1908.

Bardy, G., „Les Traditions Juives dans l'oeuvre d'Origene," *Revue Biblique*, XXXIV (1925), 217-252.

Barthélemy, D., and Milik, J. T., *Discoveries in the Judean Desert*. Vol. I: *Qumran Cave I*. Oxford: Clarendon Press, 1955.

Beck, E., *Ephraems Hymnen über das Paradies* (Studia Anselmiana 26). Rome: Herder, 1951.

Berry, G. R., "The Interpretation of Gen. 6: 3," *American Journal of Semitic Languages*, XVI (Oct., 1899), 47-49.

Bert, G. (tr.). *Aphrahat's des Persischen Weisen Homilien* (*Texte und Untersuchungen zur Geschichte der altchristlichen Literatur*, III. 3 and 4). Leipzig: J. C. Hinrichs'sche Buchhandlung, 1888.

Blank, S. H., *Prophetic Faith in Isaiah*. New York: Harper, 1958.

Bousset, W., and Gressmann, H., *Die Religion des Judentums*. Tübingen: J. C. B. Mohr, 1926.

Bréhier, É., *Les Idées Philosophiques et Religieuses de Philon d'Alexandrie*. Paris: Librarie Philosophique J. Vrin, 1950.

Bright, J., "Has Archaeology Found Evidence of the Flood?" *The Biblical Archaeologist*, V (1942), 55-62.

Brown, F., Driver, S. R., and Briggs, C. A., *Hebrew and English Lexicon of the O.T.* Oxford: Clarendon Press, 1952.

Cayre, F., *Manual of Patrology*. 2 vols. Paris: Desclee and Co., 1927.

Charles, R. H., *Apocrypha and Pseudepigrapha of the O.T. in English*. 2 vols. Oxford: Clarendon Press, 1913.

——, *The Book of Enoch*. Oxford: Clarendon Press, 1912.

——, *The Ethiopic Version of the Hebrew Book of Jubilees*. Oxford: Clarendon Press, 1895.

——, *The Book of Jubilees or The Little Genesis*. London: A. and C. Black, 1902.

Closen, G. E., *Die Sünde der „Söhne Gottes" Gen. 6: 1-4*. Rome: Päpstliches Bibelinstitut, 1937.

Colson, F. H., Whitaker, G. H., and Marcus, R., *Philo* (Loeb Series). Cambridge: Harvard U. Press, 1929-1953.

Danby, H. (tr.). *The Mishna*. London: Oxford U. Press, 1950.

Daniélou, J., *Origen*. New York: Sheed and Ward, 1955.

——, „Deluge, bapteme, jugement," *Dieu vivant*, VIII (1947), 97-111.

——, *Sacramentum Futuri*. Paris: Beauchesne et ses Fils, 1950.

David, M. V., „L'épisode des oiseaux dans les récits du déluge," *Vetus Testamentum*, VII (April, 1957), 189-190.

Dawson, J. W., "Sons of God and Daughters of Men," *The Expositor*, Ser. V, IV (1896), 201-211.

Dietrich, E. L., „Die Religion Noah's ihre Herkunft und ihre Bedeutung," *Zeitschrift für Religions- und Geistesgeschichte*, I (1948), 301-315.

Dillmann, A., *Genesis*. 2 vols. Edinburgh: T. and T. Clark, 1897.

Dölger, F. J., *Sol salutis. Gebet und Gesang im Christlichen Altertum*. Münster in Westf.: Aschendorffschen Verlagbuchhandlung, 1925.

Driver, S. R., *The Bk. of Genesis* (Westminister Commentaries). London: Methuen, 1909.

Drummond, J., *Philo Judaeus*. 2 vols. London: Williams and Norgate, 1888.

Ephraem Syri, v.s. Tonneau, R. M., *S. Ephraem Syri*.

Epstein, I. (editor) *The Babylonian Talmud*. 34 vols. London: Soncino Press, 1935.

Finegan, J., *Light From the Ancient Past*. Princeton: Princeton U. Press, 1946.

Fairbairn, P., *The Typology of Scripture*. Philadelphia: W. S. and A. Martien, 1859.

Feinberg, A. J., "Noah," *The Universal Jewish Encyclopedia*, VIII, 224.

Field, F., *Origenis Hexaplorum Quae Supersunt sive Veterum Interpretetum Graecorum in Totum Vetus Testamentum Fragmenta*. 2 vols. Oxford: Clarendon Press, 1925.

Fink, Josef, *Noe der Gerechte in der Frühchristlichen Kunst*. Münster/Köln: Böhlau-verlag, 1955.

Foakes Jackson, F. J., and Lake, K., *The Beginnings of Christianity*. 5 vols. London: Macmillan, 1920-1933.

Freedman, H., and Simon, M., *Midrash Rabbah*. 10 vols. London: Soncino Press, 1951.

Frankel, Z., *Ueber den Einfluss der palästinischen Exegese auf die Alexandrinische Hermeneutik*. Leipzig: Joh. Ambr. Barth, 1851.

Frazer, J. G., *Folklore in the Old Testament*. 3 vols. London: Macmillan, 1919.

Frost, S. B., *Old Testament Apocalyptic*. London: Epworth Press, 1952.

Funk, F. X., *Didascalia et Constitutiones Apostolorum*. 2 vols. Paderbornae: Lib. Ferdinandi Schoeningh, 1895.

Funk, S., *Die haggadischen Elemente in den Homilien des Aphraates*. Wien: Selbst-verlag des Verfassers, 1891.

Gerson, D., *Die Commentarien des Ephraem Syrus im Verhältniss zur jüdischen Exegese*. Breslau: Schletter'schen Buchhandlung, 1868.

Gifford, E. H. (editor). *Eusebius's Preparation for the Gospel*. Pts. I and II. Oxford: Clarendon Press, 1903.

Ginzberg, L., *The Legends of the Jews*. 7 vols. Philadelphia: Jewish Publication Society, 1909-1955.

——, *Die Haggada bei den Kirchenvätern und in der apokryphen Literatur*. Berlin: S. Calvary and Co., 1900.

——, "*Mabul shel Esh*," *Hagoren, Abhandlungen über die Wissenschaft des Juden-thums*. S. A. Horodezky (editor). Berditschew: Scheftel, 1911, VIII, 35-51.

Goldfahn, A. H., „Justinus Martyr und die Agada," *Monatschrift für Geschichte und Wissenschaft des Judentums*, XXII (1873), 49-60, 104-115, 145-153, 193-202, 257-269.

Goodenough, E. R., *By Light, Light*. New Haven: Yale University Press, 1935.

——, *Jewish Symbols in the Greco-Roman Period*. 3 vols. N.Y.: Pantheon Books, 1953.

Goodrick, A. T. S., *The Bk. of Wisdom*. N.Y.: Macmillan Co., 1913.

Goodspeed, E. J., *Die ältesten Apologeten*. Göttingen: Vandenhoeck and Ruprecht, 1915.
——, *A History of Early Christian Literature*. Chicago: University of Chicago Press, 1942.
——, *Index Apologeticus*. Leipzig: J. C. Hinrichs'sche Buchhandlung, 1912.
——, *Index Patristicus*. Leipzig: J. C. Hinrichs'sche Buchhandlung, 1907.
Goppelt, L., *Typos, Die typologische Deutung des alten Testaments im Neuen*. Gütersloh: C. Bertelsmann, 1939.
Gordon, A. R., *The Early Traditions of Genesis*. Edinburgh: T. and T. Clark, 1907.
Grant, R. M., *Second Century Christianity*. London: SPCK., 1946.
Green, W. H., *The Unity of the Book of Genesis*. N.Y.: Scribner's, 1895.
Guillaume, A., "A Note on the Meaning of Gen. 6: 3," *American Journal of Semitic Languages*, LVI (Oct., 1939), 415-416.

Hamburger, J., „Noachiden," *Real-Encyclopädie für Bibel und Talmud*. Strelitz: J. Hamburger, 1883, II, 863-866.
Hanson, R. P. C., *Allegory and Event*. London: SCM. Press, 1959.
Harris, J. R., "Two Flood-Hymns of the Early Church," *The Expositor*, VIII, 2 (1911), 405-417.
——, "The Thirty-Eighth Ode of Solomon," *The Expositor*, VIII, 2 (1911), 28-37.
Hatch, Edwin., *Essays in Biblical Greek*. Oxford: Clarendon Press, 1889.
Heidel, A., *The Gilgamesh Epic*. Chicago: Chicago U. Press, 1954.
Heinisch, Paul, *Der Einfluss Philos auf die älteste Christliche Exegese*. Münster i. W.: Aschendorffschen Buchhandlung, 1908.
Heras, H., "The Crow of Noe," *Catholic Biblical Quarterly*, X (April, 1948), 131-139.
Hershman, R. M., *The Code of Maimonides*, Bk. 14, *The Bk. of Judges* (Yale Judaica Series). New Haven: Yale U. Press, 1949.
Hilaire de Poitiers, *Traité des Mystères* (Sources Chrétiennes 19). Paris: Éditions du Cerf, 1947.
Hirsch, E. G., and Muss-Arnolt, W., "The Flood," *The Jewish Encyclopaedia*, V, 410-415.
Hort, F. J. A., "Apelles," *A Dictionary of Christian Biography*, W. Smith and W. Wace (editors). I, 127-128.
Hoskyns, E., and Davey, N., *The Riddle of the N.T.* London: Faber and Faber, Ltd., 1958.

James, M. R., *The Biblical Antiquities of Philo*. London: SPCK., 1917.
——, *The Lost Apocrypha of the O.T.* London: SPCK., 1936.
Jastrow, M., *A Dictionary of the Targumim, the Talmud Babli and Yerushalmi, and the Midrashic Literature*. 2 vols. N.Y.: Pardes Pub. House, 1950.
Jellinek, A., *Bet ha-Midrasch*. 3 pts. Leipzig: C. W. Vollrath, 1855.
Jonge, M. de, *The Testaments of the Twelve Patriarchs*. Assen: Van Gorcum, 1953.
Josephus, v.s. Thackeray and Marcus, *Josephus*.

Kaplan, C., "The Flood in the Book of Enoch and Rabbinics," *Journal of the Society of Oriental Research*, XV (1931), 22-24.
Katz, P., *Philo's Bible*. Cambridge: Cambridge U. Press, 1950.
Kasher, M. M., *Torah Shelemah*. Vol. II. Jerusalem: *Defos ʿAzari'el*, 1929.
——, *Ency. of Bib. Interpretation*. Vols. I and II. New York: American Biblical Ency. Society, 1953.
Kautzsch, E., and Cowley, A. E. (editors). *Gesenius' Hebrew Grammar*. Oxford: Clarendon Press, 1952.
Kay, D. M., "Noachian Precepts," *Ency. of Religion and Ethics*. Jas. Hastings (editor). New York: Scribner's, 1917, IX, 379-380.

Koehler, L., and Baumgartner, W., *Lexicon in Veteris Testamenti Libros*. 2 vols. Leiden: E. J. Brill, 1953.

Koehler, K., "Memra," *Jewish Encyclopaedia*. I. Singer (editor). N.Y.: Funk and Wagnalls, 1905, VIII, 464-465.

Kraeling, E. G., "The Earliest Hebrew Flood Story," *Journal of Biblical Literature*, LXVI (Sept., 1947), 279-293.

——, "Xisouthros, Deucalion and the Flood Traditions," *Journal of American Oriental Society*, LXVII (July, 1947), 177-183.

——, "The Significance and Origin of Gen. 6: 1-4," *Journal of Near Eastern Studies*, VI (1947), 193-208.

——, "The Interpretation of the Name of Noah in Gen. 5: 29," *Journal of Biblical Literature*, XLVIII (1929), 138-143.

Kraus, F. X., *Real-Encyklopaedie der Christlichen Altertümer*. 2 vols. Freiburg im Breisgau: Herder'sche Verlagshandlung, 1886.

Krauss, S., "The Jews in the Works of the Church Fathers," *Jewish Quarterly Review*, V (1893), 122 ff.; VI (1894), 82 ff., 225 ff.

——, "Sibyl," *Jewish Encyclopaedia*. I. Singer (editor). N.Y.: Funk and Wagnalls Co., 1905, IX, 319b-323b.

Lake, K. (tr.). *The Apostolic Fathers*. 2 vols. Cambridge: Harvard U. Press, 1946.

Lampe, G. W. H., and Woollcombe, K. J., *Essays On Typology*. London: SCM. Press, 1957.

Lauterbach, J. Z. (editor). *Mekilta de Rabbi Ishmael*. 3 vols. Philadelphia: Jewish Publication Society, 1949.

Lawson, J., *The Biblical Theology of St. Irenaeus*. London: Epworth Press, 1948.

LeClercq, H., „Arche," *Dictionnaire d'Archéologie Chrétienne et de Liturgie*, F. Cabrol (editor). Paris: Letouzey et Ané, 1907, I, 2, col. 2709-2732.

Levene, A., *The Early Syrian Fathers on Genesis*. London: Taylor's Foreign Press, 1951.

Lewis, J. P., "An Intro. to the Testaments of the Twelve Patriarchs." Unpublished Ph.D. dissertation, Dept. of History, Harvard University, 1953.

Loewe, R., "The Jewish Midrashim and Patristic and Scholastic Exegesis of the Bible," *Studia Patristica*. K. Aland and F. L. Cross (editors), Berlin: Akademie Verlag, 1957, pp. 492-514.

Lundberg, Per., *La Typologie Baptismale dans L'ancienne église*. Leipzig: Alfred Lorentz, 1942.

Maas, A. J., "Deluge," *Catholic Encyclopedia*, IV, 702-706.

Maimonides, v.s. Hershman, A. M., *The Code of Maimonides*.

Malan, S. C., *The Book of Adam and Eve, also called The Conflict of Adam and Eve with Satan*. London: Williams and Norgate, 1882.

Marcus, R., "Introduction to Philo's Questions and Answers on Genesis," *Philo*, Supplement I. R. Marcus (tr.). Cambridge: Harvard University Press, 1953.

Martin, J.,"Famine Element in the Story of the Flood," *Journal of Biblical Literature*, XLV (1926), 129-133.

Mayor, J. B., *The Epistle of St. Jude and the Second Epistle of Peter*. London: Macmillan, 1907.

Mekilta, v.s. Lauterbach, J. Z. (editor). *Mekilta*.

Ps.-Melito, *Apology* in *Spicilegium Syriacum*. W. Cureton (editor). London: F. and J. Rivington, 1855, pp. 50-51.

Midrash, v.s. Freedman, H., and Simon, M. *Midrash Rabbah*.

Mielziner, M., *Introduction to the Talmud*. Cincinnati: Block Pub. Co., 1894.

Milburn, R. L. P., *Early Christian Interpretations of History*. N.Y.: Harper, 1954.
Milik, J. T., "The Dead Sea Scrolls Fragment of the Book of Enoch," *Biblica*, XXXII (1951), 393-400.
Mishna, v.s. Danby, H. (tr.), *The Mishna*.
Montefiore, C. G., and Loewe, H., *A Rabbinic Anthology*. London: Macmillan, 1938.
Moore, G. F., *Judaism in the First Centuries of the Christian Era*. 3 vols. Cambridge: Harvard U. Press, 1930.
Morgenstern, J., "A Note on Genesis 5: 29," *Journal of Biblical Literature*, XLIX (1930), 306-309.
Ben-Mordecai, C. A., "*Be'saggam*: An Obscure Phrase in Gen. 6: 3; Reply to A. Guillaume," *American Journal of Semitic Languages*, LVII (July, 1940), 306-307.
Moulton, J. H., *A Grammar of N.T. Greek*. 2 vols. W. F. Howard (editor). Edinburgh: T. and T. Clark, 1919.
Murphy, C. C. R., "What is Gopher Wood?" *Asiatic Review*, N.S. XLII (January, 1946), 79-81.

Noth, M., „Noah, Daniel und Hiob in Ezekiel XIV," *Vetus Testamentum*, I (Oct., 1951), 251-260.

Oesterley, W. O. E., "The Dove with the Olive-leaf (Gen. 8: 8-11)," *Expository Times*, XVIII (1906-1907), 377-378.
Origenes, *Homilies sur la Genèse*. Translation and notes by L. Doutreleau. Intro. by P. Henri de Lubac (Sources Chrétiennes 7). Paris: Éditions du Cerf, 1943.

Pfeiffer, R. H., *A History of N.T. Times*. N.Y.: Harper, 1949.
Parrot, André, *The Flood and Noah's Ark*. London: SCM. Press, 1955.
Peake, H., *The Flood*. London: Kegan Paul, Trench, Trubner and Co., 1930.
Philo, v.s. Colson, Whitaker, and Marcus. *Philo*.
Pick, B., "Philo's Canon of the O.T. and His Method of Quoting the Alexandrian Version," *Journal of Biblical Literature*, IV (1884), 126-143.
Poulet, Donat, "The Moral Causes of the Flood," *Catholic Biblical Quarterly*, IV (Oct., 1942), 293-303.

Quasten, J., *Patrology*. 2 vols. Westminster, Maryland: The Newman Press, 1953.

Rahlfs, A. (editor). *Septuaginta*. Stuttgart: Privilegierte Württembergische Bibelanstalt, 1952.
Rahmer, M., *Die hebräischen Traditionen in den Werken des Hieronymus*. Breslau: Schletter'schen Buchhandlung, 1861.
Rappaport, S., *Agada und Exegese bei Flavius Josephus*. Wien: Alex. Kohut Memorial Foundation, 1930.
Redlich, E. B., *The Early Traditions of Genesis*. London: G. Duckworth, 1950.
Rehm, B. (editor). *Die Pseudo-Klementinen I, Homilien*. Leipzig: J. C. Hinrichs, 1953.
Reider, J., "Prolegomena to a Gk.-Hebrew and Heb.-Gk. Index to Aquila," *Jewish Quarterly Review*, N.S. IV (1913), 321-356, 577-620; VII (1916-1917), 287-366.
Reicke, Bo, *The Disobedient Spirits and Christian Baptism*. KøBenhavn: E. Munksgaard, 1946.
Revel, H., "Noahide Laws," *Universal Jewish Encyclopaedia*, VIII, 227-228.
Richardson, Alan, *Genesis 1-11* (The Torch Bible Commentaries). London: SCM. Press, 1953.
Robinson, J. A. (tr.). *St. Irenaeus, The Demonstration of the Apostolic Preaching*. London: SPCK., 1920.

Robert, C., „Les Fils de Dieu et les Filles de l'Homme," *Revue Biblique*, IV (1895), 340-373, 525-552.

Roberts, B. J., *The Old Testament Texts and Versions*. Cardiff: University of Wales Press, 1951.

Romanoff, Paul, "A Third Version of the Flood Narrative," *Journal of Biblical Literature*, L (1931), 304-307.

Rönsch, H., *Das Buch der Jubiläen*. Leipzig: Fues's Verlag, 1874.

Rost, Leonhard, „Noah der Weinbauer. Bemerkungen zu Gen. 9:18 ff.," *Geschichte und Altes Testament, Festschrift A. Alt*. W. F. Albright (editor). Tübingen: J. C. B. Mohr, 1953.

Ryle, H. E., *The Early Narratives of Genesis*. London: Macmillan, 1892.

——, *Philo and Holy Scripture*. London: Macmillan, 1895.

Salmon, G., "Melito," *A Dictionary of Christian Biography*. W. Smith and H. Wace (editors). III, 895.

——, "Heracleon," *A Dictionary of Christian Biography*. W. Smith and H. Wace (editors). II, 897-901.

Sandmel, S., "Philo's Environment and Philo's Exegesis," *Journal of Bible and Religion*, XXII (1954), 251-252.

——, *Philo's Place in Judaism*. Cincinnati: Hebrew Union College Press, 1956.

——, "Philo and His Pupils: An Imaginary Dialogue," *Judaism*, IV (1955), 47-57.

Scherer, J. (editor). *Entretien d'Origene*. Le Caire: Institut Français de Archéologie Orientale, 1949.

Schmidt, Nathaniel, "The Apocalypse of Noah and the Parables of Enoch," *Oriental Studies Published in Commemoration of the 40th Anniversary of Paul Haupt*. C. Adler and A. Ember (editors). Baltimore: Johns Hopkins Press, 1926.

Schürer, E., *Geschichte des Jüdischen Volkes im Zeitalter Jesu Christi*. Vol. III, 4th ed. Leipzig: J. C. Hinrichs'sche Buchhandlung, 1909.

Seligson, M., "Noah in Apocryphal and Rabbinical Literature," *The Jewish Encyclopedia*, IX, 319-321.

Selwyn, E. G. ,*The First Epistle of St. Peter*. London: Macmillan, 1947.

Surfelt, J. E., "Noah's Curse and Blessing, Gen. 9: 18-27," *Concordia Theological Monthly*, XVII (Oct., 1946), 737-742.

Siegfried, K., *Philo von Alexandria als Ausleger des Alten Testaments*. Jena: Hermann Dufft, 1875.

Simon, Marcel, *Verus Israel*. Paris: E. de Boccard, 1948.

Simpson, A. C., *The Early Traditions of Israel*. Oxford: B. Blackwell, 1948.

Skinner, J., *A Critical and Exegetical Commentary on Genesis*. N.Y.: Scribner's, 1910.

Speiser, E. A., "YDWN, Gen. 6: 3," *Journal of Biblical Literature*, LXXV (June, 1956), 126-129.

Spicq, C., *L'Epitre aux Hébreux*. 2 vols. Paris: Librairie Lecoffre, 1953.

Spitta, F., *Der zweite Brief des Petrus und der Brief des Judas*. Halle a. S.: Verlag der Buchhandlung des Waisenhauses, 1885.

Starcky, J., "Cave 4 of Qumran," *Biblical Archaeologist*, XIX (1956), 96.

Stein, E., *Die allegorische Exegese des Philo aus Alexandrein*. Giessen: Alfred Töpelmann, 1929.

——, *Philo und der Midrasch*. Giessen: Alfred Töpelmann, 1931.

Steinmueller, J. E., *Some Problems of the Old Testament*. N.Y.: The Bruce Publishing Co., 1936.

Strahan, J., "Noah," *A Dictionary of the Apostolic Church*. J. Hastings (editor). Edinburgh: T. and T. Clark, 1918, II, 91-92.

Strack, H. L., und Billerbeck, P., *Kommentar zum Neuen Testament aus Talmud und Midrasch*. 4 vols. München: C. H. Beck, 1928.

Strugnell, J., "Cave 4 of Qumran," *Biblical Archaeologist*, XIX (1956), 96.

Sukenik, E. L., *Ancient Synagogues in Palestine and Greece* (Schweich Lectures, 1930). London: Humphrey Milford, 1934.

Swete, H. B., *An Intro. to the O.T. in Greek*. Cambridge: Cambridge U. Press, 1902.

Talmud, v.s. Epstein. *The Babylonian Talmud*.

Thackeray, H. St. John, *The Septuagint and Jewish Worship* (The Schweich Lectures, 1920). London: Humphrey Milford, 1923.

Thackeray, H. St. John, and Marcus, Ralph, *Josephus* (Loeb Series). Cambridge: Harvard University Press, 1927-1957.

Terry, M. S. (tr.). *The Sibylline Oracles Translated from the Greek into English Blank Verse*. N.Y.: Hunt and Eaton, 1890.

Thomas, D. W., "Textual Criticism of the O.T.," *The O.T. and Modern Study*. H. H. Rowley (editor). Oxford: Clarendon Press, 1952.

Tonneau, R. M., *Sancti Ephraem Syri in Genesim et in Exodium Commentarii* (Corpus scriptorum christianorum orientalium 72). Louvain: L. Durbecq, 1955.

Torrey, C. C., *The Apocryphal Literature*. New Haven: Yale U. Press, 1948.

Ullendorff, E., "The Construction of Noah's Ark," *Vetus Testamentum*, IV (Jan., 1954), 95-96.

Weill, J., *Oeuvres complètes de Flavius Josèphe*. Paris: Ernest Leroux, 1900.

Wolfson, H. A., *Philo*. 2 vols. Cambridge: Harvard U. Press, 1948.

Woods, F. F., "Flood," *A Dictionary of the Bible*. J. Hastings (editor). Edinburgh: T. and T. Clark, 1899. II, 16-23.